# Pacific and Southeast Asian Cooking

# Pacific and Southeast Asian Cooking

by
Rafael Steinberg
and the Editors of
**TIME-LIFE BOOKS**
photographed by
Anthony Blake, Larry Burrows,
Eliot Elisofon, Fred Lyon
and Co Rentmeester

TIME-LIFE BOOKS, ALEXANDRIA, VIRGINIA

## FOODS OF THE WORLD
EDITOR: Richard L. Williams
*Series Chief Researcher:* Helen Fennell
EDITORIAL STAFF FOR PACIFIC AND
SOUTHEAST ASIAN COOKING:
*Associate Editor:* Harvey B. Loomis
*Picture Editor:* Kaye Neil
*Designer:* Albert Sherman
*Assistant to Designer:* Elise Hilpert
*Staff Writers:* Gerry Schremp, Ethel Strainchamps
*Chief Researcher:* Sarah B. Brash
*Researchers:* Joan Chambers, Doris Coffin, Barbara Ensrud,
Brenda Huff, Cornelia Kubler, Ellen Leiman, Lilla Lyon,
Joan Mebane, Lyn Stallworth
*Test Kitchen Chef:* John W. Clancy
*Test Kitchen Staff:* Fifi Bergman, Sally Darr, Leola Spencer

EDITORIAL PRODUCTION
*Production Editor:* Douglas B. Graham
*Operations Manager:* Gennaro C. Esposito,
Gordon E. Buck (assistant)
*Assistant Production Editor:* Feliciano Madrid
*Quality Control:* Robert L. Young (director), James J. Cox
(assistant), Michael G. Wight (associate)
*Art Coordinator:* Anne B. Landry
*Copy Staff:* Susan B. Galloway (chief), Grace Hawthorne,
Eleanore Karsten, Celia Beattie
*Picture Department:* Joan Lynch
*Traffic:* Jeanne Potter

CORRESPONDENTS: Elisabeth Kraemer (Bonn); Margot
Hapgood, Dorothy Bacon (London); Susan Jonas,
Lucy T. Voulgaris (New York); Maria Vincenza
Aloisi, Josephine du Brusle (Paris); Ann Natanson
(Rome). Valuable assistance was also provided by:
Bob Gilmore (Aukland); David Greenway, Peter Simms
(Bangkok); John Vile (Fiji); John Saar (Hong Kong);
Amir Daud (Indonesia); Timothy D. Allman (Laos);
Carolyn T. Chubet, Frank McCulloch, Marcia Gauger,
Miriam Hsia (New York); Guillermo Santos
(Philippines); Robert F. Rankin (Samoa); Peter Lim
(Singapore); Ernest Shirley (Sydney); James E.
Boyack Jr. (Tahiti).

THE AUTHOR: Rafael Steinberg (*above, right*) first crossed the Pacific in 1951 as a correspondent heading for the Korean War. Later he lived in Japan as a Time correspondent and as Tokyo bureau chief for *Newsweek*. He traveled 21,000 miles gathering material in the vast region covered by the present volume. His other books include *Japan, Postscript from Hiroshima* and the FOODS OF THE WORLD volume on *The Cooking of Japan*.

THE CONSULTING EDITOR: The late Michael Field (*above, left*) supervised the adapting and writing of recipes for this book. One of America's foremost culinary experts and teachers, he wrote many articles for leading magazines. His books include *Michael Field's Cooking School* and *All Manner of Food*.

THE CONSULTANTS: George Lang (*above, center*) established the Indonesian Theatre Restaurant for the government of Indonesia at the 1964 New York World's Fair and brought Chef Fritz Schild-Tameng (*above, left*) from Djakarta to be head of the kitchen. Mr. Lang, president of the George Lang Corporation, has been a consultant on several FOODS OF THE WORLD volumes. Mr. Schild-Tameng, a native of Surabaja, on Java, cooked for many visiting heads of state as palace chef in Djakarta. "Trader Vic" Bergeron (*above, right*) was consultant on the Polynesian chapters. Founder of an international restaurant chain, he has written several books, including *Trader Vic's Pacific Island Cookbook*. Other consultants for this volume are identified on page 208.

THE PHOTOGRAPHERS: Five photographers contributed to this volume. Their pictures appear on page 208.

THE COVER: Arranged on a glossy ti leaf are Indonesian *saté*—skewered tidbits of broiled meat with a dipping sauce—and a freshly opened coconut.

# Contents

The Recipe Booklet that accompanies this volume has been designed for use in the kitchen. It contains all of the 52 recipes printed in this book plus 75 more. It also has a wipe-clean cover and a spiral binding so that it can either stand up or lie flat when open.

# Where Many Foods Are Strange
# and Some Are Wonderful

Some of my friends have asked me what business I have writing a book about food. Their puzzlement would be justified if this were a book about familiar foods of the West, for I do not cook, and as my wife and daughters know, I have never been noted for any eagerness to help out in the kitchen.

But for the exotic foods of the Pacific and Southeast Asia I can claim understanding. Since I was a boy growing up in New York City and enjoying Jewish, Italian, Chinese and Russian cooking, I have had an inquisitive palate. "Try anything once," my father used to tell me, and so I learned early that many "strange" foods are worth tasting not just once, but again and again. My parents had a friend who had lived many years in China and he always knew in which restaurants of Manhattan's Chinatown the best chefs were working at any given moment. To these establishments, often tiny and sinister-looking—and always mysterious and exciting to a boy of 10 or 12—my parents' friend would lead us, and, speaking in fluent and what seemed to me majestic Chinese, would summon forth from the kitchen a pageant of magnificent foods with flavor combinations that I had not known existed. Later, with the ready smugness of youth, I would sneer at the chop suey and chow mein my own friends thought was Chinese food, and would lead them through Chinatown on quests for remembered delights.

Not until I lived in the Orient myself did I begin to find such fare again. During 10 years as a foreign correspondent in East Asia I traveled through many of the countries covered in this volume, eating local foods as often as I could. Thus when I set out on a five-month gastronomic exploration of the region to gather material for this book I already had a fair idea of what I would encounter.

By and large, in the countries of this vast area, native foods were not in the past considered appetizing to Westerners. Generations of snobbish colonials and timid tourists have convinced the people of these lands that it is impossible for anyone with a white skin to eat and enjoy the starchy poi of Hawaii, the spicy *lawar* of Bali, or the *miti hue* (fermented coconut milk) of Tahiti. Again and again during my tour of the region my request to be served local foods "just the way you eat them" met with resistance and disbelief.

In Tahiti it was literally headline news that I had partaken of the pickled fish dish called *fafaru*, while the acknowledged leading epicure of Apia, in western Samoa, refused to believe I was serious until I joined him in a glorious lunch of strange sea creatures plucked fresh from the sparkling lagoon. And at Ambon, in the Spice Islands, I observed out of the corner of my eye the entire kitchen staff of the Hotel Anggrek peering at me through the serving window and giggling gleefully as I struggled with my portion of *popeda,* which must be gobbled directly from the bowl without a spoon. Even President Suharto of Indonesia was surprised, and his wife was flattered, when they realized how much I was enjoying the food at one of their weekly family picnics on a tiny islet near Djakarta. Mrs. Suharto, one of the best cooks in Indonesia, had provided some of the President's favorite foods: a gingery, peppery fish soup, a spicy concoction of vegetables in coconut milk and a charcoal-grilled fish with a chili sauce. They were all marvelous.

After eating my way from Honolulu to Bangkok I can only feel sorry for the colonial who never dined out of his club and the tourist who still sticks to hamburgers or his hotel's dining room. A wide and exciting range of taste experiences awaits the traveler with an adventurous spirit—and the stay-at-home cook with an eager palate. To be sure, there are some individual dishes that, if served to your more nervous friends, may frighten them off. Further, the spices and hot chilies of some of these places must be handled with care and respect lest the unwary diner rise gasping from his seat, grabbing desperately for a glass of water. But these hazards are easily avoided, and this book will endeavor to chart their positions so that the timid may steer clear and the daring may have their fling.

All the countries I visited are fertile tropic lands, blessed with abundant rainfall, rich soil and seas teeming with edible life. But where rice can be harvested twice a year, where the munificent breadfruit tree grows easily, human life proliferates as well. And it is an unhappy fact that overpopulation and human mismanagement—abetted by years of warfare in Southeast Asia—have pushed many of these areas into poverty. Perhaps millions of the people of these lands suffer from malnutrition. Many of the interesting and delicious dishes described herein can be sampled only in the homes of the wealthy, or in restaurants far too expensive for most citizens. Only at a wedding or festival may ordinary villagers enjoy the best, most distinctive foods of their region.

These distinctive dishes are produced by cooking styles ranging from the primitive ground ovens and leaf wrapping of Polynesia to the refined and exquisite court cuisine of Thailand. In between lies a vast mélange of highly developed culinary approaches, overlaid with a crumbling crust of many colonial influences. At first glance it would seem that many of these cuisines have little in common with one another; but they all depend heavily on the coconut, whose many uses are described in Chapter 3. And without spices and rice, discussed in Chapters 5 and 8, the cooking styles of Southeast Asia could not be what they are.

Although many of the foods of the region might seem as mysterious to mainland Americans as those Chinatown dinners of 30 years ago seemed to a wide-eyed boy, they are everyday fare in Hawaii, America's own polyglot Pacific state. And so that is where I began an unforgettable exploration of the tropic opulence, the Oriental variety and the exciting spicery of the foods of the Pacific and Southeast Asia.

*—Rafael Steinberg*

# I

# *Hawaii: Where Polynesia Begins*

Arriving in the verdant islands of Hawaii, where coconut palms grace the shoreline and mountain apples and taro grow wild on the volcanic slopes above the pineapple plantations, visitors from less tropical climes quickly experience a series of happy surprises: benign sun and thunderous surf, bright unfamiliar flowers, breezy informality, an intriguing racial mix. Even things that seem to look the same as elsewhere turn out to be subtly changed.

A housewife from the mainland, for instance, can feel right at home parking her car in a crowded Honolulu supermarket lot, grasping a wire shopping cart and wheeling her way past whirring cash registers into the aisles of the fluorescent-lighted store. Row upon row of familiar products—all the friendly national brands she depends on back home—meet her eye.

But wait. Suddenly, at the vegetable counter, she comes upon a huge mound of fresh coconuts, a pile of outlandish purple taro bulbs and a dozen odd-looking roots, fruits, leaves and snakelike beans that she has never seen before. In the freezer section she finds, next to her favorite frozen orange juice, cans of frozen coconut milk, passion-fruit punch, guava-flavored yoghurt and a large selection of frozen noodles. Next to the lamb chops at the meat counter, packages of bright red *char siu* (sweet-and-sour pork) make her blink. Farther on she notes with wonder that other shoppers are buying rice in 25-pound and 50-pound sacks instead of in two-pound boxes. And where she might expect to find potato chips, as at home, she confronts a long stretch of counter stocked with

At least one tropical fruit goes into each of the refreshing Hawaiian drinks on the opposite page. Orchids and gardenias, to be had for the picking in Hawaii, are optional decorations. From the top, clockwise, the drinks are banana cow, scorpion, *kamaaina, mai tai* and Cooper's Ranch punch. Mixing instructions are in the Recipe Booklet.

China

Burma

Iwo Jima

Laos

● Hong Kong

● Hanoi

Chiang Mai ●

Thailand

*Chao Phraya Basin*

Vietnam

● Banaue

Luzon

Manila ●

Bangkok ●

Cambodia

Philippines

●Ho Chi Minh City

*Mekong River Delta*

Mindanao

● Banda Atjeh

Siau Is.

Kuala Lumpur ●

M a l a y s i a

Malacca ●

● Manado

● Ternate

Singapore

Kalimantan
(Borneo)

Ternate Is.

Bukittinggi ●

I N D O N E S I A

M O L U C C A S
I S L A N D S

Padang ●

*Sumatra*

● Palembang

Sulawesi
(Celebes)

● Ambon

Ambon Is.

West Irian

*Java Sea*

Madura

Djakarta ●

Surabaja ●

● Makasar

*Banda Sea*

Java

Jogjakarta ●

Bali

*Indian Ocean*

| 0 | 500 | 1000 | 1500 | 2000 miles |

Australia

a bewildering array of chips and crackers made from taro, breadfruit, bananas, soybeans or wonton.

Perhaps the strangest sight of all is the rack laden with plastic bags containing a purplish starchy paste—Hawaii's famous poi. Little tags label the poi as fresh or one-day-old or two-day-old, all at the same price, and just as many customers reach for the darker older stuff as for the new. Nor is this their only choice; on a nearby shelf stand bright-colored cans labeled: "Ready mixed poi. Good for baby feeding."

If the *malihini* (newcomer) leaves the supermarket and ventures afield in the food marts of Honolulu, she will encounter a great number of foods vital to the cooking not just of Hawaii but of the whole Pacific and Southeast Asian region. She will find raw fish and barbecued pig, sour tamarinds and a sweet freak coconut the Filipinos call *makapuno* and the Indonesians know as *kopior,* a strong fish sauce that millions of Southeast Asians use like salt, and fragrant East Indian spices in their natural, unprocessed form.

Long before the tourists came, emigrants from East and West were set-

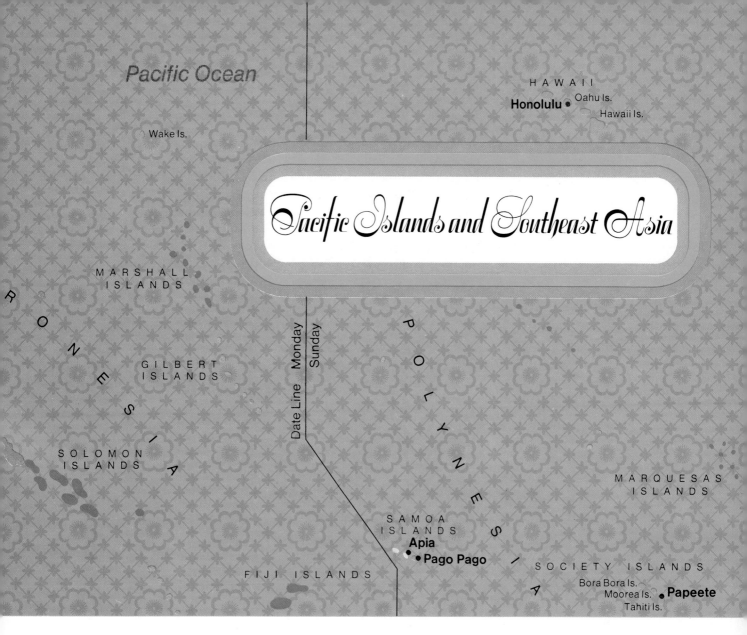

Pacific Ocean

H A W A I I
Honolulu • Oahu Is.
Hawaii Is.

Wake Is.

M A R S H A L L
I S L A N D S

G I L B E R T
I S L A N D S

S O L O M O N
I S L A N D S

Date Line Monday Sunday

P
O
L
Y
N
E
S
I
A

MARQUESAS
ISLANDS

S A M O A
I S L A N D S
Apia
• Pago Pago

SOCIETY ISLANDS

F I J I  I S L A N D S

Bora Bora Is.
Moorea Is. • Papeete
Tahiti Is.

tling in what Mark Twain once called "the loveliest fleet of islands that lies anchored in any ocean." Whether lured by climate and scenery and the promise of paradise, or ambitious to make a fortune, or heeding a call to save heathen souls, each group of *malihinis* that arrived stubbornly insisted on eating the foods they were used to at home. Thus they bequeathed to the islands a fascinating range of ingredients and cooking styles that today blends deliciously; the newest newcomer, though, is still bound to be bewildered when he finds six different cuisines represented at one meal and may wonder just where in the Pacific he is.

This culinary mixing process began with the first Hawaiian settlers, who came from Tahiti and elsewhere, across the thousands of miles of Pacific Ocean that separate the scattered islands of Polynesia. The voyagers carried with them the breadfruit and taro and pigs and coconuts that would feed them and nourish their heirs for a thousand years. In the early 19th Century, New England missionaries and whalers and traders introduced corned beef, salt fish, stews, chowders and corn bread. Chinese plantation workers brought in rice, the stir-fry method of cooking, and

The tropic region embracing the territory of this book sweeps a third of the way around the globe. It encompasses the Pacific island groups of Polynesia (including Hawaii), Micronesia and the Malay Archipelago, the vast crescent of Indonesia and the islands of the Philippines. It touches two continents, Asia and Australia. Many cultures and languages divide the area, but its foods and culinary styles have a great deal in common.

11

Asian vegetables like soybeans, Chinese cabbage and lotus roots. With the Japanese sugar-cane workers came charcoal braziers (hibachi) new kinds of noodles, a taste for seaweed, and the sugar and soy sauce teriyaki marinade—which remains the most popular way of preparing meat in Hawaii today. Koreans arrived with their *kimchi* (pickled cabbage) and hooked the islanders on the taste of garlic and chili, and the Filipinos introduced jack fruit, mung beans, bitter melons, and the powerful *bagoong* fish sauce. From Europe came the Portuguese, who left their mark too. The bright red-and-white vans that peddle their fluffy, sugary *malasada* doughnuts roam everywhere in Honolulu, especially at sporting events and festivals. A Portuguese bean soup, thick, spicy, with an insistent taste of sausage and garlic, has also become a favorite among Hawaiians of every ethnic background. Even the Scots, who arrived in smaller numbers as sugar technicians and plantation overseers, added their special touch to Hawaii's menus: scones and shortbread.

The native Hawaiians of a century ago probably could not understand why the *haoles* (white men) preferred New England salt cod and jerked beef to the fresh fish and barbecued suckling pig of the islands. But Hawaiians today owe a debt of gratitude to the conservative palates of the old missionaries and traders, for two of Hawaii's finest delicacies evolved directly from imported Yankee foods.

The whalers' jerked beef now turns up as *pipikaula,* a tasty dried meat tidbit essential to every well-planned luau, or Hawaiian feast. And the salt fish dear to the missionaries has been transmuted into the excellent *lomi lomi* salmon. *Lomi* means massage in Hawaiian, and *lomi lomi* salmon in its basic form consists of thin salted salmon fillets that have been squished in water by hand to remove some of the salt and break down the fibers. Onions and tomatoes are then added, and the mixture is "massaged" again. The result, served often with poi or by itself as an appetizer, provides one of the great taste treats of Hawaii. To a New Yorker like myself it recalls the finest smoked salmon from Delancey Street, but it is far more tender and juicy.

By the early years of this century, native Hawaiian foods had made their way into most *haole* homes. Frequently they were introduced by the Hawaiian women who had married into families from the mainland. Some *haole* women themselves, faced with the high cost of imported meat and potatoes, turned increasingly to local food products. Out of this trend grew a cooking style known as *hapa haole,* or half *haole,* which soon included taro cakes, poi stews, curries, coconut desserts, foods cooked in the broad leaves of the ti plant—and eventually even the transplanted foods of China and Japan.

One contributor to this gastronomic integration was the unknown Japanese culinary genius who hit upon the idea of adding pork to *ramen,* a Japanese rendition of a Chinese noodle dish. His brainstorm became *saimin,* a richly flavored, uniquely Hawaiian noodle concoction that is today the most popular quick-lunch snack in the islands. The Honolulu baseball team is the only ball club in the United States that buys chopsticks by the gross—for the booming *saimin* stand that does as much business as the hot dog concession.

*Opposite:* The contents of the cart this housewife is unloading at the check-out counter of a Honolulu supermarket illustrate the strongly international character of the state's cuisine. An eclectic offering of imports ranging from Japanese noodles to Battle Creek's corn flakes, and such local products as poi, papayas, rice and coconut syrup emphasize the islands' cultural mix.

Today the cross-culinary blend is complete. At the posh Pacific Club in Honolulu, blue-blooded *haoles* happily sit down every Wednesday to a lunch of poi and taro-leaf *laulau*. Both "chicken long rice" (a Chinese dish containing long, thin, transparent "cellophane noodles") and New England prune cake have somehow worked their way onto the menus of most Hawaiian luaus, while drive-ins and hot dog stands throughout the islands offer teriyaki-burgers; and almost every island housewife uses coconut milk in her sauces, soups and desserts.

The blend manifests itself at parties of every description. Combining a traditional variety of Hawaiian snacks called *pupu* with numerous Asiatic delights, the caterers and hostesses of modern Hawaii have developed a range of cocktail snacks that has become famous throughout the world. At a cocktail party in a mansion at Diamond Head, with a distant view of the surfers on Waikiki, I had an opulent assortment to choose from: cherry tomatoes stuffed with salmon *(Recipe Index);* chunks of roasted pork to be dipped into poi; *cho cho,* bits of grilled steak on bamboo skewers *(Recipe Index);* coconut chips *(Recipe Index);* canned litchis stuffed with cream cheese and chopped ginger; crisply fried wonton for dipping into soy sauce; the steamed Chinese dumplings known as *dim sum;* and Portuguese sausage with bacon.

I came across an even clearer example of the culinary mix, on a more plebeian level, at lunch one day at the Honokaa Club Hotel on the "Big Island" of Hawaii. The hotel is a small, unpretentious establishment in the sleepy little town of Honokaa, near a cattle range on the northern slope of Mauna Kea volcano; its menu includes all the cuisines of Hawaii's eight inhabited islands, but most of the dishes have been altered to suit local tastes. In the middle of the dining room stood a self-service salad cart, and patrons could take their choice from four bowls: Chinese cabbage in a strong vinegar dressing; *tsukemono,* Japanese pickled cucumber and radish; Korean *kimchi* and ordinary American potato salad. What did most of the diners take? A bit of each.

The absence of a native Hawaiian element from the salad tray does not mean that pure Polynesian foods are vanishing in Hawaii; on the contrary, among Hawaiians and *haole* old-timers alike, the best and proper way to celebrate anything is still a luau, the famous Hawaiian feast.

The ancient Hawaiians feasted to celebrate special occasions and to honor and propitiate their gods. Only men could participate in these festivities: the old Polynesian taboos barred women from eating with men and even forbade them to touch men's food or watch their husbands eat. All that has changed in Hawaii, but the male tradition is perpetuated: only men prepare the pig and all the other foods that go into the *imu,* the underground oven. And in other Polynesian islands, like Samoa, the roasting of the pig for a feast is still an event of high protocol in which each guest knows exactly which cut of meat he is entitled to receive, according to his rank and seniority.

To distinguish the modern informal feast from the traditional religious ceremony, Hawaiians took to calling it a luau, which simply means the leaf of the useful taro plant—the same plant whose root is pounded into poi. By extension the word luau came to mean the particular dish cooked with these leaves as well as the feast at which it is eaten. Two taro-leaf dishes, *luau* and *laulau,* still appear at every genuine feast, and the Hawaiians do not seem to be at all confused by eating *luau* and *laulau* at a luau—although nowadays when the party is on a small scale, more and more of them tend to call the occasion a poi supper. In Tahiti, where the Polynesian language survives in a purer state, the leaves are *fafa* and the feast is *tamaaraa,* but *luau* (the dish) by any other name tastes just as good.

From an epicurean standpoint, Hawaii's best luau food can be found at The Willows, a Honolulu garden restaurant beside what once was the private pool of Queen Kamamalu. Giant gold and white carp now inhabit the royal waters, and in addition to the weeping willows that give the restaurant its name, plumeria (frangipani) trees, ginger blossoms, orchids and ferns fringe the flagstone terrace and surround the rambling thatch and bamboo buildings. Over all looms a huge monkeypod tree, its twisting branches casting weird baroque shadows in the glow of colored spotlights. In such a romantic setting one could almost forget about the food—if it were not so good.

For an evening luau celebrating the 80th birthday of a prominent Honolulu businessman, the proprietress of The Willows, Mrs. Kathleen Perry, decked the open-walled banquet pavilion with orchids and plumeria and the fragrant Hawaiian *maile* leaves, which exude a scent of the forest. Early in the afternoon a dressed pig had been stuffed with hot stones and placed in the *imu,* the hole-in-the-ground oven right outside the banquet hall, and as the first guests arrived the nicely browned pork and its delicious aroma were emerging together. Sweet potatoes, too, came out of the *imu* but the other dishes—which in olden days would have been cooked underground with the pig—had been prepared in the kitchen, a break with tradition that no one who tasted the finished products could challenge.

There was first a tender fish steamed in ti leaves, and then a squid, cooked in coconut milk, that seemed to taste like lobster in one bite and chicken white meat in the next. An excellent, juicy *lomi lomi* salmon added zest to the subtle, faintly tangy taste of poi—with which most of the guests ate it.

For me, the two taro-leaf dishes, *laulau* and chicken *luau,* were the high points of the meal. The *laulau* comes to the diner as a fist-sized bundle wrapped in shiny, dark green ti leaves, warm and steamy. Unfolded, it discloses chunks of pork, lightly salted, mixed with chopped taro leaves. The packet has been steamed in a dry oven for five or six hours; the moisture for the cooking comes from the outer ti leaf, which imparts a distinctive, slightly musky aroma to the whole dish. Combined with the mild spinachlike taste of the taro leaf and the rich pork flavor, it adds up to one of the most delicious foods of Polynesia.

The *laulau* is filling, though, and most people would not want to cope with more than one of these hearty packages at a sitting. On the other hand, I could never get enough of *luau,* a light concoction of chopped taro leaves and chunks of chicken or fish, plus—and this is the heart of it—coconut milk. The smooth, creamy Willows version

# For Roasted Pig: Rocks, Steam and Patience, but No Ladies, Please

Steamy with *kalua* (baked) pig and redolent of tradition, any Hawaiian luau, even the debased version supplied on cue by hotels to tourists, is a fairly exalted occasion. In the old times it was more impressive still—a religious ceremony designed to propitiate and honor the gods. Taboos governed the preparation of the food, prayers marked the stages of the feast, and protocol determined who ate what. Women were not allowed to take part, and were even prohibited from eating pork (the main festive food), bananas, coconuts and some kinds of fish. In 1819 King Liholiho ended this discrimination by walking out of a feast and into the women's area, where he pointedly shared their fish and poi. Now, of course, women are welcomed at luaus; but even today at a proper feast the preparations are still a male prerogative. From digging the *imu* (roasting pit) to carving up the carcasses, a luau is strictly man's work.

Once the *imu* has been dug and the fires lit to heat the rocks that will do the cooking, the pigs are readied. First, the cook cleans a carcass thoroughly; then he rubs coarse salt—the only seasoning—all over the pig *(below)*. Then hot rocks are packed inside the pig, and it is placed in a wire basket and lowered onto a layer of banana leaves and stalks *(right)* in the heated *imu*. More leaves go on top, then some more hot stones and finally an insulating pile of earth.

Still in its wire basket, one of the pigs, done to a turn, is ready for serving after five hours in the *imu*.

A considerable variety of side-table delicacies customarily buttresses the main course at a luau. Along with very-well-done *kalua* pig (native Hawaiians prefer to cook it until it literally collapses upon being unwrapped), there may be several kinds of fruit, dishes of steamed shrimp or chicken, leaf-wrapped *laulau* or other cooked-in-the-pit items and, of course, poi. Poi, a starchy, porridgelike preparation of mashed taro root, is altogether as important as the pig itself. At the luau shown on these pages, held at a beach near Hana on the southeastern shore of the island of Maui, the poi was the "one-finger" type, that is, its consistency was thick enough so that a mouthful could be scooped up on one finger *(below left),* thinner preparations of poi require two or three fingers. Native mountain apples *(left)* and tiny fresh-water shrimp *(below)* were also served in the course of the feast as a change of pace from the basic pork and poi.

used chicken which had been stewed separately first, so the three tastes of fowl, coconut and taro leaf survived independently.

It is in the preparation of the *kalua* (baked) pig, the central food of the luau, that Mrs. Perry makes her only significant concession to what might be called *haole* taste. The Hawaiians like their pig not only greasy but so well done that it literally falls apart as it is taken from the *imu;* at The Willows, the pig is uncovered when it can still just be carved, with the skin golden brown and crisp, and it is served up in chunks so tender they can be cut with a fork.

Finally, there was a tidbit of *pipikaula,* jerked beef, and for dessert a sweet, sticky pudding called *haupia,* made of coconut milk and arrowroot. All in all, I felt that Queen Kamamalu herself would have enjoyed the feast at her pool.

Except for the *pipikaula,* the traditional luau dishes can be found in one form or another on nearly every island group in Polynesia; the leaf-wrapped *luau,* in fact, turns up in several remarkably similar guises as far west as Bangkok. Where they all originated is as fascinating an anthropological mystery as the much disputed origins of the Polynesians themselves; but the similarities of island cooking and eating habits —along with resemblances of language, religion and physical characteristics—prove that the peoples of the Pacific, separated by thousands of miles of water, made up a flourishing, more or less unified civilization long before Balboa first glimpsed the mighty ocean.

Civilization is perhaps not the right word for it. The Polynesians lacked metal and apparently had no written language, two elements that generally distinguish a civilization from what is merely a culture. Without metal, unable to boil food in a pot or fry in a pan, they had to invent other cooking techniques, such as poi pounding. In its original Polynesian usage the word poi (or *poe,* as it is spelled in Tahiti) meant not the product but the method of pounding fruits or roots into a pastelike pulp. In Hawaii today the word refers almost exclusively to poi made from taro. In Tahiti and the South Seas, though, *poe* generally means a sweetish dessert made of pounded guavas, papayas, bananas and other fruits. One theory holds that the original Polynesian migrants to Hawaii carried with them their poi pounders and their essential taro and breadfruit and yams, but they did not take, and they did not find in their new home, enough fruits for *poe* making. By the time fruits were introduced centuries later the Hawaiians had mostly forgotten about sweet *poe.*

The purple taro poi of Hawaii is one of the most ridiculed foods in the world—but unjustly so. There is nothing in it but the tuberous root of the taro plant, the most healthful and least fattening of all the world's staple starches. Cooked and peeled, the root is pounded with a little water into a smooth, doughlike mass called *paiai,* which is then thinned with more water to make one-, two-, or three-finger poi. To eat the thick one-finger poi you simply dip a finger into the lavender mass, lift into the air whatever sticks to the finger, twirl it around until you get it under control and then plop it into your mouth. Slightly thinner poi requires two fingers to pick up a mouthful, and so on.

*Opposite:* At The Willows, a famous Honolulu restaurant, a hostess presides over a tableful of Hawaiian specialties. Directly in front of her is a ti-leaf-wrapped packet of *laulau (Recipe Index),* a steamed delicacy of pork chunks mixed with chopped taro leaves. Also laid out among the plumeria (frangipani) blossoms are, from left: a baked yam; *haupia,* a firm coconut pudding; poi; *opihi,* a local shellfish; garnished *lomi lomi* salmon and chicken *luau.*

Poi has been described so often as "artificially colored library paste" or "mashed elephant" that many *malihinis* build up an aversion to the stuff long before they encounter it. But neither the flavor nor aroma of poi could offend the most finicky palate. Fresh poi has virtually no taste; two or three days of fermenting develop a mildly sour flavor that is, to Hawaiians as well as *haoles* who have grown up with it, just plain finger-lickin' good.

Lacking metal pots and pans, the Polynesians also used large leaves as utensils for steaming and for cooking liquid or juicy foods. When wrapped in ti leaves (which can be found in many mainland florist shops) or banana leaves, all manner of foods can be placed directly on a charcoal fire, or in an *imu,* without burning and without losing their juices; the moist, tough leaves insulate the food, and their moisture turns to steam which gently cooks the fish or vegetables within. The method is so effective that even in Indonesia, where cooking techniques are more sophisticated, good cooks frequently steam especially tasty fish in banana leaves over charcoal, to keep the juices and the flavor inside.

Simple as it sounds, leaf cooking has its tricks. The subtle, slightly musky flavor of the ti leaf enhances the taste of fish and meat but mars the clean sweet taste of fruits. Tahitians and Samoans therefore use banana leaves for cooking fruits, including *poe,* and use ti leaves, when available, only for fish. The ti leaf requires little preparation and easily adapts itself to any kind of wrapping: a big bundle tied with string if you are cooking a whole cleaned fish, for example, or a little sack to contain chunks of meat and vegetables. If you manage to get hold of a banana leaf, however, its thick central spine must be carefully removed before any wrapping is attempted, because the spine is too brittle to fold.

I learned a little about leaf wrapping and a good deal more about the Polynesian way with seafood in the Samoan Islands, 2,600 miles southwest of Hawaii. At a village called Aua beneath Rainmaker Mountain on Pago Pago Bay in American Samoa, three high school boys, at the request of their teacher, prepared some traditional Samoan dishes for me. The best of these was *palusami,* a Samoan cousin of Hawaii's *luau,* and for this not two but three kinds of leaves were used. First one young man poured some fresh coconut milk into cupped taro leaves held in his hand. Then this taro-leaf container was carefully folded in a banana leaf, and that in turn was deftly wrapped in a leaf of the breadfruit tree. The final folding of the large, many-fingered breadfruit leaf had to follow a prescribed and artistic pattern, so that the leaf stalk would break just at the point where the stem could be tucked under it to hold the whole packet intact. The wrapping completed—each bundle was a single portion—the packets went onto the glowing coals of an *umu* (as the Samoans called the *imu*), where they cooked for about half an hour. The result, eaten with chunks of roasted breadfruit, was rich and satisfying.

A few days afterward I visited the tiny independent nation of Samoa, where Robert Louis Stevenson lies buried, and observed firsthand just how important leaf cooking remains for many Polynesians. In the water-front market of Apia, the lazy, sun-drenched capital, giant clams and freshly caught squid, squirming crabs and lobsters, bananas in huge bunches and mounds of coconuts, squash and guava all lay scattered higgledy-piggledy, for every vendor seemed to be selling the fruits of both land and sea. But at nearly every stall I saw a pile of leaf-wrapped packets of different shapes and sizes. These contained fish, caught that morning in the lagoon and cooked in leaves in an *umu* by the fishermen's families. The packets sold quickly and cheaply, only a little more expensive than uncooked fish. Some townsmen bought small packets and ate them on the spot—a Samoan quick lunch. Other leaf bundles went into housewives' shopping baskets, obviously the Samoan equivalent of an American frozen dinner.

The market at Apia sticks in my mind because it was there that a big, hearty Samoan planter and businessman named Afoa Fou Vale introduced me to the marine smorgasbord that the Samoans can tuck away every day of their lives. An American on his father's side but a full-fledged Samoan chief on his mother's, Afoa Fou Vale is equally at home in either culture.

As we stood looking down at the lagoon, Afoa Fou Vale told me of the wonders it contained. Four outrigger fishing canoes were spreading nets in the shallow green water, while paddlers of other boats were beating the water to frighten the fish. Farther out a woman was bobbing up and down in the water, obviously searching for something. "She is diving for *se'a*," said the chief. "That's a sea slug . . . a great delicacy." Then, as if to challenge me, he asked, "Would you like to try some of our lagoon foods?" I would. "Let's go," said my host.

We stopped to pick up two of Chief Afoa's cronies and then drove down to the Apia market. It seemed to me that every kind of sea creature must have been represented there, but I was wrong: no *se'a*. Trying to hide his disappointment, the chief supervised the purchase of a dozen other delicacies, and we climbed back into his pickup truck.

Back at the chief's establishment the four of us sat down in a little thatch-roofed *fale,* an open-walled hut, and sipped coconut water from the shell while our host's wife and a bevy of female helpers unwrapped and prepared our purchases. All the foods came to us at once; those that had been cooked in leaves were presented on the opened leaf as if on green flowers, creating the impression that a jungle had suddenly sprouted from the table top.

Out of the leaf flowers came *faiai pusi* and *faiai fae*—eel and octopus in coconut milk—a lightly boiled crab and crayfish tails, which we dipped into a jug of salty coconut-milk sauce. Other shellfish we ate with chunks of taro for bread.

At this point I felt all but sated, but Afoa Fou Vale, still disappointed at not finding *se'a*, wanted to crown our lunch with something special and ordered his wife to bring out some of his precious stock of frozen *palolo,* the caviar of the South Pacific.

*Palolo* represents one of those fascinating mysteries of nature's clockwork, like the swallows that always return to Capistrano. On the first or second night of the last quarter of the moon in late October or early November, billions of the tiny creatures that produce coral reefs float

*Overleaf:* Bite-sized *pupu* are favored appetizers in Hawaii. Shown here, presented on ti leaves, are:

1 Salmon marinated in lime juice and served in cherry tomatoes
2 *Cho cho,* flank steak strips coated with a sweet-sour sauce and broiled on wooden skewers
3 Curry puffs made from shrimp and pork, deep-fried in wonton wrappers
4 Scallops marinated raw in lime juice and served in a sauce that includes sour cream, coconut milk and scallions
5 Tiny drumsticks of meat from chicken wings, deep-fried, served with apricot sauce
6 Deep-fried shrimp, dipped in flour, egg and crumbled Chinese rice-stick noodles
7 *Rumaki,* chicken livers and water chestnuts wrapped in bacon and deep-fried
8 Crab Rangoon, crab meat deep-fried in *wonton* wrappers

1                    2                    3                    4

5　　　　　　　6　　　　　　　7　　　　　　　8

their eggs to the surface—and the Samoans, in carnival mood, go out to gather them. Armed with buckets and nets and cheesecloth and lanterns, they swarm joyously out to the reef, some wading, some in canoes, to scoop up what they consider the finest seafood delicacy of all. Taken ashore, the *palolo* is fried—usually with butter and sometimes with onion—and, traditionally, the entire harvest is consumed in one day-long feast. Then *palolo* is only a memory until the next year.

The deepfreeze, however, has enabled some fortunate Samoans to enjoy *palolo* all year round, and now, though it was April, a saucerful of a shiny, dark green jellylike substance appeared on the table. With the first taste of *palolo* I understood the Samoans' love for it. Certainly it suggested a salty caviar, but with something added, a strong, rich whiff of the mystery and fecundity of the ocean depths. Shamelessly I ate more than my share, averting my eyes from my generous host. After all, I reasoned, he would still be around next October when the *palolo* would rise again.

My obvious appreciation of *palolo,* however, had made Afoa Fou Vale more determined than ever to find me some *se'a.* So two hours later three of us sallied forth to market again—one of the chief's friends having decided he needed a nap more than a second lunch. This time we were luckier. The divers in the lagoon had brought in their midday catch and a new cast of marine characters now lay wet and glistening on the market boards, *se'a* included. Chief Afoa bought a bottle of *se'a,* another containing *fuga,* a similar creature, a mess of small clams, both red and white, one football-sized clam and a few more leaf packages.

For our second lunch of the day we sat indoors, and drank beer. White wine, Afoa Fou Vale explained, may be good with oysters but it is much too pallid to stand up to the strong-tasting seafoods we were about to eat. And strong they were. This installment of the day's fare was addressed to the bold, hearty eater, not the delicate or the timid. The textures were sometimes startling, the tastes strange and compelling. It would be easy, I thought, to recoil from these foods—but just as easy to get hooked on them.

The giant clam seemed best to me. Its meat tasted like the clams I know, but stronger, bright and tingly. Some little red clams, served with soy sauce, offered a pungent flavor, and so did a tiny beach creature called *fole.* There was *limu,* a light green seaweed resembling a cluster of tiny grapes or berries that tasted powerfully of minerals, and the white *fuga,* like a cross between squid and scallop. And finally the *se'a,* Afoa Fou Vale's favorite.

The *se'a* is a small creature of many parts, almost all of them edible, and every one tasting slightly different from the others. Some parts you wrap around the stem of a coconut leaf, dip in soy sauce, and eat like spaghetti; others are best taken with slices of boiled taro to absorb and dilute the intense flavor. And some Samoans eat all of the *se'a* with banana. Most of the parts have that ripe sea taste that I usually associate with sea urchin . . . or with a deep fertile ocean of little light and less movement, of vast nourishing riches stored since ancient times and renewing themselves forever.

No matter how attached they are to seafood, for people all across the Pacific, from Hawaii through Samoa and right up to the limits of the Muslim world, the essential main dish of a feast is pig barbecued in an oven in the ground. Other foods are cooked in an *imu* as well, and in some islands an *imu* may be prepared every day even without a festive pig. But for islanders tired of fish and taro and sweet potatoes, nothing says party like pork.

In Honolulu one evening I watched the preparation of a huge *imu* for a Hawaiian school benefit luau. A dozen men had assembled to roast eight large porkers and a quantity of yams. While they salted the pigs and quaffed beer, wood blazed in a wide, shallow pit. Master *imu*-chef Clarence Hohu waited for the flaming brands to turn to charcoal and explained one of the fine points of his craft: by adjusting the thickness of a layer of banana stalks placed between the hot coals and the pigs, he can precisely adjust the temperature of the oven and determine in advance when the pigs will be done. In this case he was going to cook them all night, for the benefit luau was scheduled for the following day.

One by one the men heaved the salted pigs onto a bed of ti leaves next to the *imu*. A delicious aroma of sizzling meat filled the dusk as skilled hands stuffed the pigs with red-hot lava stones that had been heating in the pit; only well-tempered stones that would not explode inside the carcass could be used. Then the pigs and leaf-wrapped yams went onto the banana stalks in the *imu*, to be covered with ti leaves, burlap sacks and a layer of earth. The next morning everything came out just the way the Hawaiians like it: the pigs retained their shape as the ti leaves were removed but were so well done that as they were transferred into large serving tubs they collapsed into a steamy moist mass of tender delicious pork.

Although he makes his living cooking *kalua* pig for big luaus like this one, Chef Hohu misses the old-fashioned family feasts. His voice gets soft and dreamy as he recalls the way things used to be on his native island of Kauai. "The best size pig is a small one, about 80 pounds, and it doesn't come pre-dressed like these big commercial ones, so you have to roll it on the coals first to burn off the hair and blacken the skin. . . . Nowadays too many people would rather stick in the beer joints, but in the old days all the relatives, all the cousins and the calabash cousins would come to a real family luau. You bring the chicken, another one brings the meat. . . . We all go out to get taro, come back and cook the taro, make the poi. Everybody goes down to fish, we catch the fish and come home, we have our fish and poi. . . . Then we have pig. Everything goes into the *imu*, breadfruit, taro, banana, chicken, dog— anything with the back up toward the sky. . . . You make your own 'swipe,' of course, cut open a pineapple on the vine, put in a little sugar and let it ferment in the sun until it'll give you a kick. Or you go up into the mountain and get ti root, cook it three days and nights in the *imu*, and chew *that* and get drunk. . . . Everybody brings food. One whole week we celebrate. Nobody works. That's what I mean by having a good time."

To make one 10-inch pie

¼ cup cold water
2 teaspoons unflavored gelatin
4 egg yolks
½ cup sugar
½ cup boiling water
5 tablespoons dark rum
1 teaspoon finely grated fresh lemon
    peel
4 egg whites
A pinch of salt
1½ cups finely chopped
    macadamia nuts
A 10-inch short-crust pastry pie
    shell, baked and cooled *(Recipe
    Booklet)*
½ cup heavy cream, chilled
2 tablespoons superfine sugar

### *Macadamia Chiffon Pie* (Hawaii)

Pour ¼ cup of cold water into a heatproof glass measuring cup, sprinkle in the gelatin and let it soften for 2 or 3 minutes. Then set the cup in a skillet of simmering water and stir the gelatin over low heat until it dissolves. Remove the skillet from the heat, but leave the cup in the water to keep the gelatin warm.

With a whisk or rotary or electric beater, beat the egg yolks until well blended. Slowly add ¼ cup of the sugar and continue beating until the yolks are thick enough to fall in a ribbon when the beater is lifted from the bowl. Beating constantly, pour in the boiling water in a thin stream, then pour the mixture into a 1½- to 2-quart enameled or stainless-steel saucepan. Stir over low heat until it thickens into a custard heavy enough to coat the spoon. Do not let the custard come to a boil or it may curdle. Remove the pan from the heat and stir in the dissolved gelatin, then strain the custard through a fine sieve set over a deep bowl and add 3 tablespoons of the rum and the lemon peel. Let the custard cool to room temperature, stirring occasionally to prevent it from setting.

In a separate bowl, beat the egg whites and salt with a clean whisk or beater until they are frothy. Sprinkle in the remaining ¼ cup sugar

In this macadamia chiffon pie, bits of macadamia nuts appear in the filling, in the topping—everywhere but the pie crust. The macadamia tree that bears the nuts shown with the pie is native to Australia and was imported to Hawaii less than 100 years ago; but now almost all commercial production of macadamia nuts is Hawaiian. The nuts are cracked open and the kernels within are roasted in coconut oil before being marketed.

and continue beating until the egg whites form firm peaks. Stir about ¼ of the whites into the custard, then pour it over the remaining egg whites and fold them together with a rubber spatula. Fold in 1¼ cups of the nuts, pour the chiffon mixture into the pie shell and smooth the top with the spatula. Refrigerate the pie until you are ready to serve it.

Just before serving, beat the heavy cream with a wire whisk or rotary or electric beater until it begins to thicken. Add the superfine sugar and the remaining 2 tablespoons of rum; continue beating until the cream is stiff. With a spatula, spread the cream over the pie, swirling it into decorative peaks, if you like. Sprinkle the remaining ¼ cup of nuts over the top.

### Coconut Chips  *(Hawaii)*

Preheat the oven to 325°. With a small, sharp knife slice the coconut into paper-thin chips about 2 inches long. Spread the chips in one layer in a shallow baking pan and sprinkle them with the salt. Stirring occasionally, toast the chips in the middle of the oven for about 30 minutes, or until they are brown and crisp. Cool the chips to room temperature before serving. In a tightly covered jar, the chips may safely be kept for 2 to 3 weeks.

To make about 3 cups

1 fresh coconut (about 1½ pounds) shelled and peeled *(page 61)*
½ teaspoon salt

## Laulau *(Hawaii)*

TI LEAVES FILLED WITH PORK AND CHICKEN

To make 8 *laulaus*

2 pounds fresh young taro leaves or substitute *bok choy* or Swiss chard
½ pound lean salt pork, trimmed of rind and cut into ¼ inch dice
½ pound chicken breasts, boned, skinned, and cut into ½-inch cubes
1½ cups finely chopped scallions, including the green tops
16 fresh ti leaves, each about 16 inches long and 5 inches wide

First prepare the filling: With a cleaver or sharp knife, trim off the wilted leaves and heavy stalks of the taro, *bok choy* or Swiss chard and discard them. Separate the leaves and wash them under cold water. Then slice the leaves into strips ¼ inch wide and 1 inch long.

In a heavy 12-inch skillet, fry the pork over moderate heat, turning the dice about frequently with a slotted spoon until they are crisp and have rendered all their fat. Add the chicken and stir for a minute or so until the cubes are firm and white. Drop in the taro, *bok choy* or chard and, stirring constantly, cook over moderate heat for 2 or 3 minutes until the vegetable strips are limp and evenly coated with the fat. Stir in the scallions and remove the pan from the heat.

Wash the ti leaves in cold water, rubbing them with a cloth or sponge, then drying them gently with paper towels. Following the directions on the opposite page, prepare the *laulau* packages, using about ¾ cup of the filling in each one.

To cook the *laulaus,* place them in several layers in a large colander. Place the colander in a deep pot and pour enough boiling water into the pot to come to just below the bottom of the colander. Bring the water to a boil again over high heat, cover the pot tightly and reduce the heat to low. Steam the *laulaus* for 30 minutes, keeping the water at a slow boil and replenishing it with additional boiling water as it evaporates. With kitchen tongs, transfer the *laulaus* to a heated platter and serve at once. *Laulaus* are traditionally served as part of a luau.

## Lime-marinated Salmon with Tomatoes *(Hawaii)*

To serve 6 as a first course

3 medium-sized firm ripe tomatoes
1½ pounds boned and skinned fresh salmon, preferably a center cut
¾ cup strained fresh lime juice
½ cup finely chopped onions
⅛ teaspoon Tabasco sauce
1 teaspoon sugar
1 tablespoon salt
1½ teaspoons white pepper

First prepare the tomatoes: Drop them into a pan of boiling water and let them boil briskly for about 10 seconds. Run cold water over them and, with a small, sharp knife, slip off their skins. Cut out the stems, then slice the tomatoes in half crosswise. Squeeze the halves gently to remove the seeds and juices. Chop the tomatoes finely.

Lay the salmon flat on its side and, with a large, sharp knife, slice it horizontally into two sections. Holding the knife at a slight angle, cut the sections crosswise into ¼-inch-thick slices. Then lay the slices flat and cut into 1-inch squares.

In a deep ceramic or glass bowl, combine the tomatoes, lime juice, onions, Tabasco, sugar, salt and pepper and stir thoroughly. Add the salmon and turn the pieces about gently with a spoon until they are well moistened. Cover and marinate the salmon in the refrigerator for at least 6 hours, turning the pieces over every hour or so.

To serve, transfer the salmon and its marinade to a chilled deep platter or individual soup plates.

NOTE: Lime-marinated salmon can also be served as a cocktail snack, or *pupu,* in which case the marinade is made without the chopped tomatoes. Instead, the salmon slices are marinated with the other ingredients as directed, and then are rolled up and wedged into hollowed-out chilled cherry tomatoes.

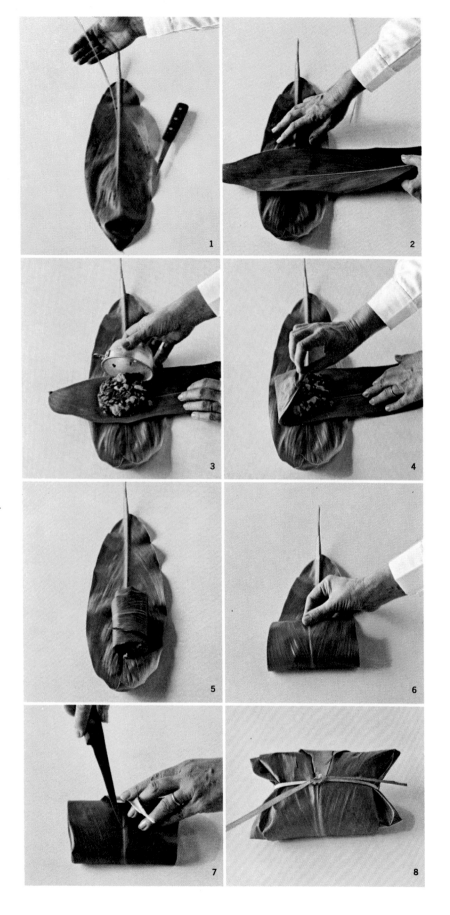

1 The first step in making ti leaf packages for *laulau (opposite)* is to prepare the leaves. Cut off the stems of half the leaves. From each of the other leaves, slice away the stiff underside of the midrib, as shown, and set the long thin pieces aside. Sharpen the remaining portion of each stem to a point.

2 For each package, lay one leaf (without stem) across another (with stem) at right angles.

3 Place ¾ cup of the filling on the top leaf, mounding it about one-third of the way from the tip.

4 Lift the tip of the top leaf and tuck it over and underneath the filling. Then roll this cylinderlike portion up into the rest of the leaf to create a neat package.

5 Place the tightly wrapped cylinder lengthwise on the bottom ti leaf, about one third of the way from the tip.

6 Fold the tip of the bottom leaf over and underneath the cylinder, then roll up the leaf toward the stem end to form a tube.

7 Wrap the stem around the tube, then cut a ¼-inch-wide slit in the leaf and insert the stem in it to hold the *laulau* in shape.

8 Wrap one of the reserved pieces of stem lengthwise around each *laulau* snugly and tie it in a knot.

31

# II

# The Bountiful Feasts of Tahiti

The eat-drink-and-be-merry spirit that Hawaiian oldtimers remember with nostalgia is still alive in such lovely islands of the South Pacific as the tropic Eden called Tahiti. One of the Society Islands group, 2,400 miles south of Hawaii, Tahiti is of middling size (600 square miles), and you can drive around most of its shoreline in a few hours. But the interior is a wilderness of dense foliage and steep mountains, with hidden silvery waterfalls where local maidens like to bathe, just as their great-grandmothers did. The beach road runs through groves of towering coconut palms, past little houses hung with bright red flowers, and beside well-tended vegetable plots. In the shade of the gnarled banyan trees, small, shy children sell bananas, a kind of chestnut and rambutan, a juicy bright red fruit; and near the island's capital, Papeete, the handsome mansions and rambling tourist hotels nestle in small private jungles of greenery.

Long before the first European explorers sailed into Tahiti's lagoons in 1767, the islanders and their neighbors on Moorea and Bora Bora had learned to love to eat and had discovered many appealing ways to cook the exotic foodstuffs that grew in such abundance around them. After the French seized the Society Islands in 1842, the islanders were introduced to the finest Western cuisine and they soon elevated their native cookery to new heights. Today without doubt Tahiti is the culinary capital of Polynesia.

I spent a week in this garden of delights and found myself wishing, as have many men before me, that I could stay much longer. On two par-

A fine morning's catch hangs from a driftwood stake planted on a Tahitian beach. The biggest prize is a brilliantly colored parrot fish, and at left are *tarao,* or rockfish. Those on the right, *iihi,* or red squirrelfish, are about to be cooked and eaten on the spot by the fishermen in the background.

ticular occasions the Tahitians found their way through my stomach to my heart. The first of these adventures began at 6 o'clock on a Sunday morning. There I was, elbowing my way through the already raucous market of Papeete. With me were a popular local saloonkeeper named Max, whose birthday we were getting ready to celebrate, and a few of his friends. Our mission was twofold: to buy the victuals for our breakfast and to purchase our contributions to the Tahitian luau, or *tamaaraa,* that would take place in the afternoon.

The entire population of Tahiti, it seemed, was engaged in similar pursuits. By open-air bus, called "le truck," by pony cart and motorbike Tahitians had come to bring in one kind of produce and take home another. Fresh bonito and other fish hung on long racks and vendors were selling fresh sea urchins in the shell, to be eaten on the spot by those too hungry to wait. I saw many kinds of taro and yams, mounds of grapefruit, and a bonanza of bananas: unripe green ones, reddish-orange plantains, yellow bananas to be eaten raw. There were taro leaves and shell leis, rambutans and tamarinds, a profusion of coconuts, bundles of cooked *poe* wrapped in banana leaves, and palm frond baskets full of tiny shellfish.

Too quickly for me to keep track of what they were buying, Max and his friends made their purchases and we squirmed out of the jostling throng, bearing odd-shaped, fragrant bundles. At Max's water-front establishment, within sight of the gleaming yachts in the harbor, we spread our prizes out upon a table and tucked into a traditional Tahitian Sunday breakfast.

First we ate sections of the large, juicy local grapefruit, which tasted enough like the grapefruit I know at home, to be sure, but had a sweetness more pronounced than a ripe tangerine; I have never had a sweeter citrus fruit. Then came stronger stuff. The murky yellow sea urchin does not ordinarily appear on breakfast tables outside Tahiti, but in this case it was seasoned with lime juice, which somehow spiked the flavor and made it surprisingly good. The best dish of all for anyone who likes cheese and shellfish, as I do, was the mixture of clams with *taioro,* a curdled coconut preparation that resembles a good sour pot cheese. Some *miti hue,* a sort of coconut buttermilk, and some strong black coffee completed the meal.

Thus fortified, we gaily set out for Paea, a village some 10 verdant, flowery miles down the coastal road. There, on the shore of the lagoon, in a grove of breadfruit and banyan trees surrounding a small cottage, a half dozen or so of Max's other friends were already at work preparing the main event of the day. One man had just slaughtered two plump suckling pigs and was cleaning them while another dug out the roasting pit, or *hima'a.* A young man was sorting out breadfruit that he had gathered and someone else was peeling taro. Standing knee-deep in the water of the lagoon, our hostess, the owner of the cottage, was casting a net for small carangid fish, and while I watched she captured a mess of them.

Earlier she had placed chunks of fresh fish in a large calabash, filled with sea water, that she keeps in her kitchen. This was for *fafaru,* a famed and fearsome dish that Tahitians demand at every feast but that Westerners are not likely to miss if it is omitted. The calabash is never emptied, though fresh brine is added as needed, and the odor of this aging broth is something not to be described in a book about food. The brine pickles and tenderizes the fish, bringing out the flavor so dear to Tahitians. The odor of the brine, I was assured, does not transfer itself to the fish; nevertheless I regarded the tightly stoppered gourd with some trepidation.

All through the hot day, with many casual comings and goings and much chatter, the preparations continued. No one seemed to be concerned as the planned time for placing the pigs in the *hima'a* came and went. Invited guests failed to show up and were forgotten, and unexpected visitors were warmly welcomed with beer or glasses of a rum punch Max concocted. At lunch time, to tide us over, our hostess served us fish fillets from a shark that had obligingly run ashore right at that spot early in the morning—the ocean's birthday gift to Max. Sautéed in garlic, salt, pepper and soy sauce, the shark fillets tasted better than a good swordfish steak.

Meanwhile, a mixture of banana and breadfruit simmered quietly in a pot, the first stage in *poe* making. On the beach, coconut husks blazed in the *hima'a,* heating the stones, and the waiting carcasses of the pigs hung from a branch, safe from wandering dogs. The youth in

At the edge of placid Cook's Bay on Tahiti's sister island of Moorea, two pit-cooking experts remove breadfruit from an outdoor oven, or *hima'a,* on the grounds of the Aimeo Hotel. In the giant clamshell in the foreground is *poisson cru,* a favorite dish at such a feast, or *tamaaraa*. The small bowls to the right of that contain fish cooked in coconut milk. The pineapple halves at right are filled with fruit salad; the girl carries *poe,* a dessert made of fruits and arrowroot. Yet to emerge from the *hima'a* is the indispensable suckling pig.

charge of breadfruit peeled and split the yellow globes and in the shade of a tree a pretty, long-legged, long-haired girl who smiled much and said little, grated coconuts.

Finally, the *hima'a* was ready and the tempo of activity quickened. The *hima'a* chef spread the pigs on banana leaves and cut them up, and the long-legged girl appeared with, of all things, a garlic press. Kneeling at the *hima'a* in her colorful *pareu,* or sarong, surrounded by breadfruit, banana leaves and near-naked children, she deftly rubbed garlic juice into the meat and stuck in slivers of garlic as well. This delightful French touch would vastly enhance the flavor of the pork—a fine example of the marriage of colonial and island cooking methods. Salt and a touch of soy sauce were smeared on the meat too.

While the chef covered the hot stones, first with palm fronds and then with banana leaves, other hands wrapped lightly salted fish in banana leaves and took them to the pit. The *poe* from the kitchen pot, now a sticky half-cooked mass, was also enveloped in banana leaves, and so were red and yellow bananas and sweet potatoes. Several people rapidly finished the preparation of the pork *fafa:* taro leaves, coconut milk and chunks from a hind quarter of one of the pigs, all mixed together in a bowl and then apportioned out into more leaf bundles. With thought and care the *hima'a* master arranged the seasoned quarters of suckling pig in the center of the steaming leaves that covered the hot stones in the pit. He put all the bundles and the taro and the peeled breadfruit around the pig, and over all he spread a thick layer of palm fronds, a small canvas covering and a layer of earth. Then he watered down the resulting mound to make it airtight and keep it from smoking.

For the rest of the afternoon there was little to do but swim and drink and sing and gossip and fish for fun. More guests arrived, learned they were early, and wandered away again—to return in good time. A few people napped. Two teenagers strummed on ukeleles, and whenever they paused you could hear in the sudden stillness the pounding of surf on the coral reef hundreds of yards across the lagoon.

Near dusk, the *hima'a* was ready and everyone converged on it as if by signal. Tau Neti, a tall and dignified police detective who is one of Tahiti's leading epicures, had arrived in his Sunday best with his queenly wife, and now he took charge with quiet authority. The moment the palm fronds were pulled away from the pit a delightful mélange of aromas arose from it. Tau insisted that I taste everything hot and fresh from the *hima'a* without waiting for the food to be spread out properly for the others. With my fingers I broke off a sliver of baked breadfruit, golden brown and tasting something like sweet potato. The long-legged girl, who now had a yellow flower in her hair, gave me a dollop of sweet, sticky *poe* as she poured it from the leaf into a pan. The pork, thanks to the sophisticated seasoning, turned out to be excellent, and the *fafa* proved a steaming reprise of the *luau* flavor I remembered from Hawaii.

Within minutes the entire contents of the *hima'a* had been spread out on a large table on a terrace under the trees. A pig's head, well browned, occupied the center; next to it appeared a bowl of *miti hue* and the covered *fafaru* gourd. We served ourselves buffet style, using our fingers, dipping breadfruit and taro into the *miti hue* for flavor, licking lips over the pork, devouring the *fafa*. And then came my moment of truth, my first *fafaru*. With Tau at my elbow, lending encouragement, and with the whole crowd watching, I plucked a piece of fish from the strong-smelling gourd, squeezed and shook it to get rid of most of the brine, smothered it in the *miti hue,* and gulped it down without bothering to savor it as the Tahitians do. I cannot, I confess, describe the taste, but I can testify that a Westerner who eats *fafaru* becomes an instant social success among the Tahitians. The atmosphere changed in a flash, everyone became my friend and all my previous inquisitiveness was forgiven. (And before I left the island, my feat of eating *fafaru* made the front pages of two Papeete papers.) In this new mood of camaraderie I went around the table for second helpings of pork and *fafa,* but by the time I felt brave enough for a second go at *fafaru* the gourd was empty. Obviously all the guests agreed with Tau that *fafaru* is "a most luxurious thing."

Neither my stomach nor my sense of taste went unsatisfied at Max's birthday *tamaaraa.* Nor did my other senses. As we began to eat, the afterglow of a wild sunset hung over the sea, a backdrop to the looming shape of the island of Moorea off in the distance. The aromas of the food slowly melted away, to be replaced by a sweet scent of night blossoms that gradually enveloped the grove. The music, sometimes soft and dreamy, then fast and loud, continued far into the night, accompanied by dancing and laughter and an unspoken suggestion that the party was just beginning and would never end, that somewhere a new *hima'a* waited to be uncovered.

A few days later, on a hillside overlooking the bay where Captain Cook, and later Captain Bligh of the *Bounty,* first dropped anchor in Polynesia, I partook of a Tahitian luncheon that for superb flavor, beauty of presentation and gastronomic satisfaction stood above anything else I found in the Pacific. The setting was the bright, airy home of Nick and Nancy Rutgers, an American couple whose presence in Tahiti is no accident. Nancy Rutgers' father was James Norman Hall, the co-author of *Mutiny on the Bounty,* who lived in Tahiti for 30 years. Nancy was born on the island and has spent most of her life there.

The first time I talked to her about Polynesian foods she began discussing breadfruit, and this I thought was fitting indeed, for had it not been for that easy-to-cultivate starchy fruit the world might never have heard of Captain Bligh, and Nancy Rutgers would not be living in Tahiti. Bligh and H. M. S. *Bounty* had picked up a cargo of a thousand breadfruit trees in Tahiti and were carrying them to Jamaica in the West Indies when Fletcher Christian and his shipmates mutinied; Christian felt Bligh lavished too much time and attention on the breadfruit, and one of the first things he did after setting Bligh afloat in a longboat was to toss the hated trees overboard.

Today, though, as Mrs. Rutgers pointed out, this large ovoid fruit is cherished all through the Pacific not only as a staple but as a delicacy. Stripped of its rough, knobby skin by means of a seashell or coconut

*Overleaf:* Using torches to dazzle the fish so that they are more easily caught, these fishermen work at dusk off the island of Au, near Papeete. Each man's gear consists solely of a homemade trident—a bamboo pole with metal prongs at one end. Plentiful and easy to spear, even in the daytime, fish—in some form—is an essential ingredient of almost every Tahitian meal.

For a party at the home of her daughter, Nancy Rutgers—an American born in Tahiti—Mrs. James Norman Hall prepares a sauce for fried chicken, squeezing fresh turmeric into coconut milk. Mrs. Hall is the widow of *Mutiny on the Bounty's* co-author.

shell (some islanders say breadfruit must never be touched with metal) and baked or boiled, the fibrous flesh of the breadfruit comes out tasting like a campfire potato or a yam. Like bread, it can be eaten with more flavorsome foods. Some of the 40 varieties are mixed with sweeter fruits and pounded into *poe.* When breadfruit *(uru* in Tahitian) begins to feel as soft as a ripe banana and when the green skin starts turning yellow and brown, then it is ripe and sweet enough to be baked as a dessert, with the core pulled out and sugar and butter poured in. In the Marquesas a potent drink called *mei* is extracted from fermented *uru,* and in Hawaii you can buy breadfruit chips, like potato chips, in cellophane bags in the supermarket. The tall, shady breadfruit tree, with its distinctive dark-green fingerlike leaves, produces so much fruit in a season that just one tree is enough to keep the bellies of a large family filled for years.

Nowadays many people boil their breadfruit or cook it in an ordinary oven, but Nancy Rutgers prefers the traditional method. When I arrived for lunch, several breadfruit, still in their skins, were roasting over a charcoal fire just outside the kitchen. When they were done, the charred black skin peeled off easily, leaving the inner flesh softer than breadfruit that has been peeled before baking.

Simultaneously, in the kitchen, a 15-pound suckling pig was coming out of the oven, its skin crisp, crackly and dark brown, and several banana-leaf-wrapped bundles of chicken *fafa* were steaming gently in a pan. Some fresh-water Tahitian shrimp were being removed from a broth of bouillon, onions, celery, salt and pepper. And Nancy and a helper were pouring coconut milk over a huge salad bowl of *poisson cru (Recipe Index),* a princely Polynesian dish that all by itself would make a trip to Tahiti worthwhile.

At heart *poisson cru (e'ia ota* in Tahitian) is a simple dish. Chunks of raw fish, usually tuna, are marinated in salted lime or lemon juice, squeezed out, then soaked and served in coconut milk. The acid juice "cooks" the fish as heat would, and the coconut milk smooths out the raw citrus bite and adds to the tender, meaty tuna a rich, creamy lusciousness that must be tasted to be understood. From island to island, and from cook to cook, the dish varies. In Fiji they call it *kokonda* and add chili. In Samoa it is *oka,* generally made with bonito. In New Caledonia it becomes a salad. Some cooks add a bit of mustard to the coconut milk, and some put onions or garlic in the marinade. The marinating time can range from 10 minutes to several hours.

In Nancy Rutgers' superb Tahitian version the French influence was apparent. She had added onions to the marinade and then had thoroughly mixed the marinated tuna with tomatoes, celery, scallions and hard-boiled egg. This gaily colored mixture was now being covered with coconut milk and garnished with parsley.

While the foods were being brought to the table, Nick Rutgers served us some rum punch and Nancy's mother, Mrs. Lala Hall, reminisced about her late husband's arising at dawn to squeeze the coconut milk for his morning coffee. Then we proceeded to help ourselves from a buffet table on the lawn and settle down to enjoy authentic prim-

40

itive Polynesian dishes that somehow had been raised to the level of sophisticated cuisine.

The tender pork, neither greasy nor dry, tasted better than any other I had in the Pacific—thanks, no doubt, to the combination of garlic, soy sauce and Hawaiian rock salt that had been applied to it before roasting. Nancy's *poisson cru,* light and cool, delivered a smooth, meaty flavor that transcended both fish and coconut milk. The soft and gentle breadfruit chunks we dipped into *miti hue.* The rich flavor of the shrimp was sufficient unto itself, but dipped in *miti hue* it changed into something entirely different.

Best of all was the chicken *fafa,* Tahiti's version of *luau.* For this, Nancy had carefully selected the leaves of Tahiti's wild *fafa* plant, which do not "scratch" as some kinds of taro leaf do. She had sautéed the chicken in butter and oil and basted it with vinegar and lime juice before pouring on the coconut cream and steaming the whole thing in banana leaves. The result was a unique and heavenly flavor, not quite coconut, not quite spinach-taro, and beyond the usual flavor of chicken.

For dessert, Nancy served us baked bananas and a Tahitian sweet *poe (Recipe Index).* As I sat back under the palm trees, stuffed and happy and ready for a siesta, I did manage to reflect contentedly on the fortunate circumstances that allowed Polynesia, France and a superb cook to combine their various gifts in so felicitous a culinary triumph.

Mrs. Rutgers' guests, most of them clad in bright Tahitian prints, help themselves to a buffet meal in her garden. Mrs. Hall, at left, is sampling the *poisson cru (Recipe Index).* Another bowl of this Tahitian raw fish specialty is at the opposite end of the table.

41

To serve 8

½ cup Japanese soy sauce
¼ cup dark brown sugar
2 teaspoons finely chopped garlic
1 teaspoon salt
½ teaspoon freshly ground black
    pepper
A 10- to 12-pound oven-ready
    suckling pig
¼ cup vegetable oil
3 or 4 ti leaves, if available

FRUIT GARNISH
16 canned litchis, drained
8 one-inch-long chunks of ripe
    banana
1 kumquat drained and cut in half
    crosswise, plus 16 whole drained
    kumquats
9 small fresh limes
8 one-inch chunks of fresh
    pineapple
1 fresh *carambola* (star fruit), if
    available, cut crosswise into ¼-
    inch-thick slices

### Roast Suckling Pig *(Tahiti)*

Combine the soy sauce, brown sugar, garlic, salt and pepper in a small bowl and stir them together until the sugar is completely dissolved. Wash the pig under cold running water and pat it completely dry inside and out with paper towels. Rub the soy sauce mixture in the cavity and all over the outside of the pig. Marinate at room temperature for at least 1 hour or in the refrigerator for 2 or 3 hours.

Preheat the oven to 350°. Crumple a sheet of aluminum foil into a ball approximately the same size as a lime and insert it in the pig's mouth to keep it open as the pig roasts. Curl the tail and cover both the tail and the ears of the pig with small squares of foil to prevent them from burning.

Place the pig on a rack set in a large, shallow roasting pan and with a pastry brush spread the vegetable oil evenly over the entire outside surface of the pig. If the head extends beyond the edge of the pan, double a strip of aluminum foil and place it on the rack under the head to catch any drippings.

Roast the pig undisturbed in the middle of the oven for 1½ hours, then remove the foil from the ears and tail and continue roasting for 15 to 20 minutes longer.

To test for doneness, pierce the thickest part of the thigh with the point of a small, sharp knife. The juice that trickles out should be a clear yellow; if the juice is still slightly pink, roast the pig for another 5 to 10 minutes.

To serve, transfer the roast pig to a large heated platter—covered with a layer of fresh ti leaves if you have them. Replace the ball of foil in the pig's mouth with one of the whole fresh limes. Use the kumquat halves to cover the pig's eyes. Let the pig rest at room temperature for about 10 minutes to make carving it easier and to allow time to prepare the garnish.

Meanwhile, thread 8 small, sharp skewers with the tropical fruits. To duplicate exactly the arrangement shown on the opposite page, string one litchi, one banana chunk, one kumquat, one lime, another litchi, another kumquat and a pineapple chunk on each of the skewers, pressing the fruits together tightly.

Insert two of the skewers of fruit into the back of the pig just behind its ears, and arrange the six remaining skewers in sets of three along each side of the body.

If you can find fresh *carambola* (or star fruit), make a ti-leaf collar for the pig and stud it with slices of *carambola*. You may also place another slice of the *carambola* at the base of the pig's tail.

To serve, display the garnished pig to your guests, then remove the skewers to a separate plate, and carve the pig as explained in the directions and illustrations on page 44. Accompany each serving with a skewer of fruit.

Bristling with *banderillas* of fruit, a freshly roasted suckling pig heads splendidly for the table. The skewered pineapple, kumquats, bananas, litchis and limes will contrast with the crisp texture of the pig's skin.

To make one 9-inch-round 2-layer cake

CAKE

10 tablespoons unsalted butter, softened
2 tablespoons plus 2 cups flour
1 cup sugar
5 eggs, lightly beaten
1½ teaspoons double-acting baking powder
¼ teaspoon salt
1 cup fresh coconut milk made from 1 cup coarsely chopped coconut and 1 cup hot water *(page 61)*
1 teaspoon vanilla extract
½ teaspoon finely grated fresh lime peel

FROSTING

1 cup sugar
1 cup water
A 2-inch piece of vanilla bean, or substitute ½ teaspoon vanilla extract
3 egg whites
⅛ teaspoon cream of tartar
¼ cup strained fresh lime juice
1 cup finely grated fresh coconut

## Coconut Cake *(Tahiti)*

Preheat the oven to 350°. With a pastry brush, spread 2 tablespoons of the softened butter evenly over the bottom and sides of two 9-inch layer-cake pans. Sprinkle 2 tablespoons of flour into the pans and tip them from side to side to spread the flour evenly. Then invert the pans and rap them sharply on the bottom to remove any excess flour.

In a deep bowl, cream the remaining 8 tablespoons of butter with the sugar, beating and mashing them against the sides of the bowl with a large spoon until the mixture is light and fluffy. Beating constantly, slowly pour in the eggs in a thin stream and continue to beat until the eggs are completely absorbed.

Sift the remaining 2 cups of flour, the baking powder and salt together and add them to the batter ½ cup at a time, beating well after each addition; add the coconut milk ¼ cup at a time alternately with the flour. Beat in the teaspoon of vanilla and the lime peel.

Pour the batter into the prepared pans and bake in the middle of the oven for ½ hour, or until a cake tester or toothpick inserted in the center comes out clean. Cool the cakes in the pans for about 5 minutes, then turn them out onto wire cake racks to cool completely.

Meanwhile, prepare the frosting in the following way: Combine the sugar, water and the vanilla bean, if you are using one, in a small saucepan and bring to a boil over moderate heat, stirring until the sugar dissolves. Boil briskly, uncovered, without stirring until the syrup thickens and reaches a temperature of 238° on a candy thermometer, or until a few drops spooned into cold water immediately form a soft ball. Remove the pan from the heat and discard the vanilla bean.

With a wire whisk or a rotary or electric beater, beat the egg whites and cream of tartar until they are stiff enough to stand in soft, moist peaks on the beater when it is lifted from the bowl. Beating constantly, slowly pour the syrup in a thin stream into the egg whites. Continue beating for 5 to 10 minutes longer, until the mixture thickens. Let the frosting cool to room temperature. Stir in the lime juice and the

## CARVING A ROAST PIG THE ISLAND WAY

The process may sound tricky if you have never done it, but is really no more difficult than carving a holiday turkey. Here is how, step by step:
1 With a sharp carving knife, cut through the skin crosswise behind the head, down the back, across the rump and inside the hind legs.
2 Peel the crisp skin away from the center cut. You can cut the skin into 1½-inch pieces and serve them, like potato chips, as appetizers.
3 From each side, scrape away and discard the layer of fat underlying the skin, exposing the meat.
4 Cut away the head, hams and forelegs.
5 Separate the halves of the pig by cutting along the backbone; the loins are then available for cutting into single- or double-rib portions; the rest of the meat can be cut into portions of the size you wish.

The most graceful way to do this is in the privacy of your kitchen. But garnish the pig and display it intact to your guests first, if you wish.

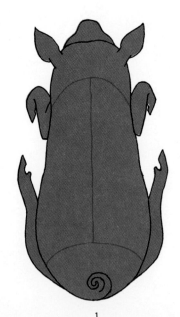

1

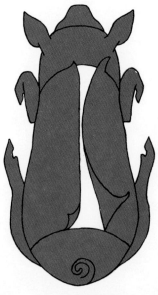

2

½ teaspoon of vanilla extract if you have not used the vanilla bean.

To assemble, place one layer of cake on a serving plate and, with a spatula or knife, spread it evenly with about ½ cup of the frosting. Sprinkle about ¼ cup of the grated coconut over the frosting, then set the second cake layer on top. Spread the top and sides with the remaining frosting and sprinkle them with the rest of the coconut.

### *Poe* *(Tahiti)*
BAKED PURÉED TROPICAL FRUITS

To serve 12

Preheat the oven to 375°. With a pastry brush, spread the softened butter evenly over the bottom and sides of a large, shallow baking dish about 14 inches long, 8 or 9 inches wide and 1½ to 2 inches deep.

If you are using vanilla beans, cut them lengthwise into halves with a small, sharp knife. Then, using the tip of a spoon, scoop out the tiny black seeds and set them aside. There should be about ½ teaspoon of seeds. (Place the pods in a 1-quart jar, fill it with 2 pounds of sugar, and cover tightly. Within 2 or 3 days the sugar will be vanilla-flavored; use it for any dessert purpose you like.)

Put the pineapple, mango, papaya and bananas through the coarsest blade of a meat grinder. Transfer the fruit pulp and its liquid to a sieve set over a deep bowl and stir until all the liquid has drained through. Measure 1 cup of it and combine it with the arrowroot in another bowl. Mix thoroughly. Then stir the arrowroot mixture into the fruit purée and add the remaining liquid, the brown sugar and vanilla seeds (or extract).

Transfer the mixture to the buttered baking dish, spreading it out evenly with a spatula. Bake in the middle of the oven for 1 hour, or until the top is golden brown. Cool to room temperature, cover with plastic wrap and refrigerate for at least 4 hours, or until thoroughly chilled.

Serve the *poe* directly from the baking dish and present the coconut top milk separately in a bowl.

2 tablespoons butter, softened
2 whole vanilla beans, or substitute 1 teaspoon vanilla extract
1 large ripe pineapple (about 4 pounds) stemmed, peeled, quartered, cored and coarsely chopped
1 large ripe mango (about 2 pounds) peeled, seeded and coarsely chopped
2 medium-sized ripe papayas (1 pound each), peeled, cut lengthwise into halves, seeded and coarsely chopped
1½ pound ripe bananas, peeled and coarsely chopped
½ cup arrowroot
1 cup light brown sugar
1 cup rich coconut top milk, chilled *(page 61)*

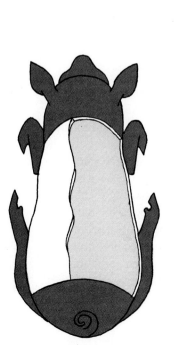

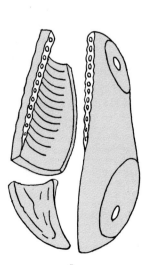

3

4

5

12 fresh ti leaves, each about 16
inches long and 5 inches wide

A 1½- to 2-pound red snapper,
cleaned but with head and tail
left on

1 teaspoon salt

½ teaspoon freshly ground black
pepper

¼ pound lean salt pork, cut
lengthwise into ⅛-inch-thick
slices

1 lemon, cut crosswise into ¼-inch-
thick slices

¼ cup rich coconut top milk (*page
61*)

## Fish in Ti Leaves *(Tahiti)*

Preheat the oven to 350°. Wash the ti leaves in cold water, rubbing
them with a cloth or sponge, and dry them gently with paper towels.

Wash the fish under cold running water and pat it completely dry
with paper towels. With a sharp knife, score the fish by making 5 diagonal slits 2 inches long and ¼ inches deep spaced about ½ inch apart
on each side. Rub the fish inside and out with salt and pepper, meanwhile massaging it gently.

To make a ti leaf envelope for the fish, first remove the stems from
all but one leaf with a cleaver or sharp knife. Trim the stem of the remaining leaf into a point. Place 3 leaves, glossy surface down, crosswise
in a shallow baking dish just large enough to hold the snapper comfortably. Overlap the sides of the leaves to make a layer that completely
covers the bottom of the dish. The ends of the leaves will stick out beyond the sides of the dish.

Then, lengthwise over the bottom row of leaves, lay the 8 remaining trimmed leaves in 2 rows of 4 each, sides overlapping, with the
tips of the 2 rows meeting in the middle of the dish and the stem ends
extending well beyond the ends of the dish. The tips of the leaves should
overlap in the center by about 3 inches.

Put the fish lengthwise in the middle of the dish. Cover it with the
salt pork and arrange the lemon slices over it in a row from head to
tail. Pour in the coconut top milk.

Lift the ends of the bottom (or crosswise) layer of leaves over the
fish, one side at a time, and tuck them snugly around it. Then fold the extending ends of the top layer of leaves back over the fish to enclose it completely. The ends of this top layer of leaves should overlap in the middle
by 2 or 3 inches.

Now carefully slide the 12th leaf under the center of the wrapped
fish. Bring the ends of this leaf around to the top and insert the pointed
stem through the center of the leaf to hold the envelope together.

Bake in the middle of the oven for 40 minutes. To serve, carefully transfer the wrapped fish to a heated platter, cut off the center "tie" and un-
fold the rest of the leaves.

2 small ripe papayas (about 12
ounces each)

½ cup sugar

¼ cup water

1½ cups fresh coconut milk made
from 1½ cups coarsely chopped
coconut and 1½ cups hot water
(*page 61*)

## Baked Papaya Dessert *(Tahiti)*

Preheat the oven to 375°. With a small, sharp knife or swivel-bladed
vegetable parer, peel the papayas. Cut them in half lengthwise and, with
a spoon, scoop out the seeds. Arrange the papayas cut side up in a shallow baking-serving dish large enough to hold them comfortably in one
layer. Sprinkle the fruit with the sugar and pour ¼ cup of water down
the sides of the dish. Bake uncovered in the middle of the oven for 1½
hours, or until the papayas are tender but still intact, basting them every
20 minutes with the syrup that will accumulate in the dish. Raise the
heat to 400° and bake for 5 minutes more until the syrup thickens and
browns to a caramel color. Turn off the heat, pour the coconut milk into
the cavities of the papayas, and let them rest in the oven for 5 minutes
until the milk is warm. Serve at once, or refrigerate and serve chilled.

## Poisson Cru *(Tahiti)*
FISH MARINATED IN LIME JUICE WITH ONIONS

To serve 6

Chill the halibut or fresh tuna steaks briefly in the freezer in order to firm the meat and make it easier to cut, but do not let the fish freeze completely. With a cleaver or large, sharp knife, cut the steaks lengthwise into ¼-inch-thick slices, then cut each slice into pieces 1½ inch square.

In a deep bowl, mix the lime juice, onions and salt together. Drop in the fish and turn it about with a spoon until the strips are evenly coated. Cover and marinate at room temperature for at least 2 hours, or in the refrigerator for 3 to 4 hours, stirring the fish occasionally.

When done, the fish will be opaque and fairly firm, indicating that it is fully "cooked." Taste to make sure; if it seems underdone, marinate the fish for an hour or so longer.

To serve, drain the fish and squeeze it slightly to remove all the excess moisture. Place the fish in a serving bowl, add the tomatoes, scallions, green peppers and hard-cooked eggs and coconut milk and toss them all together gently but thoroughly.

NOTE: The term *poisson cru* literally means raw fish. The recipe itself is similar to the *ceviche* popular in many Latin American countries which "cooks" fish in a marinade of lime or lemon juice seasoned with onions, garlic and hot chilies.

2 pounds skinned, boneless halibut or fresh tuna steaks, cut 1½ inches thick
1 cup strained fresh lime juice
½ cup coarsely chopped onions
2 teaspoons salt
3 medium-sized firm ripe tomatoes, stemmed, peeled and coarsely chopped
½ cup coarsely chopped scallions, including 2 inches of the green tops
¼ cup coarsely chopped sweet green bell peppers
2 hard-cooked eggs, coarsely chopped
1 cup rich coconut top milk, chilled *(page 61)*

*Poisson cru,* offered here in a giant clam shell, is a Tahitian marinated fish salad that retains the cool taste of the sea.

# III

# Coconuts, Friend to Half the World

Using a piece of the husk as a spoon, a young Samoan eats coconut meat that is still in its early jellylike stage. The thin hull that serves as the lining of his bowl is the part that turns brown in coconuts left to mature on the tree. The thick green husk over the hull is removed from coconuts before they are shipped.

Ever since the first European explorers sailed into the South Seas and discovered there a paradise, the graceful, swaying coconut palm has symbolized for Western man all the beauty, languor and exoticism of tropic islands. Today's travelers delight in the region's scenic glories, its mild climate, or perhaps the gentle welcome of the islanders. But what struck the hardheaded sea captains of two centuries ago was nature's generous provision for human needs—the luscious fruits that wanted only to be plucked, the fish that virtually leaped from the lagoons into waiting nets, and the coconuts that dropped like manna into waiting hands. "I thought I was transported into the garden of Eden," wrote the French explorer Louis Bougainville in 1772. "A numerous people there enjoy the blessings which nature flowers liberally down upon them." And an old South Seas proverb makes it clear that the coconut palm was the greatest of these blessings: "He who plants a coconut tree plants food and drink, vessels and clothing, a habitation for himself and a heritage for his children."

And indeed, there is nothing quite like the coconut. No other tree delivers so much to the people of so widespread an area. Coconut is the one essential ingredient in the cooking of all the countries and regions and islands from Hawaii to Bangkok. The Polynesians have no rice; the Muslims do not touch pork; the peoples of each area eat different kinds of fish, fruits, vegetables and spices, and to many of them chicken is a rare luxury. But to all of them the coconut is a necessity of life from which they receive nourishment and gustatory pleasure in many

Only a few feet from his goal, a Sumatran coconut picker completes a nimble climb up a towering trunk. He has tied a piece of cloth around his ankles, like a hobble, and will use this to brace himself when he lets go of the tree with one hand to pick the coconuts. In some parts of Sumatra trained monkeys perform the same task. Held on a leash *(opposite)*, the monkey climbs the tree, uses both hands to twirl a coconut until the stem is weakened, then bites the stem and lets the coconut drop. A monkey can be trained for the job in three months, and gathers about 75 nuts in an average six-hour working day.

forms and through an almost countless variety of dishes and tastes.

As the Southwest Pacific's one dietary constant, the coconut has had a remarkable effect on the area's otherwise dissimilar cuisines: the same coconut-based specialties turn up everywhere. Take, for instance, the dish known in Hawaii as *luau* and in Tahiti as *fafa*—that exquisitely smooth, creamy concoction of taro leaves steamed in coconut milk with chicken or fish. That all Polynesians eat it comes as no surprise, considering their common origins, but I did not expect to encounter *luau* again and again, with only slight variations, in places that have no apparent cultural or historic links with the South Sea Islands. In the Bicol region of the Philippines I discovered *pinangat*, a pork *luau* embellished with ginger, garlic and hot chilies. On my first night in Thailand I was served *hao muk*, which is simply a fish dumpling *luau* made with a tarolike leaf called *bai yaw*, ginger, chili paste and the Thais' special fish sauce *nam pla*. And one night in Jogjakarta, Indonesia, I put a forkful of a local specialty called *buntil* on my tongue and found, to my joy, that this too was fundamentally a *luau*. Although *buntil* is made with beef, which the Polynesians do not use, and supercharged with garlic, onion, salt, sugar, bay leaf and lots of chili, the smooth, creamy, well-remembered *luau* flavor of taro leaf and coconut milk came through unmistakably.

The universality of *luau*-type dishes tells only a tiny part of the coconut story. Americans who think of coconut merely in terms of candy bars or cakes or fluffy pies may find it hard to believe the many uses that coconut serves in the Pacific regions. It provides oil for cooking, a sweet refreshing water for drinking, and a sap that ferments into a liquor so potent that imbibers may wonder—afterward—whether they drank the stuff or were hit on the head by a falling nut. In Tahiti and Samoa I tasted several excellent cheeselike delicacies made of chunks of fermented coconut, and a sweetish biscuit made of flour mixed with grated coconut.

Shredded coconut baked with lots of spices and a little palm sugar goes into the filling of a marvelous stuffed fish dish called *djuku kambu*, one of the ancient traditional foods of the Makasar region of southern Sulawesi in Indonesia. Elsewhere in Indonesia grated coconut is fried and pounded, then mixed with spices to make a sauce for meat, and shredded coconut is sprinkled on fish or meat before baking or steaming. In Bali, grated coconut gets mixed with just about everything—even chopped-up pork entrails in a dish known as *lawar*.

What really brought home to me the universality of the coconut was a scene I witnessed first on the shores of a placid Tahitian lagoon, then in a Javanese dooryard at the edge of the jungle, again in a high-rise apartment house in Singapore and even in a bustling restaurant kitchen in Manila. In all these places I saw cooks picking up handfuls of grated coconut meat and squeezing out the rich, smooth milk that sets the tone of all the cuisines in the Pacific and Southeast Asia. In most of the region, tropic heat and lack of grazing land make dairy farming impractical, and the backyard coconut palm must take the place of the family cow. Coconut milk plays a more important role in every Southeast

Asian kitchen than cow's milk does in America. In some places not a single meal is ever prepared that does not have at least one dish containing coconut milk.

But coconut milk is not—as I in my temperate-zone ignorance once thought—the sweet, clear liquid found in young coconuts. This clear liquid is coconut water, or as some call it, coconut juice; it makes an excellent refreshing drink but it cannot be cooked. Coconut milk is what you get from mixing the grated flesh of the coconut with water and squeezing the liquid from the shreds. The fatty, sweetish extract has the look and feel of milk, can be used like milk in soups, sauces and dough, and behaves like milk in many ways: you have to stir it when boiling, for instance, to keep it from separating. (Conversely, the cooks of Thailand boil coconut milk without stirring, to extract oil for frying.) Sophisticated chefs even distinguish between coconut cream, the rich, thick liquid that comes from squeezing the flesh moistened by a few drops of water, and coconut milk, the thinner variety obtained when more water is added.

It is when coconut reaches this milk stage that its real versatility becomes evident. To begin with, it is the basic liquid for cooking vegetables, meat, fish and fowl. Boiled with palm sugar, it makes a sauce to be poured over fruits. Cooked with starch and butter, it becomes a white sauce for chicken and fish dishes. It finds its way into puddings, with arrowroot or cassava starch. In Indonesia the most popular refreshing drink is *tjendol,* coconut milk with different kinds of sweet-bean paste chunks. The best and most popular Balinese *saté* (barbecued meat) consists of chopped turtle meat mixed with coconut milk and spices and grilled over charcoal. Coconut milk can be whipped for icing on Western-style cakes, added to cream soups, used instead of water for steaming rice or fish and drunk with coffee. Most important of all, it is the smooth, mellow coconut milk that blends and holds the chilies and spices of Hawaiian, Thai and Vietnamese curries and the various *gulai* of Indonesia.

As if all this coconut virtuosity were not enough, the coconut tree also produces a vegetable, palmetto cabbage. This firm, greenish inner core atop the trunk, from which the leaves and nut clusters grow, is also known as heart of palm—cutting it out kills the tree. Appreciated more for its crisp texture than for its flavor, heart of palm tastes and feels something like a cross between white asparagus and bamboo shoots, and can be cooked like any vegetable. Filipinos, and some Indonesians, slice it into pencil-thin pieces to put into the dish they call *lumpia,* a version of the Chinese egg roll.

No one is certain whether the versatile coconut originated in Malaya or the Caribbean, but one reason for its appearance on widely scattered islands and continents is clear: coconuts float, and eons ago oceanic currents carried them around the globe and washed them up on beaches everywhere. Wherever the climate was warm and the rainfall adequate (the tree needs up to 70 inches of rainfall a year in order to bear fruit), the coconut palm took root and flourished, gracefully decorating tropic islands and beaches long before the arrival of man.

 *Continued on page 56*

Safe from any but the most agile predators, green coconuts cluster in bunches just beneath the crown of a lofty palm.

## *Food and Drink from a Lordly Tree*

The coconut palm, which grows in abundance in most tropical regions, is the principal source of food in the Pacific islands. Many of the world's coconut palms are "volunteers"—trees that have grown from seeds washed ashore by tides and ocean currents. But in the South Pacific, coconut groves are carefully planted and cultivated. Seeds of superior quality are selected and planted about 50 feet apart. Cultivated trees mature in seven years and grow larger than the volunteers, reaching heights of 80 to 100 feet, and yield nuts of a better quality for as long as 75 years. Every 28 days a flower spike emerges from the top of the tree and each spike bears five or six coconuts. It takes a year for them to reach maturity, at which point the brown hard-shelled nut within the fibrous husk is four or five inches in diameter, full of sweet liquid and hard, white flesh.

Six months after a coconut has begun to form, its meat starts to develop. At this early stage, the inside is jellylike and is a popular delicacy, sometimes called "spoon coconut" because it is so soft. The outer husk of the coconut is removed by striking it against a wooden stake driven into the ground *(below)*. The husked green coconut at right, with its top removed, does not have the ripe nut's dark brown shell, familiar to grocery buyers throughout the world. (Immature coconuts are not shipped.) No spoon is needed to eat the coconut from the shallow lid, as one consumer *(below right)* demonstrates.

Working out in the sunshine, a Samoan woman grates ripe coconut to be used in making coconut milk. Her grater is a metal blade with a rounded, saw-toothed outer edge, built into the bench she sits on.

Coir, the fiber from the husk of the coconut, is moistened and wrapped around the grated coconut (*above left*). It is then squeezed and twisted (*above*), just as wet clothes are wrung out, to extract the milk. Coconut milk has many of the properties of cow's or goat's milk, with fat that is more like butterfat than other vegetable fats are. In the Pacific and Southeast Asia coconut milk is used in everything from soups to desserts.

As early as the Sixth Century A.D. Egyptian merchants had discovered the coconut for the Western world along the shores of the Indian Ocean. It is not known what they thought of this large object of many layers, with its fibrous husk, hard brown shell, sweet white meat and, at the center, the even sweeter fluid. Marco Polo rediscovered the coconut on his Asian journeys seven centuries later; but not until the Spanish and Portuguese explored the Orient did what had been called the "nut of India" get its Western name: the three black spots at the end of the shell resemble the eyes and mouth of a comic face—a clown, or *coco* in Spanish and Portuguese.

Long before this, of course, the natives of Asia and the South Pacific had learned what the clown could do, and what could be done with it. They had figured out how to use the hard shell of one coconut to grate the flesh of another, and had invented an efficient method of attaching this grater to a saddle contraption that the cook sat astride while shredding the sweet meat. They had become amazingly adept at splitting open a coconut husk with one blow by striking it on a pointed stake set in the ground, and had found that the neat way to crack the inner shell into two halves without crumbling it into small pieces is to strike it with a stone along the dark line that runs between the two "eyes" of the clown's face.

They had also learned that while the ripe coconut that falls freely to the ground like an unexpected gift contains meat that is hard and nearly dry, the immature coconut provides sweet water good to drink and soft flesh that can be eaten directly—and so they learned how to pick the nuts before nature was ready to bestow them. There is scarcely an able-bodied man throughout the Pacific islands who cannot—or could not, in his youth—shinny up the impressive height of a coconut palm (they grow up to 100 feet tall) to cut off a green or yellowing nut. Samoans and some other islanders wrap their feet in a special sticky bark bandage to enable them to run up the curving tree trunks like monkeys. In Sumatra, where roads run for miles and miles through dim forests of tall coconut palms, trained monkeys actually do the dangerous job.

But manifestly it was a man, not a monkey, who discovered one day that the sap of a coconut tree could be turned into alcohol. Cut off the end of a palm blossom, let the sap drip into an empty coconut shell to ferment in the sun for a couple of days, and you get a heady wine called toddy in Micronesia, *tuba* in the Philippines—and a powerful drink in anyone's language. In the Gilbert Islands full-time toddy-tappers rig a network of bamboo poles from treetop to treetop and stay aloft all day, tending their dripping blossoms and cutting off sticky accumulations to let the sap run free (presumably abstaining from the stuff themselves until they get safely down to the ground).

Along with techniques of eating and drinking coconut, the people of the region developed complicated rules and traditions governing the growing and handling of their most important food. In Bali, Indonesia, women are theoretically prohibited from touching the coconut tree —although there seems to be no objection to their carrying huge bundles of coconuts on their heads.

Thailand, however, has no such bias. There upper-class tradition holds that coconut should be the first solid food to pass the lips of any baby, whether boy or girl. At the age of one month the Thai child undergoes a kind of baptismal ritual: The infant is bathed in water containing a coconut and then a Brahmin priest, chanting blessings, ceremonially feeds him three spoonfuls of soft young coconut meat.

It is on the remote and peaceful islands of Samoa that the uses of the coconut are broadest, and the conventions surrounding it the most complex. Samoans eat coconut at every meal: a thick, starchy soup of coconut and meat for breakfast, numerous combinations of coconut cream with breadfruit, pineapple, banana, fish and tapioca starch for their main meals, and a sweet biscuit of coconut, papaya and flour at almost any time. In American Samoa, where the steep, rugged terrain makes farming difficult, the coconut has always been protected by an elaborate set of customs and *tapui,* or taboos. A passerby must never pick up a coconut lying by the side of the road, since the fruit of every tree is strictly accounted for.

Traditionally the best way to stop someone from stealing your coconuts is to put up *tapui,* symbolic "No Trespassing" signs. And woe to anyone who disregards these warnings. A woven coconut-frond *tapui* in the shape of a platter will bring down lightning on the head of an unlawful intruder. A little basket of woven fronds, containing a bottle of medicine or a charm, will afflict a thief with an awful malady —about which he can do nothing unless he knows which medicine man concocted the charm; if he does know he may appeal to this practitioner for relief, but by doing so he confesses guilt and the medicine man will withhold any treatment until restitution has been made to the owner of the trees.

In the Philippine Islands, which produce and export more coconut oil than any other country, such effective law-enforcement procedures apparently were never worked out. Instead, in Laguna province rival factions of workers used to wage war over the possession of coconut oil or *latik,* as they called it; they no longer fight, but their battles live on in a forceful, spirited folk dance, *magla-latik,* in which teams of male dancers "attack" each other, beating out a rhythmic clickety-clack tattoo with coconut half shells that are strapped to their hands, chests, backs, thighs and knees.

The Pacific islander who refreshes himself with coconut water, gets drunk on blossom toddy and blissfully downs the myriad dishes based on coconut meat and milk is also likely to wear some coconut palm clothing, live in a house built with coconut timber or roofed with coconut fronds, burn coconut husks or shells for fuel, and fish, eat, cook, play games, make music, sweep floors and pave roads with various parts of the coconut tree. Throughout the islands and, to a lesser but still considerable extent, in Southeast Asia, I came again and again upon evidence that it is not only food that makes the coconut tree indispensable.

Flickering coconut oil lamps illuminate the dining pavilion of a prince's palace in Bali; a coconut leaf makes a natural sieve to strain the sago flour that is the vital staple of the Moluccan Islands; elsewhere the tough fiber of the coconut husk is used to make rope. At one point on my journey—in Java, I think it was—I passed three women sitting by the road beside a mound of young coconuts they were offering for sale. They squatted on a mat woven of coconut fronds, in the shade of a coconut grove, and two of them wore hats woven from the thin center spine of the young coconut leaf. The hair of the youngest shone sleekly—coconut oil. Next to them, their lunch: steamed glutinous rice wrapped in coconut leaves. Their hands worked busily, weaving baskets of coconut fronds.

From the air, flying over the Pacific islands, I saw coconuts along every beach; on the coral atolls no other vegetation is visible. Over Indonesia, Thailand, and parts of the Philippines, the light green expanses of riceland are studded with darker patches of coconut palms clustered around each village. Flying over Cambodia when the mighty Mekong River was high, I saw the flooded ricelands, shimmering, flat and unobstructed, stretching away from the riverbank for miles. Coming in for a landing in western Samoa, my plane dropped low over a dense carpet of coconut trees stretching from sea to mountain. Coconut is this island's biggest crop and—as it is for many lands of the region—the major earner of foreign exchange. "We eat about one third of the coconut we grow," my friend Afoa Fou Vale told me. "We export about one third as copra, and the beetles get the rest." (And what do Samoans do about the beetles? They construct an ingenious beetle trap out of part of a coconut trunk.)

Copra is the dried meat of the coconut, and uncounted thousands of Pacific families derive their only cash income from it. In the Philippines copra is known as the "lazy man's crop," for all a farmer has to do is split open the coconut when it falls and let the meat dry in the sun. Commercial companies turn copra into coconut oil, the primary cooking fat for most of the region's peoples, especially the Muslims, whose religion forbids the use of pork fat. Coconut oil also goes into the manufacture of soaps, perfumes, face creams, hair dressing—and nitroglycerin for explosives.

If copra growing is a lazy man's occupation, the preparation of coconut milk is not. It must be done daily (because raw coconut milk does not keep unless frozen) and it requires strong fingers and wrists. The cook cups the half shell of the nut in both hands and scrapes it over a grater. This is relatively easy; the hard part begins when enough gratings have been collected in a pan or bowl. From here on the procedures vary according to location, and depending on whether coconut cream or coconut milk is desired. Most Pacific islanders take a skein of the tough-fibered coir from the coconut husk (it looks like the excelsior Americans use for packing), stir it around in the gratings until it has picked up many of the particles, and then wring it out by hand as you would a piece of wet laundry. Another common method, for those whose hands are too tender for coconut coir, is to wring it out in cheesecloth. In either case a small amount of water may be added as a starter before the squeezing begins, without appreciably diluting the coconut cream. When the cook has wrung out all the cream that he can, he adds water to the residue of the shreds and goes through the squeezing process again to make coconut milk.

In most kitchens throughout this part of the world the distinction between coconut milk and coconut cream is sufficiently precise for all practical purposes. But the sophisticated cooking of Indonesia requires even finer classification. According to Madame S. Supit, one of Indonesia's finest cooks, there are no less than five distinct types of coconut milk. Madame Supit generally makes coconut milk with water and lets all the squeezings come together in one bowl, pressing the shreds over and over again with the liquid already obtained. Then she strains it and boils it briefly, after which a rich cream will rise to the top. This, says Madame Supit, is the best coconut cream. She skims it off with a spoon and uses it for baked fish cakes and special dishes. The liquid left when the cream is skimmed off is a thin coconut milk used for cooking vegetables and some puddings.

To cook *rendang (Recipe Index),* a Sumatran specialty of beef simmered in coconut milk, and *opor ajam (Recipe Index),* a chicken and coconut dish, and some other Indonesian delicacies, Madame Supit requires a third type of coconut milk. For this she presses out the coconut with water, as usual, but takes only the first squeezing and does *not* boil it. The fourth type of milk consists of all the pressings except that first one, mixed together; this is a common, economical and acceptable coconut milk, but one that Madame Supit herself eschews. And finally, in ordinary restaurants and the homes of the poor, one finds a cheap, thin coconut milk, the last drops of liquid that can be pressed from the coconut; by this time it is mostly water.

To make their own fresh coconut milk or cream, some modern Hawaiian cooks do not even bother to grate the coconut first. They put chunks of coconut meat, with the shell still attached, into a low oven for 20 minutes or so. The meat will shrink away from the shell and the white chunks can then go into a blender, with a little water or perhaps some cow's milk. The result, after straining, can then be boiled and skimmed for cream. Where no fresh coconut is available, according to Mrs. Perry of Hawaii's Willows restaurant, a passable coconut milk can be obtained by letting dried, shredded coconut soak in warm cow's milk for about 15 minutes and then squeezing it out through cheesecloth or a sieve. An even easier solution is the canned, frozen coconut milk that is available in Hawaiian and West Coast markets and is gradually becoming available elsewhere.

Half a world and a thousand subtle taste distinctions lie between Mrs. Perry's smooth, mild Hawaiian curry and the hot, pungent curries of Thailand. But these two basic curries have one thing in common with each other and with the chili-hot *gulai* and *rendang* and *kalio* of Indonesia. It is the presence of coconut milk or cream, a presence that blends and civilizes the most fiery, most pungent collections of spices and chilies into velvety rich, cosmopolitian flavors that somehow add up to much more than the sum of their parts. For a tree that can also charm the eye, befuddle the brain and provide the means to trap beetles, that is no mean achievement.

## *How to Buy, Open and Prepare a Coconut*

Before buying a coconut, shake it to make sure it contains liquid; the more there is, the fresher the coconut. Coconuts without liquid, or those with moldy or wet "eyes," are likely to be spoiled.

Coconuts may range from 1 to as much as 3 pounds; an average one weighs about 1½ pounds and will yield from 3 to 4 cups of chopped or grated meat.

TO OPEN THE COCONUT : Puncture 2 of the 3 eyes of the coconut by hammering the sharp tip of an ice pick or screwdriver through them. Drain the coconut water into a cup if you wish to save it. Coconut water is rarely used for cooking but may be served as a beverage.

Open the coconut as explained at right. The tapping on the shell with the cleaver in the opening process should have loosened the meat inside so that it falls away from the shell in large sections. If not, rap the shell of each piece again and cut the meat out with a knife.

TO GRATE COCONUT : With a swivel-type peeler or small, sharp knife, pare the brown skin. Then grate the meat, piece by piece, with a hand grater.

TO MAKE COCONUT MILK : Pare the brown skin and chop or break the meat into small chunks. Measure the meat required by the particular recipe and drop it into the jar of an electric blender. Add an equal number of cups of hot (not boiling) water and blend at high speed for 1 minute. Stop the machine and scrape down the sides of the jar with a rubber spatula. Then blend again until the coconut is reduced to a thick, fibrous liquid. To make the coconut milk by hand, you begin by grating the peeled coconut, piece by piece, into a bowl, then measuring the meat and stirring into it an equal amount of hot (not boiling) water.

Then proceed as follows: Scrape the entire contents of the blender jar or the bowl into a fine sieve lined with a double thickness of dampened cheesecloth and set over a deep bowl. With a wooden spoon, press down hard on the coconut to extract as much liquid as possible. Bring the ends of the cheesecloth together to enclose the pulp and wring the ends vigorously to squeeze out the remaining liquid. Discard the pulp. One cup of coarsely chopped coconut meat combined with one cup of hot water should produce one cup of coconut milk. (In the Pacific the grated coconut is often squeezed with only a few drops of water added, which produces a thicker "cream" as described in Chapter 3.)

For recipes that specify rich coconut top milk, let the milk stand at room temperature or in the refrigerator for an hour or so until the liquid separates and the richest part rises to the surface. Skim off this top milk with a large spoon. If you do not want to use the top milk separately, stir the liquid well before cooking with it. Tightly covered and refrigerated, coconut milk can be safely kept for about 5 days.

Smashing a coconut open with a rock is a messy business in the kitchen, but the nut can be opened neatly by the application of pressure in the right place. After draining the water by punching holes through the "eyes," hold the coconut as shown, and with the back of a cleaver give the shell a sharp blow a little more than a third of the way down from the top. Turn the coconut an inch or two and tap again, and keep on turning and tapping until you hear a noticeably different sound—the sound of the shell cracking. A thin but visible crack should run all around the shell at that point and the top of the nut can be pried up quite easily. The first time you try this you may have trouble finding the shell's "fault line," but keep trying; it really works.

Indonesian *urab* combines cabbage, spinach, beans and bean sprouts in an unusual salad that has a coconut dressing enlivened by chilies, lime, tamarind *(in white bowl)* and *trassi,* or shrimp paste *(in glass jar).*

To serve 6

½ pound fresh bean sprouts, washed and husks removed, or 2 cups drained canned bean sprouts
2 cups finely shredded green cabbage
½ pound fresh spinach, coarsely chopped
½ pound yard beans or fresh green string beans, trimmed, washed and cut into 1-inch lengths
5 tablespoons tamarind water *(opposite)*
4 teaspoons *sambal ulek (below)*
½ teaspoon *trassi* (shrimp paste, *see Glossary*)
½ teaspoon crushed *kentjur (see Glossary)*
2 teaspoons salt
1 coconut, shelled, peeled and coarsely grated *(page 61)*


To make about ½ cup

½ cup finely chopped fresh hot chilies *(caution: see page 69)*
2 tablespoons fresh lime juice
1 teaspoon *trassi* (shrimp paste, *see Glossary*)
½ teaspoon salt
¼ teaspoon finely grated fresh lime peel


To make about 4 cups

2 tablespoons ground coriander
1 tablespoon sugar
2 *salam* leaves *(see Glossary)*
¼ teaspoon *trassi* (shrimp paste, *see Glossary*)
½ teaspoon turmeric
⅛ teaspoon ground cumin
1 teaspoon salt
¼ teaspoon white pepper
¼ cup tamarind water *(opposite)*
¼ cup vegetable oil
1 coconut, shelled, peeled and finely grated *(page 61)*

## *Urab (Indonesia)*
### VEGETABLE SALAD WITH SPICED COCONUT DRESSING

Following the directions on page 71, steam the four fresh vegetables one at a time until they are tender but still somewhat resistant to the bite. The bean sprouts and cabbage will each need to cook for 12 to 15 minutes, the spinach for about 10 and the yard or string beans for about 30 minutes. As they are cooked, transfer the vegetables to a large serving bowl and set them aside to cool to room temperature. (Canned bean sprouts do not require any cooking.)

Meanwhile, prepare the coconut dressing in the following fashion: Combine the tamarind water, *sambal ulek, trassi, kentjur* and salt in a deep bowl and stir vigorously with a spoon until the ingredients are well mixed. Drop in the coconut and toss it about with the spoon until it has absorbed the tamarind mixture. Taste for seasoning.

To assemble the salad, add the dressing to the vegetables and mix them gently but thoroughly together. Serve the salad at room temperature or refrigerate it for an hour or so and serve it chilled.


## *Sambal Ulek (Indonesia)*
### HOT CHILI AND LIME CONDIMENT

Combine the chilies, lime juice, *trassi* and salt in the jar of an electric blender and blend at high speed for 10 or 15 seconds. Turn off the machine and scrape down the sides of the jar with a rubber spatula. Then blend again until the chilies are completely pulverized. Transfer the entire contents of the jar to a small bowl and stir in the lime peel. Cover with foil or plastic wrap and refrigerate until ready to use.

*Sambal ulek* serves as a seasoning in *urab (above)* and may also be used as a condiment with meats and poultry. It may be safely kept, covered and chilled, for 1 week.


## *Serundeng (Indonesia)*
### TOASTED SPICED COCONUT

Preheat the oven to 400°. Combine the coriander, sugar, *salam* leaves, *trassi,* turmeric, cumin, salt and white pepper in a small bowl and mix well, pressing down hard on the *trassi* with the back of a spoon to mash it to a paste. Stir in the tamarind water and oil. Then add the coconut and toss it vigorously about with a spoon until it has absorbed the spice mixture.

Spread the coconut evenly in a large jelly-roll pan or shallow baking dish and, stirring occasionally, toast it in the middle of the oven for about 45 minutes, or until it is golden brown and crisp. Taste and add more salt if necessary. Remove the pan from the oven and discard the *salam* leaves.

Let the *serundeng* cool to room temperature and serve it from a bowl or platter. It is a traditional accompaniment to *nasi kuning lengkap (Recipe Index).*

NOTE: To make *serundeng katjang,* stir ½ cup shelled unsalted peanuts into the coconut mixture before toasting it.

## Tamarind Water

Place the tamarind pulp in a small bowl and pour the boiling water over it. Stirring and mashing it occasionally with a spoon, let the tamarind soak for about 1 hour, or until the pulp separates and dissolves in the water.

Rub the tamarind through a fine sieve set over a bowl, pressing down hard with the back of a spoon before discarding the seeds and fibers. Cover tightly and refrigerate until ready to use. Tamarind water can be kept safely for a week or so.

*To make about 1 cup*

2 ounces dried tamarind pulp *(see Glossary)*
1 cup boiling water

## Onde-onde *(Indonesia)*
POACHED SWEET RICE-FLOUR BALLS COATED WITH COCONUT

Combine 1⅓ cups of the sweet rice flour, the coconut milk and ⅛ teaspoon salt in a deep bowl, and stir together until the mixture becomes a smooth, thick paste.

To shape each *onde-onde*, scoop up about 2 tablespoons of the paste and, between the palms of your hands, roll it into a ball about 1½ inches in diameter.

With your thumb or the handle of a small spoon, make a 1-inch depression in the center of the ball and fill it with ½ teaspoon of the brown sugar. Pinch and pat the openings together firmly to enclose the sugar completely.

As each ball is formed roll it in the remaining ⅓ cup of sweet rice flour and set aside on wax paper or a plate. Place the shredded coconut in a shallow bowl and stir into it a pinch of salt.

In a heavy 4- to 5-quart saucepan bring 3 quarts of water to a boil over high heat. Drop in the balls and stir them gently with a spoon to prevent them from sticking to one another or the bottom of the pot. Poach the balls over medium heat for 5 to 6 minutes, or until they rise to the surface. With a slotted spoon, transfer the balls one at a time to paper towels to drain. While they are still warm, roll the balls in the shredded coconut.

Cool the *onde-onde* to room temperature and serve them arranged attractively on a plate.

*To make about twelve 1½-inch balls*

1⅔ cups sweet rice flour *(see Glossary)*
¾ cup fresh coconut milk made from ¾ cup peeled, chopped coconut and ¾ cup hot water *(page 61)*
⅛ teaspoon salt plus a pinch of salt
2 tablespoons dark-brown sugar
2 cups finely shredded fresh coconut

Indonesia's *onde-onde,* delectable yet easily made sweetmeats, have brown-sugar cores and are coated with coconut.

# IV

# Indonesian Tour: From Hot to Sweet

Ancient kingdoms and a food from the New World meet in this scene in Central Java. The temple, at Prambanan, was built in the 10th Century to honor Siva, a Hindu deity. Corn came from the Americas centuries later via Europe. Now, more corn than ever is being grown to provide a more varied diet for Indonesia's rice-loving millions.

Java, Bali, Krakatoa—the very names conjure up visions. The Spice Islands, Sumatra, Borneo—most of us in the West have only a vague idea of where they are, but we have a feeling we know what we would find there: sensuous Balinese dancers . . . Sinbad the Sailor . . . the South Sea Bubble (or was it a bauble?) . . . the Spirit of Bandung. Out of forgotten history lessons, half-remembered romantic poems, the stories of Joseph Conrad and yesterday's headlines emerges a jumble of images adding up to our confused impression of what is the sixth most populous nation on earth, the world's biggest collection of islands, a lush, richly endowed equatorial region often on the brink of economic collapse—Indonesia.

If we are vague about Indonesia it is nobody's fault. It was only a few decades ago, in the struggle against Dutch colonialism, that the Indonesians themselves developed any sense of nationhood, and began to shape a national language out of the ancient Malay tongue. Even today, a generation after they wrested their independence from Holland in a bitter, bloody war, they are separated from one another by such great cultural differences and divided by such a lack of internal communication and transportation that in social customs, language—and even food—the people of some regions have more in common with nearby countries like Malaysia or the Philippines than with their fellow Indonesians on remote islands of their archipelago.

The distances are immense, and the contrasts startling. Straddling the equator between Australia and the Asian mainland, the 7,900 islands of Indonesia—the East Indies—stretch for more than 3,000 miles. Within this span lie hundreds of tiny coral atolls, thick uninhabited jungle, and three of the world's biggest islands; one island, Java, is the most densely populated region of its size on earth. The East Indies were what Columbus was looking for when he discovered America, and their natural treasure, systematically exploited by the Dutch for three centuries, financed the prosperity of modern Holland.

To understand Indonesia and its complex cuisine of strange and wondrous dishes it is necessary to dispel a few misconceptions. The first is that the Portuguese and Dutch explorers, when they arrived in the East Indies in the 16th Century, discovered there a simple, uncivilized people isolated from the outside world. Actually, long before then, the East Indies teemed with the competition of commerce, the conflicts of religions, the rise and fall of kings. Art and music flourished; complicated dance-dramas and written histories celebrated the feats of men and gods; elaborate rituals of food and dress and etiquette—many of which survive today—had been raised to a sophisticated level. Huge stone monuments, which could not have been constructed without great organizational skill and the tight discipline of thousands of workers, rose majestically in the fertile plains of Central Java; and ships from China, India and Arabia rubbed hulls with native proas in dozens of ports around the Java Sea, the Mediterranean of the Orient. What this polyglot, cosmopolitan area of many domains lacked in cohesiveness it more than made up for with a network of trade and cultural and religious links to every part of Asia. "Java," wrote Marco Polo in the 13th Century, "is a very rich island, producing . . . all the precious spices that can be found in the world. It is visited by great numbers of ships and merchants who buy a great range of merchandise, reaping handsome profits and rich returns. The quantity of treasure in the island is beyond all computation."

Nor had this civilization decayed when a Portuguese fleet reached the Malacca Strait, gateway to the Indies, in 1511. The Portuguese were tracing the spice routes eastward, seeking the source of the lucrative trade that canny Arab merchants had concealed from their European customers for centuries. To gain a foothold in this trade, and to control it as the Dutch eventually managed to do, took much more than merely dazzling a few innocent native chieftains with trinkets or frightening them with a show of naval gunfire. The Europeans had to use brute force, political skill and old-fashioned duplicity to subdue the rulers and displace the merchants.

The shifting forces of trade, religion and conquest that swept over the East Indies for two millennia left behind a jigsaw of exciting and sophisticated cuisines. Even on Java, the heart of Indonesia, several distinct styles of cooking can be found. The West Javanese like their vegetables raw and their meats and fish lightly and simply cooked—often in banana leaves—and they tend to add their spices after cooking. In Central Java, almost every dish that calls for chili and spices (which means most of them) also demands a generous amount of sugar; the cuisine is a mix of sweet, sour and hot flavors. The people of East Java are fond of a number of set combinations of spices and aromatic nuts and roots. And just to the east of Java lies the fabled island of Bali, its mystic Hindu culture rooted in art and music, where still another style of cooking, with different spice combinations and an abundance of pork, offers eating experiences unique in predominantly Muslim Indonesia. It is the "national" Indonesian dishes, and the cuisines of Java and Bali, that are presented in this chapter. (In the next chapter we will travel to the Spice Islands in eastern Indonesia, and in Chapter 6 we go west, to inquire into the foods of Sumatra, Malaysia and Singapore.)

Common to almost all of Indonesia is a style of eating and a dependence on rice that shape the methods and tastes of all of its cuisines. Rice for most Indonesians means more than a staple starch like bread or potatoes: it is the main course, the essential element in every meal. The housewife buys rice first and plans her meal around it, adding other foods as taste and budget dictate.

Unlike the chopstick users of China and Japan, who generally eat rice after other dishes or at least in separate mouthfuls, the Indonesians like to mix their rice with other cooked foods just before eating. It is hard to say whether this is a cause or a result of their custom of eating with their fingers. The rice comes to the table rather dry and unsticky compared to Chinese or Japanese rice (see Chapter 8), and if you tried to pick some up by hand or with chopsticks you would be bound to spill many grains. The other dishes, generally cooked with sauces, could not be eaten without a spoon. When mixed together, however, the rice absorbs the sauce and becomes sticky enough to be scooped up in the fingers, molded into a neat but substantial handful and—if you know how to do it—placed on the tongue without a single grain dribbling down the chin. Eating neatly with the hand demands at least as much practice as using chopsticks, and I must confess that I have not mastered the finger technique. I was taking notes during most of my Indonesian meals and found it hard to write with greasy fingers. As I cannot write with my left hand and as one must never eat with the "unclean" left hand in Indonesia or any Muslim, Malay or Hindu country, I had to fall back upon the fork and spoon, devices which many modern Indonesians use anyway.

A failure to understand this practice of eating almost everything mixed with rice has encouraged the Western notion that Indonesian foods are too chili-hot and spicy to cope with. The foods *are* hot, to be sure, but one must remember that every dish and every *sambal,* a ubiquitous chili-and-spice sauce *(Recipe Index),* have been designed to be spread over a quantity of bland rice. The unwary Westerner who may not be fond of rice, and even the Japanese or Chinese who wants to save his rice for afterward, may try a *sambal* by itself—and regret it.

The Indonesian rice fixation led also to the famous Dutch colonial *rijsttafel,* or rice table, which to many epicures the world over still symbolizes Indonesian cuisine. In fact, though, one cannot find a *rijsttafel,* as the Dutch knew it, in Indonesia today; the word itself makes many Indonesians wince by reminding them of past humiliation. Yet, all that *rijsttafel* means really is a rice meal, surrounded by a variety of other dishes, and this is the basic pattern of Indonesian eating. The difference lies in the way it is done. The Dutch settlers, with an abundance of servants, money and leisure, and lacking other pastimes in their remote outposts, developed the *rijsttafel* as entertainment as well as nourishment, and thereby transformed an indigenous style of eating into an ostentatious display of fine cooking, opulence and power. Since this went on in a country where most of the people lived on rice, fish and an occasional *sambal,* it is no wonder that they do not like to be reminded of it. One Indonesian told me: "There are no rice tables in Indonesia today but there is rice on every table."

For those who could enjoy it, however, the first full-scale *rijsttafel* was an unforgettable gastronomic experience, combining in a two- or three-hour meal the best dishes from all the East Indian islands. A "proper" *rijsttafel* has been described as a food parade, "a Dutch lunch that takes twenty-three men and a boy to serve." The guests—there might be anywhere from four to 100 of them—received two plates apiece. Then the procession of white-coated waiters began, each bearing rice or one of the other dishes. The diner would fill one plate with fluffy rice, and then take what he wanted from the other offerings, putting them on or around the rice and on the second plate. At a well-planned *rijsttafel* the waiters would present the dishes in a carefully orchestrated sequence worked out by some behind-the-scenes genius in the kitchen, balancing and contrasting meat and fish, spicy and bland, crisp and soft, sweet and sour, and never repeating any particular flavor. The closest thing to a *rijsttafel* in Indonesia today is a *prasmanan,* or buffet, where the guests must help themselves, and consequently, since they feel self-conscious about raiding the table again and again, eat less than they would at a rice table. Soon after my arrival in the capital of Djakarta I attended a *prasmanan* dinner of 52 dishes, arranged not as an idle feast but as a display, for my benefit, of several Indonesian cuisines. Regardless of my embarrassment, both courtesy and professional curiosity compelled me to taste every dish.

Four cooks had worked all day to prepare that meal. Each offered the principal dishes of her own region—and each brought along her whole family to help finish off the food, because 52 dishes cannot be produced in small enough quantities to make a meal for fewer than 20 or 30 people. Like an old-time *rijsttafel,* the meal required about three hours to consume, and it provided me with my first taste of many Indonesian regional dishes.

Among the 52 dishes I encountered a number of preparations that vary from place to place but are recognizable everywhere in Indonesia. First among these so-called "national" foods was *saté,* delicious bite-sized bits of skewered meat basted with soy sauce and oil, grilled over charcoal and dipped before eating into a hot sauce made of chili, spices and usually peanuts *(Recipe Index).* Saté comes in an almost endless variety; it seems that every town, if not every chef, cherishes a particular recipe for *saté* sauce and a particular method of preparing the meat for grilling. Saté originated centuries ago in Java but now, from remote villages in Malaysia to the islands of eastern Indonesia, it is eaten as part of a meal or as an any-time snack—often late at night. When the sun goes down, tiny outdoor *saté* stalls open for business along busy thoroughfares, their flickering candles and gas lanterns inviting passers-by to sit down for an inexpensive treat. In any town the itinerant *saté* vendor, ringing his bell and shuffling through the streets with all his ingredients and his charcoal brazier slung from the ends of a pole across his shoulder, seems to stay up long after everyone else has gone to sleep; one wonders where he finds customers at such hours. Throughout most of this predominantly Muslim area, beef, goat and chicken are the most common *saté* meats, but carabao *saté* appears in Makasar, shrimp *saté* turns up wherever shellfish are available, and in Chinese areas one can find *saté* made from tender chunks of pork. The Balinese produce a *saté* from a paste of chopped-up turtle meat mixed with coconut milk and spices. The mixture, kneaded onto the end of a stick for grilling, comes off the coals as one of the most heavenly concoctions I have ever tasted.

Another island-wide Indonesian dish served at my Djakarta *prasmanan* was *soto ajam,* a gingered chicken soup *(Recipe Index).* Fried shallots, garlic, lemon grass and celery leaves go into this broth, which is often poured over rice for eating. Every Indonesian cook can make it, and I must have had it several dozen times during my trip, usually taking several helpings. Alone, or even with rice, *soto ajam* often fails to satisfy a robust appetite, although many Indonesians must get along with little else at a meal; but the tart spiciness of this soup goes well with richer dishes, clearing the palate for whatever is still to come.

One of the dishes that may follow is *opor ajam,* a Pan-Indonesian chicken-and-coconut-milk preparation generally classified as a curry *(Recipe Index).* Unlike most curries, *opor* comes out with a white sauce that clings to the meat without overwhelming the chicken taste. The chicken itself is not cut up into small chunks but its cooked and served in pieces, bones and all. The *opor* sauce may contain ground-up candlenut, which adds a hefty flavor and texture.

In addition to these national dishes, the Djakarta buffet introduced me to several ingredients and condiments whose flavors, likely to be a bit strong at first for the Western palate, are essential to Indonesian cookery. Among these were *trassi,* a brick-red fermented shrimp paste used in most kinds of *sambal* and various meat sauces; *petis,* a strong, salty fish sauce; and *peté* (peh-tay), a bitter bean that grows in a footlong pod and looks like a shiny lima bean. There was also *lontong,* rice tightly wrapped and steamed in banana leaves; several kinds of fried and boiled soybean products that show up in dozens of different dishes; and an assortment of the large crispy shrimp crackers, called *krupuk* that Indonesians love so much.

As I moved along the *prasmanan* tables from different kinds of chili-hot *sambal* to peppery soups, I frequently needed something to cool my tongue and soothe my palate. My host's pretty daughter came to the rescue with glass after glass of a semi-sweet refreshing iced drink called *tjintjau.* This welcome beverage, brewed from leaves of the *tjintjau* vine and

*How to Handle Fresh Hot Chilies*

Hot chilies are cousins to the familiar green bell peppers, but they require special handling. Their volatile oils may make your skin tingle and your eyes burn. Wear rubber gloves if you can and be careful not to touch your face or eyes while working with the chilies.

To prepare chilies, rinse them clean under cold running water and cut or break the stem off if you wish to leave the seeds (which are the hottest parts) intact in the pods. If the chili is to be seeded, pull out the stem and the seeds attached to it; then break or cut the pod in half and brush out the remaining seeds with your fingers. In most cases the ribs inside are thin, but if they seem thick and fleshy you may cut them out with a small, sharp knife. Follow the instructions included in the recipes for slicing or chopping chilies.

After handling hot chilies, wash your hands thoroughly with soap and warm water.

embellished with the fruit of the sugar palm as well as a number of sweet bean-paste tidbits, tasted a bit like a mixture of ice tea and liquid fruit Jello, only better.

In such a conglomerate, loose-knit country as Indonesia the dishes at any one table can only suggest the great range of foods and tastes available in other locales. Accordingly, I set out from Djakarta, my appetite aroused and my understanding somewhat broadened, on a gastronomic tour of the country. And within an hour of leaving the capital I discovered one of the reasons why the foods of Indonesia, as well as the customs, dress and culture, vary so much from place to place.

Our car had stopped at a market town on the way to the mountain resort of Bandung. With my guide and interpreter, a resident of Djakarta, I stepped out to sample the local treats—mangoes, avocado, papaya and oranges. My companion exclaimed in glee and hurried over to a stall where some sausagelike objects hung from a rack. Explaining that he and his wife loved this *dodol,* a sticky confection of coconut milk, palm sugar and glutinous rice, he bought half a dozen and carried them back to the car, where I ate my share and more. Djakarta was only 30 miles behind us, but the shops of the national capital do not sell *dodol,* and although it can keep for months, no enterprising peddlers have thought of bringing it into town. Transportation in Indonesia is still so rudimentary that one can buy this potentially popular product only in the rural areas where it is made.

A few miles on, when we pulled up at a roadside stall to haggle for a durian, I again experienced the diversity of Indonesia. Although my interpreter spoke three or four dialects as well as the national language, he could not communicate with the wizened farmer squatting beside a pile of the brown spiky fruit. But our driver knew some of the local phrases so we were able to make our purchase without having to pay heavily for the presence of a Westerner with a camera around his neck. What struck me more, however, was the fact that a countryman who lived only a few miles from his nation's capital city had no language in common with its residents.

But he did sell good durian. Common throughout Indonesia, Malaysia and the southern Philippines, durian is one of those foods that no one can be neutral about. People who like its strong flavor and penetrating aroma (and I am one of them) cannot stop eating it once started; those not under its spell will not approach within yards of the opened fruit and will steer clear of anyone who has eaten it. Its taste is most like a robust overripe Roquefort (some people call it the cheese that grows on trees) and its aroma is mindful of overripe onions. Some airlines of the region specifically forbid passengers to take fresh durian aboard an airplane, and in an air-conditioned hotel in the Philippines I once came across a printed notice to the effect that "Firearms and durian fruit are prohibited in the rooms." None of this discourages durian-lovers. With gusto, they cut open the prickly soccer ball-sized fruit and dig out with their fingers the sticky yellow pulp—often bantering as they do so and trading anecdotes about durian's supposed aphrodisiacal value.

I would not eat durian before attending a diplomatic reception, but on that day, driving through the thick greenery of West Java's fruit-growing plain, zipping past pony carts and brightly painted *betjak* (the three-wheeled pedicabs of Indonesia), passing banana and coconut groves and ripening rice fields and rubber plantations, I ate it greedily. Our driver —his nickname was deservedly "Happy"—kept one hand on his horn, and drove as if cyclists, peasants bearing loads of oranges on poles across their shoulders, and women with bundles of pandanus leaf on their heads had no right to the road at all. Enveloped in our durian cloud, with our horn blasting chickens and pedicabs aside, we drove past ribbon villages stretched out for miles along the road as it climbed terraced hills. At the top of one rise we saw below us a lush picture-book landscape, rural, if crowded, peaceful but teeming with the labor of man and beast; the valley was laid out in allotted sections for ripening rice fields, well-laden coconut palms, thick banana groves and busy villages clustered under red clay roofs. Every field had its crop, every tree its fruit—and every few yards someone was doing something. All at once I understood how Java, even though it has only three real cities, could be so thickly populated.

Still farther up in the mountains we halted for a late lunch at the Nikmat Restaurant, which specialized in West Java food. The spare, rustic establishment was perched on a quiet hillside, surrounded by fish ponds stocked heavily with gold and white and yellow carp; the only sound was the rush of water and the splashing of the fish. A waiter plunged his hands into a pond and captured some fat carp for our inspection. We chose a golden one and watched it disappear, flapping wildly in a bucket, into a dark kitchen where charcoal fires glowed cozily in tiny brick ovens and smiling girls ground chilies and spices in stone mortars. Our fish was cleaned quickly, skewered from tail to mouth on a bamboo spit and placed whole in one of the ovens, to be grilled without seasoning. The spices would meet it later.

On the outdoor dining terrace we sat down at a plain wooden table and gazed across a little valley at a steep flight of rice fields, and at mountains rising mistily in the background. Our meal began with fresh green coconut split in half but still in the husk, served Dutch style with ice and a little orange syrup poured into the open shell. We dug out the soft, sweet coconut meat with spoons, sipped iced tea and listened to the faint clatter from the kitchen.

At last, with what may have been an effort to echo the *rijsttafel* style of serving, four waiters filed out to the terrace with our meal, each one bearing one or two dishes. Our carp appeared, charred almost black on the outside but tender and juicy within, and spread with a thick red tomato-and-chili sauce tasting of onion, ginger and other spices. With the fish came a charcoal-grilled chicken drenched in a sauce containing all of the same condiments plus soy sauce, nutmeg and pepper. We ate these hot foods with steamed white rice from a graceful conical basket, and then turned to the *lalab,* a simple but typically West Java dish of raw vegetables—including cabbage, cucumber, eggplant and the bitter *peté* bean—eaten with a specially prepared, fiery *sambal*

## How to Steam Vegetables

*Pacific cooks, like good cooks everywhere, often steam leafy or green vegetables to preserve their flavor, color and texture as well as their nutritional value. Many kinds of special steaming pans are available. Whether manufactured in the United States, Europe or the Orient, they generally are made up of two pans stacked one on another like a double boiler —but with perforations or slots in the lower part of the top pan. The bottom part contains boiling water, the top part the food that is to be cooked by the steam rising beneath it. There also are collapsible steaming baskets on legs which simply stand inside any kind of large pan with a tightly fitting cover. Or, you can improvise a steamer by standing a colander in a big pot.*

*Pour water into the lower part of the steamer to within about 1 inch of the top pan; or, if you have improvised, pour water into the pot to within an inch of the bottom of the basket or colander. Bring the water to a full boil before you set the perforated container over it. Immediately cover the pot and cook over high heat; cooking times vary, of course, but steaming vegetables takes a little longer than boiling them. When done they should be tender, but still somewhat crisp.*

made with *trassi.* I wrapped up the greens in a cabbage leaf, dipped the bundle into the *sambal,* and bit into it with caution. Seldom has a salad tasted so wildly adventurous. The *sambal* was so strong that my taste buds desperately needed the cooling, crisp freshness of the vegetables. (I had the same feeling again in Singapore, where cucumber is served at *saté* stalls and the customers spear a slice or two with their skewers and wolf it down to quench the spice-fire in their mouths.)

The West Javan fondness for salads and simple foods expresses itself also in two salads that I first sampled at the big Djakarta *prasmanan.* One of them, *asinan (Recipe Index),* often turns up in modern, Westernized Indonesian meals as an appetizer. It is a refreshing combination of cucumber, cabbage and bean sprouts, seasoned only with a simple sauce of vinegar, salt, chili and shrimp paste. Fried peanuts and cracker crumbs are sprinkled on top of it, giving the salad a crunchy texture to match the clean astringency of vegetable and vinegar.

Another favorite salad is *gado-gado (Recipe Index)*—gado² is the way the Indonesians write it. One finds it almost everywhere, but the West Javanese (who call it *lotek*) seem to eat it more often and in my opinion prepare it best. To the assorted vegetables of *lalab* they add bean sprouts and shallots, as well as *ketupat,* rice wrapped tightly and steamed in palm fronds. The *ketupat* is firm, like a cake, and can be cubed, and the lightly boiled vegetables are cut up too. All these are then mixed with a hot sauce of chili, peanuts and spices. The peanut flavor predominates in a good *gado-gado.* I had some as a lively late-morning snack in the same market town where my guide had found his candy-like *dodol,* and that night, in a restaurant in Bandung, my dinner included a *gado-gado* made without the *ketupat,* since we were eating rice with it anyway.

By the time I got to Central Java I had already enjoyed enough *gado-gado* to be thoroughly familiar with its taste; and so when I tried a Central Java version of it I immediately realized that I had crossed a culinary boundary line. Central Java represents Indonesia's sweet tooth; I spent several days eating a great variety of dishes noteworthy for the generous amounts of palm sugar in them. But although the sweetness of this new *gado-gado* surprised me at first bite, I realized as I tried a little more that I was penetrating a more sophisticated cuisine, that another element besides mere sweetness was involved in a play of flavors subtler than any I had encountered in West Java. In the *gado-gado,* a fairly simple dish no matter how you mix it, this added element was easy to identify: vinegar and tamarind had been added as well as the sugar, producing a sweet-sour spiciness.

But in some of the more complex cooked foods of Central Java—dishes demanding an array of chilies and spices and several cooking procedures—it was difficult to determine by just what stroke of ancient kitchen magic the presence of sugar produced something more than added sweetness. Although I did not expect to enjoy sweetened meats and vegetables, I confess that I did; it seemed that the sugar in these dishes somehow got the fires of chili and spices under control without actually quenching them, and enabled me to recognize and appreciate a

*Opposite:* Indonesian Chef Fritz Schild-Tameng, one of the consultants for this book, demonstrates the techniques of an itinerant *saté* vendor. Fanning the coals in the broiler, he grills *saté* made of beef chunks; the bowl contains curry sauce. The far tray holds *saté* of fish, pork, chicken and lamb, with shallots and red chilies to be used for seasoning. The vendor's equipment, called a *pikulan,* is portable. He carries the yoke on his shoulder, and the bells clang together to announce him.

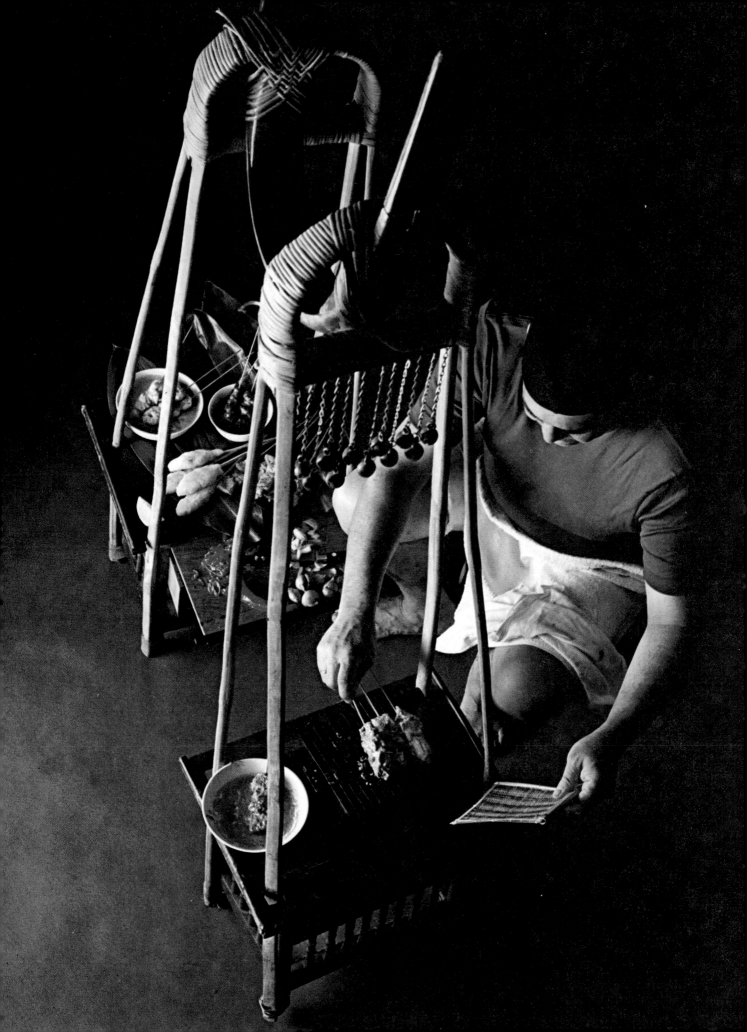

spectrum of flavors I might otherwise have missed. But whether the Central Javanese use an abundance of sugar in order to bring out other flavors, or have devised their complex cuisine to balance and leaven a basic sweetness they cannot do without, is a gastronomic secret that lies buried with cooks long gone.

Nor is anyone quite sure just where this culinary quirk originated. For centuries, even under Dutch colonial rule, Central Java, with its capital of Jogjakarta, enjoyed a measure of independence under its powerful sultanate and conducted its own commerce with China, India and other nations—any one of which might have provided the inspiration for Central Javanese cooking. Even now, under the Republic of Indonesia, the Central Javanese retain a measure of autonomy; at the time I was there, the Sultan was Indonesia's minister of development and one of the triumvirate ruling the nation. The people of Jogjakarta have a full-fledged tradition of art, music and dance that is second only to Bali's in richness; they speak a more refined dialect than their neighbors to the east and west, and they are proud of their *kain,* the plaid sarong that both men and women wear. They are masters of their own culture and guardians of their own cuisine.

One dish that the Central Javanese can truly call their own is *gudeg.* It is found elsewhere only rarely, although jack fruit, its chief ingredient, turns up throughout Indonesia, the Philippines and Malaysia. In Jogjakarta, *gudeg* was served to me three times in 30 hours, at each of the meals I ate in the city; luckily I liked it. When eaten raw, the firm, yellow, melonlike flesh of the ungainly jack fruit tastes something like a mild cheese; in *gudeg,* cooked with coconut milk, coriander, a variety of other spices and, of course, palm sugar, the jack fruit slices develop a rather delicate meaty flavor that can best be described as a cross between artichoke and mushroom. Purists always cook *gudeg* in an earthenware pot, claiming that enamel and metal fail to bring out the proper "warmth." Hard-boiled eggs go into some versions, a single bitter *peté* bean into others.

Ordinarily, *gudeg* is a side dish, eaten alone and not in the same mouthful with rice. But at a lavish banquet in Jogjakarta I found something called a "complete" *gudeg* containing chicken, bean curd, egg and a hot fried *sambal* as well as the usual jack fruit and coconut milk. Served with rice, this kind of *gudeg* often makes a complete meal-in-a-casserole in Central Java homes.

It was at this banquet that I sensed the wealth of subtle tastes underlying the surface sweetness of the Central Java foods I had first eaten at the Djakarta buffet. In Djakarta, for instance, I had tried a gay little dish called *ikan atjar kuning,* a lightly marinated fried fish served in a thick, bright yellow sauce of pickled spices and palm sugar. It looked pretty and had tastes to match: a happy rainbow of sweet, sour and hot flavors that vanished from tongue and memory almost immediately. Authentic as it may have been, it only began to hint at the memorable tastes I found in Jogjakarta itself.

The sweet tooth of the Central Javanese demands a wide variety of snacks and tidbits sweeter and more complex than similar delights in other parts of the country. Almost all these cakes and candies depend on a standard set of four ingredients—sugar, coconut, glutinous rice and cassava (tapioca) starch—but they come out in a delightful variety of sizes, shapes, textures and tastes. One of the best is *budjang di-dalam selimut,* a fluffy pancake colored green with pandanus leaf and folded over a mixture of coconut and palm sugar. (The whimsical name for this dish translates as "bachelor wrapped in a blanket.") Then there are coconut bonbons, dried cassava cakes flavored with coconut, and glutinous rice cakes sprinkled with sesame seed. Central Javanese eat these and other sweets not only for dessert but before and during a meal as well.

The Jogjakarta banquet taught me a great deal about the ceremonial importance of food to the Malay peoples of Java. Centuries ago they worshiped a pantheon of deities who were said to live on a sacred mountain, and they periodically offered food to appease the evil spirits and honor the benevolent ones. Though the rulers of Java became in succession Buddhist, Hindu and finally Muslim, the aboriginal animistic beliefs and customs survived. Today, although most Indonesians pray to Allah and follow his prophet Muhammad, they also remember the ancient gods. And even the Sultan of Jogjakarta, whose authority derives from the prophet Muhammad, celebrates Muslim holidays by offering a *tumpeng,* a rice cone symbolizing the immemorial sacred mountain.

Indonesians cherish their *tumpeng* rice cone; in one form or another it is central to their religion, as important as matzoh is to the Jews or the Eucharist to Catholics. The difference—and it tells much about the difference between Asian and Western religions—is that a *tumpeng* is also good to eat. I had already discovered this back at the Djakarta buffet, where the first thing that caught my eye as I entered the room was a foot-high cone of steamed rice dominating one of the tables. Long green beans decorated the sides of this *tumpeng* and a bright red chili pepper had been stuck in the top of it, pointing up. The cone stood in the center of a flat bamboo basket, surrounded by symmetrical fields of small fried salted fish, boiled eggs, fried soybean curd, mung bean sprouts and numerous boiled vegetables mixed with spiced grated coconut. Although designed for appearance and ceremony, the *tumpeng* and its accessories presented a stimulating variety of natural, basic tastes: smooth coconut, salty fish, aromatic basil leaves, hot chili and the rather rugged flavor of *kentjur,* a pungent root vaguely akin to ginger. As a man, I could serve myself directly from the *tumpeng* tray, but women must not touch the sacred rice cone or invade its precincts. More of the *tumpeng* accessories had been placed in a banana leaf-lined dish beside the basket and the women guests demurely helped themselves from that.

It is obvious from the taboos surrounding the *tumpeng* that it has phallic as well as religious significance; this is particularly true of the chili pepper on top, which can be placed in varying positions depending on the nature of the occasion. But as in many Oriental customs the full meaning is rather obscure. As my Jogjakarta banquet host, a history professor, described it, the sultan used to celebrate Muhammad's birthday by offering massive man-tall *tumpeng* at the local mosque. As many as eight

*Continued on page 84*

75

# Ancient Ritual in a Modern Feast

Religious ceremonies and taboos governing the preparation of food have had an important effect on Indonesian culture. A ritual feast called the *slametan* combines elements of a pagan religion of ancient Java with touches of the Hinduism that was introduced about 400 A.D. and of Islam, which came about a thousand years later. Today the *slametan* is still a significant religious ritual held for a number of reasons—to assure the health of a baby, to appease the spirits, to create a sense of communal fellowship. It can also be an almost secular affair, a get-together of neighbors and friends that has few religious aspects. In any case the abundant food at a *slametan* feast has not changed; it provides an extensive sampling of the traditional dishes of Indonesia.

Participants in a modern *slametan,* some of them wearing characteristic Indonesian hats, bow their heads in prayer before beginning the feast. The men, along with their families, are guests of Dr. Soewadji, a Djakarta neurosurgeon, at his holiday bungalow in Puntjak, a resort area 50 miles south of Djakarta. The gathering of the men in prayer around a mat and the absence of women are survivals of religious ritual. After this solemn beginning the feast assumes a purely social tone. A small daughter of one of the guests *(below),* unperturbed at her exclusion from the central proceedings, gets a head start on the meal, eating rice with her fingers in the Javanese manner.

Three women *(above)* begin
preparing the food in the morning
on the day of the party.
(Traditionally a *slametan* is held
after sundown, but this one was
set for midday.) The two women
on the left are cutting up onions
and red and green chilies for use
in various types of fiery *sambal,*
while their companion squeezes and
strains freshly grated coconut
through a wicker sieve to produce
the coconut milk needed for some
kinds of *sambal* and other dishes.
Meanwhile a man and his little
helper *(right)* see to the roasting
of the young ram that will be the
main dish of the feast. Their brazier
is supported on a bamboo frame
and their spit is a bamboo pole.

Preparing *saté* is part of the morning's work. The Southeast Asian form of kabob, *saté* may be made of any kind of meat, fish or fowl but never includes vegetables. Here the party guests themselves skewer lamb, already cut into bite-sized chunks, on bamboo sticks. The tray in the foreground holds *lontong,* which is rice wrapped in banana leaves and then steamed

Cooking the *saté* is part of the fun. Several grills, with room enough for everyone to find a place around them, are set over containers of charcoal, and the guests, using sections of banana stalks as handles, broil the skewered lamb to their own taste. Bowls of hot sauce made of chilies and spices have been set out, and the broiled *saté* is dipped in the sauce for seasoning. *Saté* of various kinds can be found all over Indonesia, and it turns up in the most grand and the most humble surroundings.

A daughter of Dr. Soewadji, one of the hostesses at the party, finishes a *nasi kuning* by adding a red chili to the tip of its cone. The cone has already been decorated with vertical strips of shredded beef, red chilies, a row of cooked egg, and, in the center, a row of peanuts. *Nasi kuning* was originally a ceremonial food, prepared according to strict protocol, but it now appears in various forms as part of any festive meal.

*Overleaf:* The meal is served, buffet-style, in Dr. Soewadji's garden. Among the many dishes are *(left to right, front row):* fried chicken and tomatoes; *nasi tumpeng,* a white rice cone with garnishes; *lontong,* rice-stuffed banana leaves. Middle row: *gulai,* a lamb curry; crisp, fried whole eggs; tomatoes; chicken livers with paprika; *gudeg,* a jack-fruit dish. Back row: steamed rice; *asinan,* a salad; *gurami,* fish garnished with hard-boiled eggs; another *nasi tumpeng;* and bananas. Some guests help themselves while others, in the background, tend the roast.

people were required to carry each one from the palace in a lavish, solemn procession. These giant *tumpeng* always went in pairs, a large one representing man and a slightly smaller one symbolizing woman. Both rested on blue and white cloths which were intended to ward off evil spirits and disease. The cones themselves were often garnished with foods of different colors: red for anger, yellow for greed, black for violence. As long as the whiteness of the rice, signifying purity, balanced these three colors, the *tumpeng* was believed to assure the mastery of reason over passion.

At the mosque, religious leaders would divide the *tumpeng* into three parts: one for the evil spirits, one to be blessed, then eaten by the donors of the *tumpeng,* and one to be tossed to the common people who would scramble in the dust for the sacred scraps—a form of almsgiving. Although such displays no longer take place, ordinary Indonesians still make *tumpeng* to offer at the mosque on Muslim holidays, or to celebrate particularly happy events, or as a private pledge to the gods. In 1966, to mark the peaceable end of the "confrontation" between Indonesia and Malaysia, the Indonesian government produced a mammoth *tumpeng*—and high officials of both nations gathered round to be photographed amiably eating from it.

Other felicitous occasions in Indonesia rate *nasi kuning,* or yellow rice boiled with turmeric in coconut milk *(Recipe Index)*. Although the color yellow stands for greed in the *tumpeng* spectrum, it signifies happiness when used alone. Indonesian cooks will rustle up a *nasi kuning* for weddings, births and such events as a baby's first taste of solid food. Traditionally, the ingredients in *nasi kuning* were rigorously determined by the nature of the occasion; nowadays it has become an all-purpose festive dish, and almost anything may go into it. One I remember was decorated with a sunburst design of bamboo shoots and symmetrically garnished with peanuts, vegetables and bean curd; it looked as if a large sunflower had sprouted through the table.

Of all the regions of Indonesia, it is in Bali that ceremonial foods attain their most ornate and complicated forms. On this lovely green isle just east of Java, in a setting exquisitely balanced between the tropical beauties of nature and the cultivated gardens and arts of man, nearly a million proud and seclusive Hindus preserve an ancient culture and a self-contained way of life. India's Jawaharlal Nehru once called Bali "the morning of the world," implying, I think, that the Balinese live in a kind of Eden, a state of unspoiled blessedness in which all of man's needs, physical, spiritual and aesthetic, can be satisfied.

But for all its loveliness, Bali is no paradise. In the blood bath that drenched Indonesia after the attempted Communist coup in 1965, the Balinese massacred a greater proportion of their neighbors—about one in twenty—than did the people of any other part of the country. But that merely may have proved the Balinese to be more intensely committed to age-old traditions than their countrymen, which is not surprising in the light of their stubborn survival as a Hindu island in an Islamic sea.

Bali was just a backwoods corner of Madjapahit, the last great Hindu-Javanese empire, when the advancing tide of Islam broke up the Hindu domains in the 15th Century. Refusing to accept Allah, a prince of Madjapahit gathered a group of priests, artists, dancers, musicians— and cooks—and fled east to Bali to save what he could. Nourished by the island's rich soil, protected by seas and mountains from invaders and left more or less alone even by the enterprising Dutch until the 20th Century, the Javanese Hindus established a living relic of their once-mighty civilization.

Religion is the force that meshes every element of Balinese life with every other. It is not merely the skill and verve of Balinese dancers that has made them world-famous, nor the psychedelic liveliness of a *gamelan* orchestra, but the total unity of sound and movement. Every gesture of eye and hand, every chime and gong, fit together exquisitely, so that the whole performance runs like some divine apparatus. Yet none of the performers is professional. Entire villages participate in such dance dramas, and there are communities where everyone paints, or where every small boy learns how to carve the stone lions that guard the temple gateways. Everyone has a talent and employs it to honor the gods and also to gratify his community. A villager may earn his livelihood as a farmer or a storekeeper or a mender of bicycles, but he or she is known to the neighbors as a dancer or a woodcarver or a musician —or a maker of *bebanten*.

The *bebanten* is the Balinese temple food offering, but it resembles the Javanese *tumpeng* about as much as a peacock resembles a robin. You first notice the *bebanten* from afar, as tall, bright towers that seem to float over the heads of a crowd converging on a temple for a religious festival. A closer view reveals the towers to be intricate constructions of fruits and cakes, flowers and varicolored sweets, gracefully balanced on the heads of solemn maidens. The *bebanten* approach from all directions, joyous with color even in the lantern glimmer of an evening ceremony, so hypnotically attractive that one cannot decide whether to watch them or the shy, clear-eyed, smooth-skinned girls who bear them with such ease and dignity. The girls file through the temple gates and stoop so two attendants can lift each *bebanten* and place it before a chanting priest who blesses it and dedicates it to the spirits. After the spirits have accepted the "essence" of the gift, and after the community has admired the rainbow array of *bebanten* in the temple courtyard, the lissome girls appear once more and carry the offerings back, so the families that presented them can partake of the blessing while happily consuming the oranges and bananas, the pink and yellow rice cakes, the yellowing mangoes, the *salak* fruits and *pomelo,* the columns of white rice in split bamboo, and the whole roast suckling pig that is sometimes included.

The same love of color and design that goes into the gorgeous displays of the temple offerings also shows up in the presentation of foods at banquets. At Sanur Beach, near the modern and touristy Bali Beach Hotel, a small restaurant named Tanjung Sari specializes in such ornate arrays. At one unforgettably lavish luncheon buffet at Tanjung Sari, half a dozen vegetable, fish and meat dishes were served up in intricately carved melons, some shaped like grinning fish with chili pep-

pers inserted for teeth, and some in the shape of baskets. Garlands of brilliant red and yellow flowers were looped around the melon vessels, a huge bowl of fruits and flowers stood behind the display, and white and gold painted statues of mythical Balinese animals held parasols over the table to shield it from the noonday sun. With coconut palms and the wash of the sea in the background, the setting seemed too beautiful for the foods to be real; but they were, and excellent too.

In fact, it could be said that the exuberance of Bali's dances, the bright, childish colors of the *bebanten,* and the flowered tables have their counterparts in the tastes of the island's food. The Balinese like their spice flavors vivid, the tastes of other ingredients clear and recognizable. The sweet subtleties of Central Java cooking are too subdued to move the Balinese.

At the core of the Balinese taste is a favorite combination of spices called *bumbu megenep,* which is used in so many dishes that I suspect the original cooks who took it from Madjapahit to Bali must have endowed it with an almost ritualistic importance. It contains salt, pepper, chili, ginger, onion, garlic, turmeric, sesame seed, bay leaf, a chili-like seasoning called *tabia bun,* and the two pungent roots called *kentjur* and *laos.* So famous is the Balinese fondness for this one spice mixture that the cooks of neighboring East Java have worked out a milder but similar combination which is known throughout Indonesia as *bumbu Bali.* Balinese epicures demand the original.

At the Puri Ubud, a prince's palace where I stayed my first few days in Bali, I was served a particularly memorable *bumbu megenep* dish called *guran asam ajam,* a hot, sour chicken stew. It was the best of a series of magnificent dishes that emerged in steady succession from the primitive open-air kitchens of the palace. My host, Prince Tjokorda Agung, wore a gold-trimmed sarong and an embroidered red turban on his head, a sign that he was entertaining important guests. All afternoon his kitchen staff had been busy slicing and grinding spices, pounding turtle meat for *saté penyú,* roasting a suckling pig on a spit and cutting up pork for a dish of coconut milk, spices and marinated meat called *lawar.* Now the guests were assembled under flickering coconut oil lanterns in the dining pavilion. A small *gamelan* group squatted on the floor and played strange and haunting music. We devoured the exquisite mild turtle *saté* and gingerly tasted the fiery hot *lawar* rife with strong, primeval flavors. Perhaps the lantern light playing on the huge ruby embedded in the handle of the Prince's ceremonial *kris* mesmerized me, or maybe it was the exotic music, or the scent of blossoms from the courtyard, or the smiles and conversation of the beautiful people, Balinese and foreign, whom chance had brought together on what seemed a magic night; or perhaps the *guran* stew really was that good. As I let the first forkful spread over my tongue, its many-layered flavors of *megenep* spices sang to me of ancient secrets steeped in Hindu philosophy, of dark Balinese mysteries never to be solved, of gods and goddesses looking down on us from Bali's sacred mountains. . . . Perhaps I should add that before the meal Prince Agung had served us some *brom,* Bali's potent rice wine.

*Opposite:* In the Balinese village of Serongga, three girls carry towering food offerings called *bebanten* from a temple where they have been presented at the shrine of Batari Durga, goddess of death. The *bebanten,* which can take days to prepare, are constructed mainly from fruits, cakes and rice balls, and are decorated with flowers and carved palm fronds. They will now be returned to the families that donated them, and will be consumed at a ceremonial feast.

To make about 16 *saté*

1 teaspoon finely chopped garlic
1 teaspoon salt
⅛ teaspoon white pepper
2 tablespoons *ketjap manis (page 106)*
2 teaspoons strained fresh lime juice
2 twelve-ounce chicken breasts, skinned, boned and cut into 1-inch squares
2 tablespoons vegetable oil
*Katjang* sauce *(page 93)*

## Saté Ajam *(Indonesia)*
### BROILED SKEWERED MARINATED CHICKEN

Combine the garlic, salt and pepper in a deep bowl and with the back of a spoon mash them to a paste. Mix in the *ketjap manis* and lime juice. Add the chicken and toss the pieces about with a spoon until they are evenly coated. Marinate at room temperature for at least 30 minutes or in the refrigerator for 2 hours, stirring occasionally.

Light a layer of coals in a charcoal broiler or hibachi and let them burn until a white ash appears on the surface, or preheat the broiler of the oven to its highest point.

Remove the chicken from the marinade and thread it tightly, 4 or 5 pieces at a time, on small skewers—preferably Oriental wooden skewers about 6 inches long. (Protect the exposed ends of wooden skewers with foil.) Brush the oil evenly over the chicken. Broil about 3 inches from the heat, turning the skewers occasionally, for 5 minutes or until the chicken is crisp and brown. Serve at once directly from the skewers, accompanied by the *katjang* sauce presented separately in a bowl.

This Javanese *gado-gado,* with vegetables, egg, bean curd and a complex, spicy sauce, is one of many Indonesian versions.

## Gado-Gado (Java)

RAW AND COOKED VEGETABLES WITH PEANUT AND COCONUT MILK SAUCE

To serve 6 to 8

First prepare the sauce in the following way: In a heavy 4- to 6-quart casserole, heat the oil over moderate heat until a light haze forms above it. Drop in the onions and garlic and, stirring frequently, cook them for about 5 minutes, or until the onions are soft and transparent but not brown. Watch carefully for any sign of burning and regulate the heat accordingly.

Add the *trassi* and mash it with the back of a spoon until it is well blended with the onions. Pour in the 2 cups of water and bring to a boil over high heat. Stir in the peanuts, brown sugar, chilies, *salam* leaves, ginger root and salt.

Then reduce the heat to low and add the coconut milk and ¼ cup of tamarind water. Stirring occasionally, simmer for about 15 minutes, or until the sauce is thick enough to hold its shape lightly in a spoon. Taste for seasoning and set the pan aside off the heat.

To prepare the vegetables: place the bean curd cakes and ½ teaspoon of salt in a bowl, pour in ¼ cup of tamarind water, and let the cakes soak for at least 10 minutes, turning them over occasionally. Drain the bean curd cakes and set them aside on paper towels.

Drop the new potatoes into enough lightly salted boiling water to cover them completely and boil them until they are almost tender and show only slight resistance when pierced with the point of a small, sharp knife. Drain the potatoes in a sieve or colander and pat them completely dry with paper towels. Then cut them crosswise into ¼-inch-thick slices.

Following the directions on page 71, steam the yard beans or string beans for 30 minutes; the fresh bean sprouts for 12 to 15 minutes; the *kang kung* or spinach for 12 to 15 minutes. When done, the vegetables should be tender but still somewhat crisp to the bite. After they are steamed, set the vegetables aside separately.

While the vegetables are steaming, pour about 3 cups of vegetable oil into a 12-inch wok or fill a deep fryer or large, heavy saucepan with oil to a depth of 3 inches. Heat the oil until it reaches a temperature of 375° on a deep-frying thermometer.

Drop in the bean curd cakes and, turning them gently with a slotted spoon, deep-fry for about 2 or 3 minutes, or until they are crisp and golden brown. Drain the bean curd cakes on a double thickness of paper towels, then cut them crosswise into strips about ¼ inch wide and 1½ inches long.

Add the potato slices to the hot oil and, stirring them gently about with the slotted spoon, fry them for about 4 minutes, or until they are crisp and golden brown on both sides. Transfer the potato slices to paper towels to drain.

To serve, mound the *kang kung* or spinach in the center of a large serving plate; arrange the bean curd strips, potatoes, bean sprouts, yard or green beans, hard-cooked eggs, lettuce and cabbage attractively in rows on each side of the mound. Line the edges of the plate with the cucumber, overlapping the slices slightly.

Serve the sauce at room temperature from a bowl or sauceboat.

### SAUCE

3 tablespoons vegetable oil
½ cup finely chopped onions
1 teaspoon finely chopped garlic
1 teaspoon *trassi* (shrimp paste, *see Glossary*)
2 cups water
4 cups shelled unsalted peanuts, pulverized in a blender or with a nut grinder
3 tablespoons light brown sugar
1 tablespoon finely chopped fresh hot chilies (*caution: see page 69*)
2 *salam* leaves (*see Glossary*)
½ teaspoon scraped, finely grated fresh ginger root
1 teaspoon salt
4 cups coconut milk made from 4 cups coarsely chopped coconut and 4 cups hot water (*see page 61*)
¼ cup tamarind water (*page 63*)

### VEGETABLES

2 fresh bean curd cakes (*see Glossary*)
½ teaspoon salt
¼ cup tamarind water (*page 63*)
4 small new potatoes, peeled
1 pound yard beans or fresh green string beans, trimmed, washed and cut into 3-inch lengths
1 pound fresh bean sprouts, washed, and husks removed, or substitute 2 cups drained, canned bean sprouts, washed in a sieve under cold water
1 pound fresh *kang kung* (*see Glossary*), or fresh spinach, trimmed, washed and coarsely chopped
Vegetable oil for deep frying
2 hard-cooked eggs, cut crosswise into ¼-inch-thick slices
1 cup finely shredded iceberg lettuce
2 medium-sized cucumbers, scrubbed but not peeled, scored lengthwise with the tines of a table fork and cut crosswise into ¼-inch-thick slices

To serve 4 to 6 as a main course
  or 8 as part of *nasi kuning
  lengkap*

2 teaspoons finely chopped garlic
2 teaspoons salt
½ cup tamarind water
  *(page 63)*
2 teaspoons ground coriander
1 teaspoon sugar
¼ teaspoon white pepper
A 3- to 3½-pound chicken,
  chopped into 12 serving pieces
Vegetable oil for deep frying

## *Ajam Ungkap* (Central Java)
### DEEP-FRIED TAMARIND-MARINATED CHICKEN

In a deep bowl, combine the garlic and salt and mash them to a paste with the back of a spoon. Mix in the tamarind water, coriander, sugar and white pepper. Add the chicken and turn the pieces about with a spoon until they are well coated with the marinade. Marinate the chicken for at least 1 hour at room temperature, or 2 hours in the refrigerator, turning the pieces over occasionally.

Preheat the oven to the lowest setting, then line a large, shallow baking pan with a double thickness of paper towels and place it on the middle shelf of the oven.

Pour about 3 cups of vegetable oil into a 12-inch wok or fill a deep fryer or large, heavy saucepan with oil to a depth of about 3 inches. Heat the oil until it reaches a temperature of 375° on a deep-frying thermometer. Remove the chicken from the marinade and pat it dry with paper towels. Deep-fry 3 or 4 pieces at a time, turning them frequently with tongs or a slotted spoon for about 15 minutes, or until they are crisp and richly browned. As they brown, transfer the chicken pieces to the paper-lined pan and keep warm in the oven while you fry the rest. Serve immediately. *Ajam ungkap* appears as part of the *nasi kuning lengkap (Recipe Index),* but may also be served more simply with plain boiled rice.

To make 8 *saté*

3 tablespoons vegetable oil
2 tablespoons finely chopped onions
½ teaspoon finely chopped garlic
A 2- to 2½-pound pike or other
  firm, white-fleshed fish, cleaned,
  skinned, boned and finely ground
  (about 1 cup ground)
2 tablespoons rich coconut top milk
  *(page 61)*
¼ teaspoon strained fresh lime
  juice
½ teaspoon salt
⅛ teaspoon white pepper

## *Saté Lileh* (Bali)
### BROILED SKEWERED FISH STICKS

In a heavy 6- to 8-inch skillet, heat 1 tablespoon of the oil over moderate heat until a light haze forms above it. Drop in the onions and garlic and, stirring frequently, cook for 4 or 5 minutes until they are soft and transparent but not brown. Watch carefully for any sign of burning and regulate the heat accordingly.

Transfer the entire contents of the skillet to a deep bowl and add the fish, coconut milk, lime juice, salt and white pepper. Beat vigorously with a spoon until the mixture is smooth, then cover tightly and marinate in the refrigerator for at least 1 hour.

Light a layer of coals in a charcoal broiler or hibachi and let them burn until a white ash appears on the surface, or preheat the broiler of your range to its highest point.

With a pastry brush, spread vegetable oil evenly on both sides of eight ¼-inch-wide, flat stainless-steel skewers, about 10 inches long. Divide the fish mixture into 8 portions and shape them into small cylinders. Thread each cylinder on a separate skewer, further patting the fish into a smooth, somewhat flattened sausage shape about 3½ to 4 inches long.

Brush about 1 tablespoon of vegetable oil evenly over the grill of the charcoal broiler or hibachi, or on the rack of the broiler pan. Arrange the *saté* on the grill or rack and broil them 4 inches from the heat for 3 minutes. Brush the *saté* lightly with the remaining oil and, using a metal spatula, gently turn them over. Broil for 3 minutes more, or until they are firm and delicately browned. Serve at once.

Rising like a golden mountain from its foothills of side dishes, *nasi kuning lengkap,* or yellow rice complete *(Recipe Index),* is a spectacular party dish. Shown here on a bed of ti leaves, it is set off by cucumber slices and dyed hard-boiled eggs. Reading clockwise from top right, the side dishes *(Recipe Index)* are: *sambelan goreng kentang,* deep-fried potato rounds; *serundeng katjang,* toasted spiced coconut; *rempah,* coconut patties; *atjar kuning,* yellow pickles; *udang asam garem,* tamarind shrimp; *rempejek,* peanut wafers; and *ajam ungkap,* deep-fried tamarind chicken.

## To serve 4

A 2-pound mackerel, cleaned, with head and tail removed

4 cups plus 2 tablespoons vegetable oil

1½ cups finely chopped onions

2 medium-sized garlic cloves, peeled and thinly sliced

2 tablespoons finely chopped fresh hot green chilies (*caution: see page 69*)

1½ teaspoons scraped, finely grated fresh ginger root

¾ cup yellow bean paste or thick bean sauce (*see Glossary*)

1 teaspoon sugar

1½ cups fresh coconut milk made from 1½ cups coarsely chopped coconut and 1½ cups hot water (*page 61*)

1 large green bell pepper, seeded, deribbed, and cut into thin rings


## To serve 4

DRESSING

¼ cup finely chopped fresh hot chilies (*caution: see page 69*)

½ teaspoon scraped, finely grated fresh ginger root

½ teaspoon finely chopped garlic

¼ cup distilled white vinegar

2 cups cold water

3 tablespoons sugar

½ teaspoon *trassi* (*see Glossary*)

1 tablespoon salt

SALAD

1 cup fresh bean sprouts, steamed for 12-15 minutes (*see page 71*) and cooled, or substitute 1 cup drained, canned bean sprouts

3 fresh bean curd cakes, cut into ½-inch cubes

1 cup thinly shredded green cabbage

1 cup thinly sliced radishes, preferably icicle radishes

1 cup coarsely chopped pickled mustard greens (*see Glossary*), or substitute sauerkraut

1 cup shelled peanuts


## *Pesmol* (*Java*)
FRIED AND BAKED MACKEREL WITH GREEN-PEPPER-AND-CHILI SAUCE

Ask the fish dealer to bone and flatten the mackerel, or do it yourself in the following way: Wash the fish under cold running water and pat it completely dry with paper towels. Spread the fish open, then cut along both sides of the backbone and when it is free from the flesh lift it out. Place the mackerel between 2 sheets of wax paper and pound it gently with the side of a cleaver to flatten it.

In a heavy 12-inch skillet, heat 4 cups of the oil over high heat until it is very hot, but not smoking. The oil should be at least 1 inch deep; if necessary, add more.

Place the fish skin side down in the hot oil and fry it for 5 minutes. Turn it gently with a slotted spatula, and continue frying for about 5 minutes longer, or until it is richly browned on both sides. Transfer the fish to paper towels to drain.

Preheat the oven to 350°. Pour off the frying oil and wash and dry the skillet thoroughly. Add the remaining 2 tablespoons of oil to the skillet and heat it over moderate heat until a light haze forms above it. Drop in the onions, garlic, chilies and ginger and, stirring frequently, cook for about 5 minutes, or until the onions are soft and transparent but not brown. Watch carefully for any sign of burning and regulate the heat accordingly.

Add the bean paste and sugar and stir for 2 or 3 minutes. Mix in the coconut milk and cook, stirring frequently and regulating the heat so that the sauce does not boil rapidly, until the mixture is thick enough to hold its shape lightly in a spoon.

Place the fish flesh side up in a shallow baking-serving dish large enough to hold it comfortably. Arrange the green pepper rings in a long row on top of the mackerel, overlapping them slightly, and pour the simmering sauce over them. Bake uncovered in the middle of the oven, basting the fish occasionally with the sauce, for 15 to 20 minutes, or until the fish is tender but still intact and the sauce very thick. If the sauce seems to be thickening to a paste, thin it by adding up to ¼ cup boiling water, a few tablespoons at a time.

Serve the fish directly from the baking dish, accompanied if you like by hot boiled rice.


## *Asinan* (*West Java*)
VEGETABLE, BEAN CURD AND PEANUT SALAD WITH HOT CHILI DRESSING

Combine the chilies, ginger root, garlic and vinegar in the jar of an electric blender and blend at high speed for 20 or 30 seconds. Then turn the machine off and scrape down the sides of the jar with a rubber spatula. Blend again until the mixture is a smooth purée.

Add the 2 cups of cold water, the sugar, *trassi* and salt to the chili mixture and blend for a few seconds longer until all the ingredients are well combined. Taste for seasoning.

To assemble the salad, arrange the bean sprouts, bean curd, cabbage, radishes, mustard greens or sauerkraut, and peanuts in attractive mounds on a large platter. Pour the sauce evenly over them and serve at once.

## Ikan Bumbu Bali *(Java)*
DEEP-FRIED MACKEREL IN RED SWEET-AND-SOUR SAUCE

Combine the bell peppers, chilies and ½ cup of the water in the jar of an electric blender and blend at high speed for 20 or 30 seconds. Turn off the machine, scrape down the sides of the jar with a rubber spatula, and blend again until the mixture is reduced to a smooth purée.

In a heavy 8- to 10-inch skillet, heat ½ cup of vegetable oil over moderate heat until a light haze forms above it. Drop in the onions and garlic and, stirring frequently, cook for about 5 minutes, or until they are soft and transparent but not brown. Watch carefully for any sign of burning and regulate the heat accordingly.

Add the ginger, *laos* and *trassi* and mash the *trassi* with the back of the spoon until it blends into the onion mixture. Stir in the *salam* leaves, brown sugar and 1 teaspoon salt, then add the tamarind water, *ketjap manis* and remaining cup of water and bring the sauce to a boil, stirring frequently. Remove the pan from the heat.

Wash the fish under cold running water and pat it dry inside and out with paper towels. With a sharp knife, score the fish by making 4 diagonal slits 2 inches long and ¼ inch deep spaced about ½ inch apart on each side of the body. Rub the fish inside and out with 1 teaspoon of salt.

Pour 4 cups of oil into a heavy 12-inch skillet and heat it over high heat until it is very hot but not smoking. The oil should be at least 1 inch deep; if necessary, add more. Add the fish and, turning it once with a slotted spatula or spoon, fry it for about 15 minutes, or until it is richly browned on both sides.

Pour off all the frying oil, add the sauce and turn the fish over with a spoon until it is well coated on all sides. Basting constantly, cook over high heat for 5 minutes, or until most of the liquid in the pan has evaporated and the sauce is very thick.

To serve, transfer the fish to a heated platter and pour the sauce over it. *Ikan bumbu Bali* is traditionally accompanied by hot boiled rice.

## Katjang Saos *(Indonesia)*
SPICED PEANUT SAUCE

In a heavy 8-inch skillet or sauté pan, heat the oil over moderate heat until a light haze forms above it. Drop in the shallots, or scallions, and garlic and, stirring frequently, cook for 3 or 4 minutes, or until they are soft and transparent but not brown. Watch carefully for any sign of burning and regulate the heat accordingly. Add the *trassi* and mash it thoroughly with the back of a spoon.

Pour in the chicken stock and bring to a boil over high heat. Stirring constantly, add the peanuts, *ketjap manis,* lime juice, ginger and chilies. Reduce the heat to low and, stirring occasionally, simmer uncovered for 10 minutes, or until the sauce is thick enough to coat the spoon heavily. Serve at once.

(If necessary, the sauce may be prepared ahead and reheated. In this event it may thicken as it stands. Thin it if necessary with a tablespoon or more of water.)

*Katjang* is traditionally served with *saté ajam (Recipe Index).*

To serve 4

SAUCE
½ cup coarsely chopped sweet red bell peppers
½ cup coarsely chopped fresh hot red chilies *(caution: see page 69)*
1½ cups water
½ cup vegetable oil
2 cups finely chopped onions
1 teaspoon finely chopped garlic
2 teaspoons scraped finely grated fresh ginger root
1 teaspoon powdered *laos (see Glossary)*
1 teaspoon *trassi* (shrimp paste, *see Glossary)*
2 *salam* leaves *(see Glossary)*
1 tablespoon dark brown sugar
1 teaspoon salt
¼ cup tamarind water *(page 63)*
1 tablespoon *ketjap manis (page 106)*

FISH
A 2- to 2½-pound mackerel, cleaned but with head and tail left on
1 teaspoon salt
4 cups vegetable oil

To make about 2 cups

2 tablespoons vegetable oil
¼ cup finely chopped shallots or substitute ¼ cup finely chopped scallions, white part only
1 teaspoon finely chopped garlic
¼ teaspoon *trassi* (shrimp paste, *see Glossary)*
2 cups chicken stock, fresh or canned
½ cup shelled peanuts, preferably Spanish peanuts, pulverized in an electric blender or with a nut grinder or mortar and pestle
1 tablespoon *ketjap manis (page 106)*
1 teaspoon strained fresh lime juice
¼ teaspoon scraped, finely grated fresh ginger root
¼ teaspoon finely chopped fresh hot chilies *(caution: see page 69)*

# V

# *Treasures of the Spice Islands*

The setting sun brightens the Celebes Sea to the west of Manado, the main port of northern Sulawesi and one of Indonesia's chief spice-growing centers. Among the silhouetted trees are teakwoods used in local shipbuilding; but it is the cloves and nutmegs growing in the surrounding hills, and exported around the world, that make Manado commercially important.

From the sea, sometimes, when the season and the winds are right, one can still sniff the fragrance that lured countless mariners to triumph —or to death. From the air, the islands look primeval: a carpet of green forest runs down to the water's edge, hiding the narrow roads and the thatch and bamboo houses perched on stilts. There are few signs of cultivation, for the forest itself produces the islands' wealth. Dark-skinned men wearing breechcloths and carrying primitive hand-made tools trudge the roads and the forest trails. In the towns, chickens and cattle wander the quiet streets in the sleepy noontime and the townsfolk move with unhurried grace.

These are the Moluccas, the Spice Islands of the East Indies, for thousands of years the only source of the world's nutmeg, cloves and mace. The Moluccas are the most remote of the fabled spice-producing lands of Asia: Sumatra (white pepper), India (turmeric and ginger), Ceylon (cinnamon), Java (black pepper) and Vietnam (cassia). Empires were built on their resources, nations warred to possess them, and in the race to find them continents were discovered, the peoples of the world came to know each other, and a few previously insignificant kingdoms in Europe were able to spread their culture and their power around the globe. Today, even Indonesians regard the distant Moluccas, 1,500 miles east of Djakarta, as the end of the earth; once upon a time they represented the end of the rainbow.

To get to the Moluccas one flies first to Makasar in southern Sulawesi (formerly known as Celebes) and waits for a seat on one of the

95

An expert spice sorter, her face protected from irritating dust by sago-palm flour, separates whole webs of mace from the less desirable broken webs. Mace is the red covering of the seed of the nutmeg fruit *(above)*; the nutmeg itself is inside the shiny black shell.

two planes a week that make the 600-mile flight across the Banda Sea. In Makasar itself, the massive battlements of old Fort Rotterdam are crumbling and banana trees grow atop the walls, but the high, sloping Dutch-style roofs and the dormer windows of the houses within the fort remind the visitor that for centuries this port was a center of Holland's world-wide spice trade. Until just a few years ago spices from the Moluccas and parts of Sulawesi funneled through Makasar warehouses on their way to the kitchens of the world.

Although the Europeans dominated Makasar for a long time, the people of the area still cling to their traditional foods, and one sultry night, while waiting for my flight, I had a chance to try some of them. My hostess was the wife of a former mayor of the town; four of her stunning daughters—all but one wearing the long, colorful saronglike skirts of Makasar—added a note of gaiety as they giggled nervously at this Westerner trying their foods. As it turned out, they need not have been concerned. The six or seven main fish and beef dishes spread out on the long dining table, and the bright, fruity desserts served with coffee afterward, made me glad there had been no direct plane connections to the Moluccas. The best dish of the night was a traditional preparation, usually reserved for wedding feasts, called *djuku kambu*. The flesh of a tender rockfish had been extracted without breaking the skin, then ground up and seasoned with pungent roots and a bit of palm sugar, then stuffed back into the skin to be baked in grated coconut.

The smooth stuffing, ever-so-slightly sweet, made an exquisite pâté. We ate it with a slightly sour beef-liver stew, and it occurred to me that there was hardly a flavor in the world that was not represented in the multifarious and cosmopolitan foods on this table.

The next day I boarded the plane on my way to see some spices actually growing—and to find out what I could about the islanders' own cuisine. My destination was Ambon, the capital and principal port of the Moluccas. Soon after landing, I was introduced to Z. M. Sitanala, a local spice planter. He led me to one of the trees that started it all and showed me a nutmeg, a complex plum-sized fruit. Inside a thin, yellow-green skin, a soft fleshy pulp (which the Indonesians use to make candy) cushioned a bright red, weblike membrane, which in turn covered a glistening inner shell. The membrane is the pungent spice called mace; the shell within it, about the size of a pecan, holds the fragrant, meaty nutmeg itself. As I admired this many-layered marvel, a young boy shinnied up another tree nearby and descended with a fistful of fresh cloves—the red buds of a pinkish-green flower, plucked before they blossom. He also handed me some dried cloves, picked a few days earlier and now at nearly full flavor. I stood in the glade with the sharp-sweet clove on my tongue and the ripe nutmeg in my hand and pondered. . . . The grower must have read my thoughts. "It is because of these cloves and nutmegs," he said with a smile, "that Columbus discovered your country. Looking for these, I think."

Long before Columbus, cloves and nutmegs from the Moluccas were among the varied spices of the East making their way through India and Arabia to the Mediterranean Sea and westward to command fantastic prices in the markets of Europe. During the first millennium B.C. the Arabs dominated the western end of the spice route, buying cheap in Indian ports, which served as export terminals for Eastern spice growers, and selling dear in Egypt; the Roman historian Pliny complained in the First Century that pepper was selling in Rome at a hundred times its original cost. To protect these profits and keep their customers away from their suppliers, the Arab traders cannily reported that the spices came from Africa, and they spread fantastic stories about fierce birds and beasts that guarded the trees and pounced on unwary spice hunters. But about 100 A.D. the Greeks and Romans learned the truth after they discovered how the Arabs were able to sail back and forth to carry on the trade. The Indian Ocean's monsoon winds change direction twice a year; riding them, a ship could sail from the Red Sea to southern India and return to Egypt within a year.

Once Mediterranean sailors learned to follow Arab routes, the Arab monopoly disappeared; spice prices dropped, and the Roman Empire was flooded with the luxuries that eventually contributed to its downfall. The Romans wrote books on spice cooking, drank spiced wine, slept on saffron-filled pillows to avoid hangovers and bathed in aromatic oils. The Emperor Nero is said to have burned a year's supply of cinnamon at the funeral of his wife.

With the fall of Rome and the rise of Islam the spice trade passed back into Arab hands. As Muhammad himself was a trader in spices, it

was natural for his missionaries to seek spices as well as converts, and it is no coincidence that the trail of Muslim conquest followed the spice routes eastward.

Within a few centuries the religious and commercial heirs of Muhammad had taken over the spice trade and most of the spice-growing areas in India and Indonesia. By 1475 they had established sultanates within the Moluccas themselves and were extorting fantastic prices for their goods in Alexandria, where Venetian and Genoese ships loaded for the last leg of the trip to Europe. In the West spices were so valuable that peppercorns were used as currency to pay taxes in England, and a pound of nutmeg could buy seven fat oxen in Germany. At one point, eunuchs and white female slaves from Europe were traded for cinnamon, cloves and pepper. But when Marco Polo described the wealth of the Orient and told of the abundant spices of Java and India, Europe awoke to the exciting possibility that the hated Saracen and his profit taking at the eastern end of the Mediterranean could be bypassed and the Venetian middlemen eliminated if only the Spice Islands could be reached by a sea route circling around the land obstacles.

Convinced that the world was small (many people realized it was round), Christopher Columbus set out to find a shortcut to the East by sailing west. Again and again in his voyages through the Caribbean he sent his men out with samples of spices to ask the natives where they grew, and he brought back everything he could find that resembled or tasted like the spices he was familiar with. But he never saw a nutmeg tree, and never realized why.

Meanwhile the Portuguese made their way step by step around Africa seeking an eastward sea route. They found it in 1498 when Vasco da Gama reached India and returned with a cargo of gems and spices and the news that Indian spice merchants were willing to sell to the Portuguese. European spice prices plummeted, the Venetian traders and their Muslim suppliers could no longer compete, and the center of economic power in Europe shifted almost overnight to Lisbon.

Combining religious zeal with commercial advantage, the Portuguese moved swiftly to wipe out the Muslim spice trade. Within 10 years they had sunk enough dhows and raided enough Muslim ports to control the spice commerce of India and Ceylon, and were roving eastward to find the nutmegs and cloves. In 1511 they won control of the Malacca Strait at the tip of the Asian mainland, thus blocking the Muslims from the sea gateway to the East Indies. By 1514 the Portuguese had established a permanent trading post at Ternate in the north Moluccas. For the first time, cloves and nutmegs could travel from their source to Europe in the ships of one nation. And the Portuguese chronicler Tomé Pires could gloat: "Whoever is lord of Malacca has his hand on the throat of Venice."

The Portuguese remained a power in Indian trade into the 20th Century, but they were unable to hold on to their Indonesian outposts. Their rule was marked by violent oppression, and the Muslims rose against them. By 1580 the Portuguese had been driven back to one last Moluccan foothold, a fort at Ambon, and they soon lost that to the Dutch.

With the capture of Malacca in 1641 and Makasar in 1668, the

*Opposite:* In a warehouse on the island of Siau, north of Sulawesi, women and children sort nutmegs according to size, discarding the culls. At this stage the nutmegs, oval and averaging about an inch long, have been removed from their shells, in which they were allowed to dry. The workmen at the left pour the sorted nutmegs into burlap sacks to be sent by sea to Manado, where they undergo still more sorting before being exported.

99

In a cassia grove near Padang, on the west coast of Sumatra, a worker peels away a strip of bark that will be cleared of its splotches of fungi, dried and ground into cassia powder, to be sold in the United States as cinnamon. Bark like this from the trunk contains the cassia's most essential oils. Cassia sticks, or quills ("cinnamon sticks"), come from the trees' branches.

Dutch gained control of the Indonesian islands and held on to them for the better part of three centuries. During the first 150 years or so, by means of a policy as ruthless as any the Portuguese ever conducted, the Dutch created a monopoly and forced up the prices of cloves and nutmegs. They destroyed three fourths of the spices trees in the Moluccas, strictly limited the number under cultivation, and decreed a death penalty for anyone selling or cultivating or even possessing cloves or nutmegs illegally. They ruled the market, and the world paid . . . until, in the 18th Century, a clever Frenchman smuggled out of the Dutch colonies some clove, nutmeg and cinnamon plants and got them growing in French tropical colonies. And that was the end of the last of a line of spice monopolies.

Monopoly or no, the Indonesian islands still account for nearly 70 per cent of the world's production of nutmeg and mace. Tiny outrigger boats called proas, laden with sacks of nutmegs and mace, still sail into the spice ports of Manado, in Sulawesi, and Ambon, in the Moluccas. There, in dim, dusty warehouse buildings known as godowns, hundreds of chattering young girls squat over brimming baskets, cracking the nutmeg shells, removing the nuts and skillfully sorting them out by grade. Hard-sinewed coolies, their backs bent almost flat under bulging 165-pound sacks, emerge from the gloom at one end of the sorting room and make their way through the aisle. Over all hangs a fine, fragrant haze of nutmeg dust. Nearby is another room, brighter, with a tint of red in the air, where the mace sorters separate the bright red bits of the fruit membrane from the duller orange pieces, which bring a lower price. Since nutmeg and mace come from the same plant they are somewhat alike. Ground mace, a dusty orange color, has a warm, piquant flavor and deep aroma; the tan ground nutmeg, sweeter and more delicate, tends to cool the tongue.

The glories of these sensual spices are lost upon the islanders who grow them. The Indonesians themselves use very little nutmeg or mace, and most of the produce of the godowns winds up in Europe and the United States. The best goes to Europeans, who are willing to pay more than Americans for the top grades. And today much American nutmeg comes from Grenada, in the West Indies, which grows a coarser, oilier product. Housewives desiring good nutmeg should pass up the powdered concoctions and buy whole nuts—the best are those that are smooth, plump, hard and heavy. Mace can be purchased only in ground form.

The other native Moluccan spice enfolds a mystery of its own. Clove trees do not blossom fully every year but in cycles of two years, or in some places four. In the good year, all the trees in an area bear heavily, and in the lean years they all perform poorly. No one seems to know why. As the clove buds must be cut off just before they bloom, the harvest season is short, and thousands of pickers swarm to the groves. For a few weeks, from dawn to dusk, the islands pulsate with activity, and then for two or four years calm returns.

But few of these rich, oily cloves ever get into England's apple tarts or America's baked hams. The Indonesians themselves use nearly all

the cloves they grow, but not in food (they almost never cook with cloves, any more than they do with nutmeg and mace). The bulk of the Indonesian clove crop is dried and mixed with cheap tobacco to make the sweet *kretek* cigarettes that are the country's most popular smoke. As a result, most of the world's best cloves are sweetly, fragrantly going up in smoke every day.

Nutmeg, mace and cloves are the only international spices growing in the Spice Islands themselves, but other parts of Indonesia produce pepper—the most important spice—and cassia, often confused with cinnamon. Cassia and cinnamon, essential baking spices, come from the aromatic barks of two similar but distinct varieties of the laurel family. Most "cinnamon" sold in the United States is actually cassia from Sumatra and Vietnam. True cinnamon, grown mostly in Ceylon, now known as Sri Lanka, consists of only the thin inner bark of the cinnamon tree; it has a subtle flavor and delicate aroma preferred by European connoisseurs. The coarser cassia—once considered a poor man's cinnamon—has a more intense aroma and can be pungent on the tongue.

Cooking foods with aromatic spices such as nutmeg, cloves or cinnamon is a little like dressing Cinderella in fine gowns of silk and satin; the foods take on a soothing fragrance, a sweet grace and ele-

A basket of red chilies is the brightest item in this Sumatran street vendor's display. It will also be the first basket emptied, for hot chilies are the most popular condiment for many Indonesian staple foods. The vendor's wares also include dried fish, in the baskets next to the chilies; potatoes and shredded coconut *(left);* and rice, in the packages at lower right.

101

These dark peppercorns, grown on vines in the Lampung district in Sumatra, will eventually be ground into black pepper, either in a local factory or in somebody's kitchen. Berries for black pepper are picked before they are ripe, dried in the sun and ground up. The same kind of berry is used for white pepper, but it is allowed to ripen fully; then the outer hull is removed and the inner core is bleached.

gance. But pepper performs another function entirely. Pepper wakes up the tongue and stimulates the appetite; it enhances the flavor of the food itself, and its tang provides a general air of excitement—like decking Cinderella out in a low-cut blouse and miniskirt, with spangles.

Pepper, a berry from a climbing vine grown on Java and Sumatra, is the world's most popular and universal spice. Native to India, it was mentioned in Sanskrit literature 3,000 years ago, and over the years has become involved in more confusion than even cassia and cinnamon. At one time Roman writers thought that black and white pepper came from different plants (white, preferred by Europeans, is the ground inner kernel of the berry; black, a bit stronger, is the ground whole berry). As late as the 14th Century, a scholarly friar took great pains to explain that white peppers were scorched black when the pepper pickers of India started fires to ". . . chase away the serpents . . . [that] keep the woods that peppers groweth in."

These misconceptions were minor compared to the errors that Columbus introduced. He was after pepper, naturally, since it was the spice most in demand. When he and his men came across capsicum pods, the hot chilies of the New World, and found they burned the mouth like the spice they were seeking, they confidently named them "pepper." Within a century or so of Columbus' voyages, chili peppers from the New World had been planted in the East Indies. Ironically, it is these imported chilies rather than indigenous condiments that have become traditional spices in the cooking of the Spice Islands and Southeast Asia.

Today, in Indonesia, Malaysia, Thailand and parts of the Philippines, hot chilies, red and green, appear in the majority of dishes, and vast displays of them, spread out on straw mats, decorate every marketplace. Housewives buy them whole, picking them out pod by pod, then chop or grind them—or put them out on the table for brave diners to nibble on as Americans might eat olives.

The Indonesians' favorite chili recipes are those for the fiery relish called *sambal (Recipe Index)*. Javanese attach so much importance to *sambal* that one proverb declares even an ugly girl will find a husband if she can brew good coffee and mix up a good *sambal*. Most *sambal* makers start with lime juice, shallots (or onions) and garlic—and of course chili. In west Sumatra, noted for vigorous food, I came to grips with *lado,* a stark, blazing *sambal* of chili, salt, tamarind and shallots, which is guaranteed to arouse dull palates and sleepy dinner companions. *Lado* is one of the *sambal* that are frequently stir-fried with seafood, boiled eggs or vegetables to become the more substantial *sambal goreng (Recipe Index)*.

Chili is also the spice that often puts the heat in curry, an Indian invention that has spread throughout Southeast Asia and even to Polynesia. Another essential curry spice is turmeric, the starchy rhizome, or underground stem, of a plant related to ginger. Grown on Java, it thickens the curry sauce, giving a taste like a mild mustard, a clean aroma similar to that of ginger, and the color of saffron—with which it is often confused.

102

In many parts of Indonesia, curry is considered a party dish, for special occasions. The everyday equivalent is *gulai,* or *gulé,* made with the thinner, second squeezings of the coconut milk and with fewer spices than curry. Chili, salt, onion and turmeric are the basic spices of a Sumatran *gulai,* with other condiments to be added depending on the main ingredient. A fish *gulai,* for example, needs ginger to neutralize its fishiness, plus basil and lemon grass for accents.

The Indonesians do wonderful things with several richly flavored nuts that are little known outside of this region. One of these is the *keluak;* in the *rawon* of East Java this slightly bitter, black nut comes into its own, contributing to a complex, heavily spiced beef dish, a unique taste that I can characterize only as single-minded and masculine. *Kemiri,* or candlenut, is a condiment favored for vegetables and *sambal;* it has a mild taste like a macadamia nut and can be particularly useful as a thickener for sauces.

In the Molucca Islands themselves, a third tasty nut provides the basis for the best local dishes. This is the *kenari,* akin to the almond; ground up with vinegar, chili, onion and salt it makes a thick yellow dipping sauce for charcoal-grilled fish. The nut played a role in an unforgettable dish that I had on my last night in Ambon. I had been invited to dinner by Mrs. Sinai, the manageress of the hotel, and she arranged a special party not in the forlorn hotel dining room but in her private quarters, a cheery place decorated with porcelain figurines of Dutch milkmaids and sentimental paintings of windmills.

The main dish was called *tjolo-tjolo (Recipe Index):* a whole *bobara* fish baked right in the dipping sauce made from the ground *kenari.* From this simple nut and its carefully chosen companions came a new and extra taste that blended magically with the tender flesh of the *bobara.* It was as if the fish had been plucked from some ambrosial pond and baked over burning spice leaves.

Along with this delicacy, Mrs. Sinai offered a sample of everyday fare, a dish made of sago flour, the staple starch extracted from the inner pulp of the trunk of the sago palm. She served it in its most popular version, *popeda,* a soft, wet, sticky dough immersed in a sort of vegetable soup. No spoon or implement is provided; you eat *popeda* directly, bending over your plate and slurping it up as best you can.

I insisted on trying it, and to the vast amusement of my hostess and her guests, I managed to get some down. But I reflected, as I wiped soup from my face, that *popeda* eating must be easier for people of the Malay race, whose noses tend to be flatter than mine.

At the meal's end the *kenari* appeared again, in an old traditional form. Our hostess passed around sweet little crispy balls, tasting faintly of almonds, a familiar flavor. . . . This is a Molucca candy made of *kenari* and sugar, I was told; you find it nowhere else. But when I heard its name I suddenly felt that I had touched the ancient spice routes, the sultanates, the outrigged proas, the camel caravans and the bustling Near East bazaars where nutmegs and cloves from this island of Ambon were once traded perhaps for a candy like the one in my hand—a "Moluccan" candy called *halvah.*

These chilies ripening on a bush in Sumatra will not be picked until they all turn red. The change of color—from original yellowish green—begins at the tip. The plants are grown from seeds and can reach a height of six feet. There are hundreds of kinds of chilies and countless variations of flavor and hotness, but they are all of the Capsicum family, which also includes bell and sweet red peppers.

# A Sextet of Spicy Condiments

1 Sambal iris
2 Sambal badjak
3 Sambal goreng
4 Atjar kuning
5 Sambal ketjap
6 Dabo dabo lilang

*Recipes on next pages
and in Recipe Booklet*

6

5

To make about 2 cups

1 medium-sized onion, peeled, cut
in half lengthwise and sliced
lengthwise into ⅛-inch-wide
strips
1 small firm ripe tomato, washed,
stemmed, cut in half lengthwise
and cut into ¼-inch dice
1 small fresh hot red chili, about 1
inch long, stemmed, seeded and
cut lengthwise into ⅛-inch-wide
strips *(caution: see page 69)*
1 small fresh hot green chili, about
1 inch long, stemmed, seeded and
cut lengthwise into ⅛-inch-wide
strips *(caution: see page 69)*
¼ cup strained fresh lime juice
Lime rind

To make about 1 quart

2 cups dark brown sugar
2 cups water
1½ cups Japanese soy sauce
¾ cup dark molasses
½ teaspoon ground *laos (see
Glossary)*
½ teaspoon ground coriander
½ teaspoon freshly ground black
pepper

To make about ½ cup

3 tablespoons vegetable oil
1 teaspoon finely chopped garlic
¼ teaspoon *trassi* (shrimp paste,
*see Glossary*)
⅓ cup finely chopped shallots, or
substitute ⅓ cup finely chopped
scallions, white parts only
¼ cup finely chopped fresh hot
chilies including the seeds
*(caution: see page 69)*
¼ teaspoon salt

## Sambal Iris *(Northern Sulawesi)*
CHILI, ONION AND LIME JUICE CONDIMENT

*"Sambal," like those shown on the preceding pages and described in
the recipes below, are fiery blends of fresh hot chilies and other seasonings used as relishes or condiments throughout Indonesia. There are scores
of "sambal"; some raw, some cooked. A "sambal" is served in much the
same way a Western housewife uses piccalilli or Tabasco. Related to
"sambal" is "sambelan" (Recipe Index), a kind of hot chili sauce in
which raw or cooked food is simmered before serving.*

Combine the onion, tomato, red and green chili strips, lime juice and
rind in a bowl and mix them together thoroughly. Let the *sambal iris*
stand at room temperature for 30 minutes or so before serving.
   NOTE: *Sambal dabo dabo lilang* is made the same way, but with the
addition of 1 teaspoon finely cut fresh basil leaves. *Sambal dabo dabo
bakasans* is also made the same way, but 1 teaspoon *trassi* is dissolved
in the lime juice before it is added to the other ingredients.

## Ketjap Manis *(Indonesia)*
INDONESIAN SWEET SOY SAUCE

*The ubiquitous American tomato ketchup, or catsup, gets its name but
not its ingredients from the Malaysian "kechop" (in Chinese, "ketsiap")
which originally was a pickled fish brine. "Ketjap manis" is like soy sauce
and is used in Indonesia in stews and "sambal."*

Combine the sugar and water in a 2- to 3-quart enameled or stainless-
steel saucepan and bring to a boil over moderate heat, stirring until the
sugar dissolves. Increase the heat to high and cook briskly, uncovered,
for 5 minutes, or until the syrup reaches a temperature of 200° on a
candy thermometer. Reduce the heat to low, stir in the soy sauce, molasses,
*laos,* coriander and pepper, and simmer for 3 minutes. Strain the sauce
through a fine sieve set over a bowl. Tightly covered, *ketjap manis* may
be kept at room temperature for 2 or 3 months.

## Sambal Goreng *(Indonesia)*
FRIED CHILI, SHALLOT AND SHRIMP-PASTE CONDIMENT

In a heavy 8- to 10-inch skillet, heat the oil over moderate heat until a
light haze forms above it. Drop in the garlic and stir it for 1 minute,
add the *trassi* and mash it completely with the back of a spoon. Stir in
the shallots or scallions and cook for a minute or so longer. Add the chilies and salt and, stirring frequently, simmer for about 5 minutes, or
until most of the liquid in the pan has evaporated and the mixture is
thick enough to hold its shape almost solidly in a spoon. Cool the *sambal
goreng* to room temperature before serving. Covered and refrigerated,
it may be safely kept for 1 or 2 weeks.

## Tjolo-Tjolo *(Moluccas)*
### BROILED FISH AND VEGETABLES WITH 3 SAUCES

First prepare the three sauces in the following way: for the almond-and-coconut-milk sauce, preheat the oven to 350°. Spread the blanched almonds in one layer in a large shallow baking pan and, stirring occasionally, toast them in the middle of the oven for 8 to 10 minutes, or until they are lightly and evenly browned.

Combine the toasted almonds and 1 cup of water in the jar of an electric blender and blend at high speed for 20 or 30 seconds. Turn off the machine, scrape down the sides of the jar with a rubber spatula and blend again until the nuts are completely pulverized and the mixture is reduced to a smooth purée.

In a heavy 8- to 10-inch skillet, heat 3 tablespoons of vegetable oil over moderate heat until a light haze forms above it. Drop in the onions and, stirring frequently, cook for 5 to 8 minutes, or until they are a delicate golden brown. Watch carefully for any sign of burning and regulate the heat accordingly.

Add the *trassi* and mash it with the back of a spoon until it is well blended with the onions. Add the *djeruk* leaf. Stir in 2 tablespoons of chilies and the garlic and cook for a minute or so.

Then, stirring constantly, add the *sereh,* coconut milk and almond purée. Simmer for 5 minutes, stirring occasionally, then add the tamarind water, 1 teaspoon of salt and the pepper. Taste for seasoning and transfer the almond-and-coconut-milk sauce to a serving bowl.

To prepare the tomato-and-red-chili sauce, combine the chopped tomato, chilies, lime juice and salt in a serving bowl and toss gently but thoroughly together with a spoon.

To prepare the *ketjap* sauce, mix the *ketjap manis* and 1 tablespoon of lime juice in a serving bowl.

Set the three sauces aside at room temperature until you are ready to serve them.

Arrange the tomato wedges, cucumber slices, carrot slices, string beans, shredded cabbage, celery leaves, and eggplant cubes (if you use them) attractively on a platter in concentric circles or in rows or in a ring of individually mounded vegetables. Cover the platter tightly with a strip of aluminum foil or plastic wrap and set the raw vegetables aside in the refrigerator.

Set the broiler rack 4 inches from the heat and preheat the broiler to its highest point. Wash the mackerel under cold running water and pat it completely dry with paper towels. Then season it inside and out with 1 teaspoon of salt and the white pepper.

With a pastry brush, spread 1 tablespoon of the melted butter evenly over the broiler grid and lay the fish on it. Then brush the fish with a tablespoon of the butter.

Basting it every 3 or 4 minutes with the remaining 4 tablespoons of butter, broil the fish for about 10 minutes on each side, or until the skin is crisp and golden brown and the fish feels firm when prodded gently with your finger.

With a wide metal spatula, transfer the fish to a heated platter and serve it at once, accompanied by the vegetables and the three sauces.

### ALMOND AND COCONUT MILK SAUCE
1 cup blanched almonds
1 cup water
3 tablespoons vegetable oil
1 cup finely chopped onions
1 teaspoon *trassi* (shrimp paste, *see Glossary*)
1 *djeruk* leaf *(see Glossary)*
2 tablespoons finely chopped fresh hot chilies *(caution: see page 69)*
1 teaspoon finely chopped garlic
¼ teaspoon powdered *sereh (see Glossary)*
½ cup fresh coconut milk *(page 61)*
2 tablespoons tamarind water *(page 63)*
1 teaspoon salt
⅛ teaspoon white pepper

### TOMATO-AND-RED-CHILI SAUCE
3 medium-sized firm ripe tomatoes, stemmed and finely chopped
¼ cup finely chopped fresh hot chilies *(caution: see page 69)*
¼ cup fresh lime juice
¼ teaspoon salt

### "KETJAP" SAUCE
½ cup *ketjap manis (page 106)*
1 tablespoon fresh lime juice

### VEGETABLE GARNISH
1 large firm ripe tomato, cut lengthwise into 6 to 8 wedges
1 medium-sized cucumber, scrubbed but not peeled, scored lengthwise with the tines of a fork and cut into ¼-inch-thick rounds
3 medium-sized carrots, scraped and cut into ¼-inch-thick rounds
¼ pound fresh green string beans, cut into 1-inch lengths
1 cup finely shredded green cabbage
½ cup finely cut celery leaves
1 small eggplant, peeled and cut into ½-inch cubes (optional)

### FISH
A 3-pound mackerel, cleaned but with head and tail left on
1 teaspoon salt
⅛ teaspoon white pepper
6 tablespoons melted butter

# VI

## *Crossroads of Asia: Sumatra & Malaysia*

For nearly 2,000 years, most of the spices that the East Indies sent to the Western world traveled around the Southeast corner of Asia through the sultry, jungle-lined waterway known as the Strait of Malacca. Unlike modern seafarers who can steam through it at will, the ancient merchants from Araby, Persia and India had to stop in this strategic passage to wait for favorable winds, to take on supplies, to trade their goods for those that had entered the strait from the opposite direction, or at times to pay tribute to the pirates or more legitimate nabobs who controlled the area. As commerce increased, early trading posts established along the strait developed into powerful international business centers with permanent colonies of foreigners who brought along their own customs, religions and eating habits. By the time the Portuguese captured Malacca in 1511, the shores of the Strait had become one of the most cosmopolitan centers in all the Orient.

Today the Malacca Strait is an international boundary. On one side. lies Indonesia's huge and sparsely populated island of Sumatra, where tigers and elephants still roam wild through vast tracts of rain forest, little disturbed by the pipelines and drilling rigs that tap the oil fields under the jungle floor. On the other side lie the great port of Singapore, now an independent nation, and, at the heart of Malaysia, the Malay Peninsula. This is a tight land of rubber plantations, tin mines, paved highways with traffic lights, and crowded *kampongs*, clusters of thatched bamboo houses. But despite their quite different colonial experiences, the Malay peoples who inhabit both sides of the Strait

The swooping roof line of this west Sumatran farmhouse, mirrored in an unplanted rice field on the Menangkabau plateau, echoes the curving horns of the water buffalo, or carabao, Southeast Asia's ubiquitous work animal. The ducks in the rice field will end up in *gulai,* a kind of curry, or in other favorite Sumatran dishes.

speak the same languages, share a single ethnic heritage, and have learned many of the same cooking lessons from the generations of foreigners who have lived among them.

The alien influences have so overlapped each other that it is impossible to say for sure whether it was the Arabs or the Indians, for instance, who introduced such spices as nutmeg, cloves, anise, cinnamon, coriander and cardamom into the cooking of the area, or who taught the Malays various pilau-type methods of cooking rice with meats and seasonings. What is clear is that these spices and cooking techniques have taken stronger root along the Malacca Strait than anywhere else in East Asia, and they seem to be most popular in localities where great trade centers once flourished or where Islam is strongest.

If the foods of this area merely imitated those of India and the Middle East we would not linger over them. But a vigorous and imaginative local element, stimulated and enriched by Arab and Indian ideas, has imbued the cooking of Sumatra and Malaysia with a distinctive taste. This culinary genius resides in the enterprising Menangkabau people who come from the mountains of west Sumatra and who can now be found as traders and cooks throughout Malaysia and Indonesia. It is their tendency to leave home to find their fortune that sets them off from other Indonesian peoples.

One finds Menangkabau cooking at its finest at Padang, on the west coast of Sumatra. Entering the dusty city, the first thing you notice is the throng of tiny pony carts clogging the streets—and then you realize that there are no *betjaks,* pedicabs, in sight. Not even the poorest Menangkabau would demean himself by hauling another human being around for pay like a beast of burden.

Obsessed with trade, proud of the independence and individualism that make them unwilling to follow any stranger's orders, the Menangkabau are fond of relating the legend that gives them their name. The word Menangkabau means "victorious carabao," and the story goes that in ages past two rival clans decided to settle a land dispute by having two water buffalo fight it out for them. One clan hid a *kris* in the mouth of a hungry baby bull and sent it into battle. When the calf tried to suckle the enemy animal, the knife inflicted a fatal wound and the calf was declared the victor. Some people might be ashamed of such ancestral trickery, but the "victorious carabao" people glorify the event as proof that even a big power will succumb to wit and wisdom —that a David can indeed conquer a Goliath. Whether the Menangkabau conduct their business in the same spirit today is not a subject to be discussed here, but they do enjoy a reputation as the only Indonesians who can compete successfully in trade with the Chinese. Certainly the resourcefulness that placed a knife in the mouth of the calf centuries ago puts a varied and exciting fare in the mouth of anyone who walks into a Padang restaurant today.

The Djaja (Great) Restaurant is Padang's best, but it has no menu. The dishes of the day are set out in a tempting display at the door, where much of the cooking is done. If you are not too hungry, you stop on your way in and indicate what you want. The usual procedure, however, especially if you are in a party of four as I was, is to walk directly to a table and wait—but you do not wait for long.

We were barely settled, still shifting our chairs and looking about us at the crowded, chatter-filled room, when a team of waiters surrounded us, plunked down a rice bowl at each place and then deposited on our table in no particular order a varicolored assortment of cooked foods, each in its own little dish, each different from the others. We started in, mixing the spicy preparations into our rice and bringing it to our lips with our fingers. Some of the dishes contained chili, some pepper (the west Sumatrans seldom use both chili and pepper in the same concoction), and most were hot, piquing the tongue, enticing us to eat as fast as the locals around us were doing.

Of the dozen or so dishes I sampled that day the best, and the most typically Menangkabau, was *rendang (Recipe Index)*, bite-sized chunks of beef loin which had been cooked in spices and coconut milk until all the sauce had dried up. The heavily spiced *rendang*, I was told, can keep for three or four days without needing refrigeration; Menangkabau traders and peddlers in the old days would carry some with them on long trips through the jungle, to eat with their *lontong*, rolls of rice steamed in banana leaves. Yet, thanks to the intricate combination of such "native" spices as *laos (lengkuas)* and such "Indian" spices as cumin, cinnamon and coriander—plus chili, lime leaf, bay leaf and lemon grass—the *rendang* was impressive enough to hold its own at a sit-down meal.

Then there were several kinds of *gulai,* the west Sumatran version of curry. (To the west Sumatrans, *gulai* means anything cooked with coconut milk and retaining its sauce.) A surprisingly good *gulai* was made of tripe, seasoned with pepper and other spices and doused with a thick turmeric-yellow sauce. A milder *gulai* of tender fish fillets, containing just the barest touch of chili, contributed the sourness of tamarind as a change of pace.

*Lado,* a stock red-hot Sumatran *sambal,* appeared twice at our meal, a powerful version served by itself to season fried beef and barbecued fish, and a milder version that came with hard-boiled eggs. This was my first encounter with *lado* and I confess I preferred the milder version. (In south Sumatra, the function of *lado* is taken over by a strong sauce called *sambal tempojak,* made from fermented durian fruit, coconut milk, and an arsenal of spicy ingredients. I confounded my guides by being able to eat more of this durian *sambal* than I could of the simpler *lado.*)

Some plain fried chicken and a couple of vegetable dishes rounded out my first Padang meal, but these were less memorable: the Menangkabau obviously lavish the greater part of their culinary art on fish and meat creations.

We had eaten freely, calling for additional portions of some dishes we enjoyed and leaving others untouched. When we had finished, and drunk a frothy sweet tea-and-egg concoction to soothe our burning tongues —and had loosened our belts—the headwaiter strolled over and surveyed the ruins of our feast. Silently he removed the untouched food and returned it to the kitchen pots. Then, frowning and mumbling, he counted the empty dishes, apparently determining from the color and consistency of the smears of sauce left in each plate just what it had contained; and eventually he presented us with our bill.

In the next few days I discovered that my meal at the Djaja Restaurant had provided the merest introduction to the varied fare of west Sumatra. I learned, for example, that it includes not only pure Menangkabau foods but also local versions of several Indian dishes, such as *korma,* a mild beef curry, and a chicken curry brilliantly blending such contrasting spices as garlic, cumin, nutmeg and pepper. A half-baked *rendang* turned up at one private dinner; known as *kalio (Recipe Index),* this Menangkabau specialty is prepared exactly like the usual *rendang* but is removed from the fire before it dries up. It will not keep as long as *rendang,* and would be somewhat untidy to carry around in a knapsack, but the version I had at this dinner, made with beef liver and dressed in a thick brown sauce, was excellent.

Just about every meal in Padang included a *gulai* of one type or another, some with vegetables, several smooth and mellow examples made with calf's brains, and a sturdy, smoldering number containing tender chunks of goat meat. There was even a duck *gulai,* cooked—in defiance of the standard definition—in oil instead of coconut milk, with generous amounts of both pepper and chili to stand up to the gamy flavor of the fowl.

For between-meal snacks and breakfasts the Sumatrans produce a spectrum of light tidbits little known in other places. My favorite was the west Sumatran *dadih,* a pudding-like mixture of buffalo milk yoghurt, glutinous rice and dark palm sugar; the sour-sweet combination of yoghurt and sugar proved a delight. But to Sumatrans, as to all Southeast Asians, *saté* is the king of snacks. The Javanese pay Padang the compliment of calling their hottest, most popular *saté* by the name of *"saté* Padang" *(Recipe Index),* but when I got to Padang I found the genuine *saté* of the area to be even hotter. I tasted it in a tiny restaurant that doubles as a grocery store. The thick, peppery, red-brown sauce blended magically with the tender beef chunks—and this was no accident, I learned, because the beef had been boiled briefly before grilling and the stock mixed with an assortment of spices to make the sauce. Happily, I found some relief then and there for my pepper-scorched lips and tongue. On the grocery shelves above our table I noticed tall bottles labeled, "Grief Fruit a Go Go." I was fascinated and bought a bottle. It turned out to be lime syrup; with water and ice it became a sweet drink that quenched the fires of the sauce. But no one could explain the name.

Although *saté* came from Indonesia, it is on the narrow busy streets of Singapore, across the Strait, that it really flourishes. The residents of this tropical cosmopolis love to eat outdoors, and there is nothing more compelling, when evening drains the heat from the city, than the aroma of barbecued meat and fowl rising from hundreds of tiny charcoal fires. Down the street from the ornate old Raffles Hotel, or in the swarming passageways around the Bugis Street market, or amid the plate-

112

*Continued on page 118*

A Sumatran farmer pauses in a small village on his way to the market at Bukittinggi, 50 miles north of Padang. His distinctive carabao cart is a model of utility. Inside is his produce for the market. His sleeping roll is stowed at the back, underneath a protective layer of banana leaves. Piled on top of the leaves and the roof is fodder for his carabao.

# A Bustling Weekly Market High in the Sumatran Mountains

The Menangkabau people seem to live for trade, and Bukittinggi, a city tucked in a mountain basin at an altitude of 3,000 feet, is a major trading post. Every Wednesday thousands of buyers and sellers from all around the sculpted hills converge on this highland center. They come by pony cart, carabao cart *(above)*, automobile, truck, bicycle and on foot. The market has several levels. The top level is in the town itself, where residents shop daily for food. But on Wednesdays the market spills down the hillside, first onto narrow steps or terraces, and then out onto a lower level that sprawls for acres under tin-roofed sheds. All day the market bustles furiously with women carrying huge bundles on their heads, men struggling with handcarts and little girls selling handfuls of chilies. The following week it will be just the same all over again.

113

Foods to eat on the spot and foods to take away are spread out for sale in the Bukittinggi market place. The spectacular array at left includes small, pale green eggplants in the top row and dark green limes in all three rows, along with such local specialties as *djeruk-manis,* sweet oranges *(front row),* and the black, mushroomlike *djamur kuping,* or "cloud ears" *(middle row),* used in soups. Ready-to-eat *lemang,* rice baked in banana leaves, is offered in the picture above; it is usually eaten plain as a dessert. The women *(opposite, top),* wearing *slendang,* or scarves, thrown gracefully over one shoulder are selling a heavily aromatic, acidic fruit called *djenkol.* The bright green vegetables on sale at right are *peté* beans.

*Overleaf:* White paper umbrellas blossom over vendors' tables on the steps connecting the upper and lower levels of the Bukittinggi market. But there is not enough room for everybody under the umbrellas, and many of the vendors have to sell their wares directly from mats on the ground.

glass-and-concrete office buildings of fashionable Orchard Road, the *saté* vendors do business from dusk to nearly dawn. Chinese can find pork *saté,* the Muslim Malays buy sticks of skewered goat meat, and both take chicken—all with various hot sauces containing, as a rule, peanuts, ground dried chilies, garlic, onion and *laos (lengkuas).*

Some of the outdoor eating areas, of course, offer much more than *saté.* On Orchard Road a daytime parking lot transforms itself every night into a glittering carnival of food. Within minutes after the last car has departed, tables and stools have been set out, signs and stalls and lights have been installed, charcoal and kerosene fires have been lit, and dozens of vats and pots and Chinese woks, or fry pans, are bubbling and sizzling. Here one can sample Javanese fried rice and Sumatran *gulai* and all kinds of noodles, a peppery Indian mutton soup or Chinese roast pork, hot curries and tropical fruits and fresh fish and intriguing vegetable mixtures, as well as a special Singapore delicacy of river oysters fried with eggs and sweet potatoes. Throngs of jostling customers rove along the stalls until suddenly captured by an aroma, by a glimpse of an enticing morsel, or by the strident spiel of one of the sharp-eyed hawker-chefs who can tend their pots, size up their clientele, serve their food and make change while simultaneously singing their wares into the clamorous equatorial night.

Although the vast majority of the people of Singapore are Chinese, the basic home cooking of the city-state is not, strictly speaking, a part of Chinese cuisine. Nor is it Indian or Malay. The "Straits Chinese" cooks have invented a style of their own called *nonya.* With Chinese methods and implements they use local ingredients and the sweeter Indian spices to produce dishes that look like those of Malaysia and Indonesia but taste like . . . well, like *nonya.*

In *nonya* cooking (the word is the term for a Straits-born housewife), one finds many a *gulai* that tastes vaguely Chinese, along with Chinese vegetable combinations cooked in coconut milk, and such startling juxtapositions as rice noodles served with a hot chili *sambal.* The *nonya* taste prefers thinner coconut milk and less turmeric, chili and pepper than the Malays employ—but more of these ingredients than would be used anywhere in China. Pious Malays cannot eat *nonya* food, because it is cooked with lard instead of coconut oil.

The *nonya* style has also developed a line of sweet desserts, mostly based on the thick brown palm-sugar syrup known as *gula Malacca.* Coconut milk, grated coconut, gelatin and glutinous rice go into many of these sweets, which, when displayed together, present a shimmering spectrum of gay nursery colors. In at least one of them, *kuey lapis,* the color must be more important than the taste; children apparently love *kuey lapis* for its many different-colored layers of gelatin which they peel off one by one. (Green layers are colored with powdered pandanus leaf, yellow with egg yolk, white with coconut, the rest artificially.) My own favorite sweet was *naga sari,* a soft white Jello-like pudding made of mung beans, sugar and coconut milk.

I had the opportunity to compare *nonya* and pure Malay cooking in Singapore when, by chance, a *nonya* and a Malay cook each chose to pre-

118

pare her own version of prawn *sambal* for me. The *nonya* exponent was Mrs. Lee Chin-Koon, the leading cooking teacher of Singapore. In the gleaming American-style kitchen of her handsome mansion, Mrs. Lee deftly and rapidly ground chilies, *kemiri* nut, shallots and *trassi,* stir-fried them in vegetable oil, then added just the meat of the prawns. Tamarind squeezings, for sourness, and a considerable amount of sugar next entered the wok, followed by salt. After less than five minutes of cooking, the oil rose to the top and the dish was ready. Like many *nonya* dishes it tasted quite mild.

Within 24 hours, in a cramped kitchen in one of Singapore's new high-rise apartment developments, Mrs. Ali Yussuf, the plump young wife of a local newspaper photographer, cooked the original Malay version of the prawn dish for me. Mrs. Yussuf's spices included ginger, garlic, anise and a great deal more chili, proportionately, than Mrs. Lee had used; and perhaps to smooth out these seasonings, Mrs. Yussuf used coconut milk instead of oil as a cooking liquid. The prawns, moreover, went into the pan whole ("The brains are the best part," her husband said). Here was a *sambal* that would be a good deal stronger, more vigorous and less sophisticated than the *nonya* version. A lively streak of hot-sour flavor ran through the sauce, discernible within the velvet softness of the coconut milk; the prawns themselves came out soft but tingling to the tongue. Which prawn *sambal* actually tasted "better" I could not say; the two dishes differed so markedly from one another that it was not until some hours afterward that I realized that Mrs. Yussuf's offering was, in theory at least, the same dish that Mrs. Lee had prepared for me.

Of the many fine Sumatran-Malayan foods on Mrs. Yussuf's table that day the one I best remember was *ikan ketja,* a complicated dish of fish fillets fried and then boiled in pepper and soy sauce, with a paste of powdered turmeric on top. The fish absorbed and blended the essence of the spices and the soy, and came up with a new flavor that belonged to none of the ingredients alone but to all of them together.

Among the Malays of Singapore, on the mainland of Malaysia itself, and in south Sumatra, the influence of the visiting traders of long ago is even stronger than it is in west Sumatra. In Johore Bahru, Malaysia, for instance, I encountered some curries that seemed little different from the pure Indian versions, and a *lado* or two even hotter than those in Padang; yet they were cooked not by Indians but by a woman who once was employed as a chef for the Sultan of Johore. In Palembang, south Sumatra, at a luncheon in the Governor's residence, I found several Javanese dishes to which Indian spices had been freely added, thus changing their character considerably. And in the same city, the star pupil of a government-operated cooking school prepared for me— carefully observed all the while by her teacher—a wondrous *nasi samin,* a dish identified as having originated in Arabia.

For this pilau-style dish my charming young cook, Djadmilla by name, filled a cheesecloth bag with a dozen kinds of coarsely pounded spices, just about the entire Indian list, and let this bag dangle in a bubbling chicken broth so the spice flavors could seep into the stock. Then the broth, chicken and spice bag, along with raw rice, were poured into a pan where garlic and onions were frying in "camel milk oil imported from Arabia." The rice cooked in this mixture, with a little fresh-squeezed tomato juice added for color. When I sat down to taste it, the whole cooking school was watching and I wondered whether I would be able to conceal my disappointment in case Djadmilla had made some mistake. I need not have worried. The rice grains came out separate, light, and very slightly oily, and the dish had a heady flavor of nutmeg and a fragrance of cloves and coriander that matched the liveliness of my surroundings. I do not know how the teacher rated the dish but I gave Djadmilla an "A." Anyway, I always enjoy food more in the company of a pretty girl, and on this occasion there were twenty of them at the same table.

When I think back on the foods of Sumatra and Malaysia it is always those of west Sumatra that come most clearly to mind. I especially remember my visit to Bukittinggi, the mountain market town 50 miles from Padang that is the unofficial capital of the Menangkabau people. I set out for Bukittinggi, on my last full day in Indonesia, in the hope of coming upon a wedding feast so that I could observe the cooking and perhaps taste a specially prepared water-buffalo stew that bride and groom and guests traditionally eat together from a huge bowl, while a tethered buffalo stands by.

It turned out that no one was getting married that day, but my trip was worthwhile anyway. It was Wednesday, the weekly market day in Bukittinggi, and from all around people had come bringing their produce or their cash. The Menangkabau passion for trade perhaps accounts for the extraordinary breadth and bustle of this market, the epitome of an Oriental bazaar. Goods of every description were spread out for sale and there were so many vendors it seemed impossible that there would be enough customers to make it worth their while; but then I realized that every seller was a buyer too, that this was a place for the exchange of goods, as markets used to be.

Finally, there was another reason for remembering my visit to this lively town with its picturesque pointed roof-ends representing the horns of the revered carabao. All through Indonesia my friends and guides had constantly inquired whether the foods I was getting were not too hot for me, and when I politely said no and calmly swallowed another bit of a blazing *sambal* they stared in amazement. And eventually, of course, I began to get used to the chili and pepper, and missed them when they were not there. But Bukittinggi, high in the mountains, is 10 degrees cooler than the coast, and people from Padang claim that they need more pepper and chili up there to stay warm. I was aware of this, yet the dishes at the Djaja Restaurant of Bukittinggi looked like those of the Djaja in Padang, and had the same names: *gulai itik, gulai ikan, kalio* . . . and so without thinking I plunged in. With the first bite my mouth caught fire and I could not go on. I felt that all the hottest spices of the marketplace had somehow been forced down my throat in one dose. I had met my match, and not even two glasses of soothing Grief Fruit a Go Go juice could quench the fire.

## Saté Padang *(Sumatra)*
BROILED SKEWERED BRAISED BEEF WITH SPICED COCONUT MILK SAUCE

Place the beef in a heavy 3- to 4-quart saucepan and pour in enough water to cover it by 1 inch. Bring to a boil over high heat, then reduce the heat to low and simmer partially covered for 1 hour, or until the beef is tender but still intact. Transfer the beef to a plate to cool.

Meanwhile, prepare the sauce. Combine the onions, chilies, garlic, ginger and 1-3 of water in the jar of a blender and blend at high speed for 30 seconds. Turn the machine off, and scrape down the sides of the jar with a rubber spatula. Blend again until the mixture is a smooth purée.

In a heavy 10- to 12-inch skillet, heat the oil over moderate heat until a light haze forms above it. Add the contents of the blender jar and, stirring frequently, cook briskly until most of the liquid in the pan has evaporated and the mixture is thick. Stir in the coriander, turmeric, cumin and salt and cook for a minute or so. Then pour in the coconut milk, mix well and remove the pan from the heat.

Preheat the broiler to its highest point. Thread the cubes of beef tightly, 4 or 5 pieces at a time, on a small skewers—preferably Oriental wooden skewers about 6 inches long. Protect the ends of the wooden skewers by wrapping them with foil. With a pastry brush, spread a generous coating of the sauce evenly over the beef. Arrange the skewers on a large baking sheet and broil them 4 inches from the heat, turning them once or twice, for about 3 minutes, or until crisp and brown.

Arrange the skewers on a heated platter and brush the meat again with sauce. Reheat the remaining sauce and serve it in a small bowl.

## Gulai Udang Dengan Labu Kuning *(Malaysia)*
SHRIMP AND ZUCCHINI CURRY

Shell the shrimp. Devein them by making a shallow incision down their backs with a small, sharp knife and lifting out the black or white intestinal vein with the point of the knife. Wash the shrimp under cold running water and set them aside on paper towels to drain.

Put the chilies and onions through the finest blade of a meat grinder, or purée them in the jar of an electric blender. Transfer the purée to a heavy 2- to 3-quart saucepan and stir in the lemon grass, basil, turmeric, *laos* powder and 1 cup of water. Bring to a boil over high heat, reduce the heat to low and simmer uncovered for 5 minutes.

Stir in the zucchini and continue cooking for 5 or 6 minutes longer, or until the squash shows only the slightest resistance when pierced with the point of a small knife. Add the coconut top milk and the shrimp and, stirring frequently, cook for 4 or 5 minutes until the shrimp are firm and pink. Do not allow the liquid to boil or it will curdle. Remove the pan from the heat, stir in the lemon juice and salt and taste for seasoning. Serve at once from a heated bowl, accompanied if you like by hot boiled rice.

### To make 6 to 8 *saté*

2 pounds bottom round of beef, trimmed of all fat, and cut into 1-inch cubes
1 cup finely chopped onions
2 tablespoons finely chopped fresh hot chilies *(caution: see page 69)*
1 teaspoon finely chopped garlic
1 teaspoon scraped finely grated fresh ginger root
⅓ cup water
¼ cup vegetable oil
1 tablespoon ground coriander
1½ teaspoons ground turmeric
¼ teaspoon ground cumin
1 teaspoon salt
1 cup fresh coconut milk made from 1 cup coarsely chopped coconut and 1 cup hot water *(page 61)*

### To serve 4

1 pound uncooked jumbo shrimp (10 to 15 to the pound)
4 large fresh hot chilies, each about 4 or 5 inches long, stemmed, seeded and coarsely chopped *(caution: see page 69)*
1 cup coarsely chopped onions
1 three-inch blade of fresh lemon grass, crushed with the flat of a large knife or cleaver
2 fresh basil leaves
1 teaspoon turmeric
¼ teaspoon ground *laos (see Glossary)*
1 cup water
1 medium-sized zucchini squash, peeled, cut lengthwise into ½-inch-thick slices and then into ½-inch cubes
1 cup rich fresh coconut top milk *(page 61)*
2 teaspoons strained, fresh lemon juice
1 teaspoon salt

To serve 6 to 8

4 cups fresh coconut
  milk made from 4 cups coarsely
  chopped coconut and 4 cups hot
  water *(page 61)*
1½ teaspoons salt
⅓ cup vegetable oil
1 cup finely chopped onions
2 teaspoons finely
  chopped garlic
1 tablespoon ground coriander
2 three-inch-long pieces of stick
  cinnamon
½ teaspoon turmeric
¼ teaspoon ground cumin
⅛ teaspoon ground allspice
¼ teaspoon white pepper
A 4-pound boneless lamb shoulder,
  trimmed of excess fat, rolled and
  tied securely in 3 or 4 places
A 3½- to 4-pound firm ripe
  pineapple, peeled and with its
  "eyes" removed *(see directions
  on page 185)*, cut in slices
  no less than ½ inch wide

## *Patjeri Nenas*  *(Borneo)*
### BRAISED LAMB SHOULDER WITH FRESH PINEAPPLE

Preheat the oven to 350°. Prepare the coconut milk and let it stand at room temperature or in the refrigerator for an hour or so until the rich top milk rises to the surface. Skim off 1 cup of top milk and reserve it. Stir the salt into the remaining 3 cups of coconut milk and set it aside in a separate bowl.

In a heavy 5- to 6-quart casserole, heat the oil over moderate heat until a light haze forms above it. Drop in the onions and garlic and, stirring frequently, cook for about 5 minutes until they are soft and transparent but not brown. Stir in the coriander, cinnamon, turmeric, cumin, allspice and pepper. Mix well, then raise the heat. Add the lamb and turn it about with a slotted spoon for 5 minutes, or until it is lightly browned on all sides and evenly coated with the onion mixture.

Pour in the 3 cups of coconut milk and bring to a boil over high heat. Cover tightly and place the casserole on the middle shelf of the oven. (Cooking liquid should be kept at a slow simmer; check the lamb after it has been in the oven for about 30 minutes and, if the liquid is bubbling too rapidly, reduce the heat to 325°.) Braise the lamb for 1 hour, turn it over, and continue braising for 1 hour longer, or until the meat is tender and shows no resistance when pierced with the point of a small, sharp knife. Transfer the lamb to a heated platter and drape with foil to keep it warm while you prepare the sauce.

With a large spoon, skim as much fat as possible from the liquid remaining in the casserole. Bring the liquid to a boil over high heat and, stirring occasionally, cook briskly until it has been reduced to about 1½ cups. Stir in the rich coconut top milk and the pineapple slices. Reduce the heat to the lowest point, and, stirring from time to time, simmer

A pineapple top garnishes each end of *patjeri nenas,* a Bornean dish with alternating

for 15 minutes or so, until the pineapple slices are tender but still intact.

To serve, remove the strings from the lamb and carve the meat crosswise into ¼-inch-thick slices. With a slotted spoon or spatula, gently lift the pineapple out of the sauce, and arrange the pineapple and lamb slices alternately in a single row on a heated platter. Garnish each end of the row with one half of the pineapple top. Taste the sauce for seasoning and pour about ½ cup over the *patjeri nenas*. Serve the remaining sauce separately in a bowl.

### *Kalio* or *Rendang* (Sumatra)
COCONUT BEEF

Preheat the oven to 375°. In a heavy 6- to 8-quart casserole, combine the beef, onions, garlic, coriander, ginger, chili, turmeric, salt and pepper. Pour in the coconut milk and mix well.

Stirring frequently, bring to a boil over high heat. Place the casserole on the middle shelf of the oven and, stirring it every 30 minutes or so, cook uncovered for about 3 hours, or until the beef is soft enough to be easily pulled apart with a fork and the sauce is thick enough to coat a spoon lightly. At this stage, the beef and its sauce are called *kalio* and may be served immediately.

To prepare *rendang,* continue to cook the meat briskly on top of the stove, stirring it gently all the while until most of the liquid in the pan has evaporated. Be careful not to break the pieces of meat apart or shred them.

Before serving *kalio* or *rendang,* taste for seasoning and then transfer the entire contents of the casserole to a large heated bowl. Both are traditionally accompanied by hot boiled rice.

To serve 4 to 6

2 pounds lean beef chuck, trimmed of excess fat, sliced 1 inch thick and cut into 2½-by-1-inch pieces
3 cups coarsely chopped onions
2 tablespoons coarsely chopped garlic
2 tablespoons ground coriander
1 teaspoon scraped, finely grated fresh ginger root
1 teaspoon finely chopped fresh hot chili *(caution: see page 69)*
¼ teaspoon turmeric
2 teaspoons salt
¼ teaspoon white pepper
10 cups fresh coconut milk, made from 8 to 10 cups coarsely chopped coconut and 10 cups hot water *(page 61)*

slices of lamb and pineapple. The coconut sauce contains cinnamon and other spices.

# VII

# The Philippines, Outpost of the West

Bearing a dish of boiled crabs, a housewife in a coastal village near Manila heads happily for a potluck feast with her neighbors. Filipinos depend heavily on seafood for protein, yet country-wide the supply is inadequate, and as a result many fishing villagers are noticeably sturdier than their inland compatriots.

It is a wild land of typhoons and earthquakes and volcanoes, with a lively history of political gunplay, of primitive tribes and head-hunters roaming the unexplored rain forests, of pirates and smugglers still at large in the southern seas.

It is also a mild land of white beaches lined with coconut palms, of simple thatched huts smothered with blossoms, of easy friendships, fiestas and old world Spanish courtliness.

It is a Malay land of Oriental fatalism that says *"bahala na,"* "what will be will be," and assumes that tomorrow will look after itself. But it is a Christian country too—the only one in Asia.

Of all the lands of the East, the Philippines is the most Western. Not in that it is modern and industrialized—although Manila has factories, traffic jams and air-conditioned office buildings—but Western in customs and taste. Four hundred years of Spanish rule brought the country Christianity, prudery, a dollop of the volatile Latin temperament and a taste for rich desserts, breakfast sausages, olive oil and lard. Fifty years of American occupation implanted free speech, free elections, free-swinging competition, a capacity for hard work and a passion for American slang, quick results, Coca-Cola, steak and hot dogs. And two decades of independence seem to have engraved these traits indelibly on the character of most of the nearly 50 million people who inhabit the 7,000 islands of the Philippines.

Not surprisingly, the Philippine taste in foods is thoroughly compatible with a Westerner's. Nowhere in Asia can a timid American or

European tuck into a wide range of local dishes with less chance of offending his palate or his stomach. There are exceptions, of course. The bitter melon generally lives up to its name; travelers with fragile taste buds should go easy, at first, on the fishy *bagoong* sauce; those with vivid imaginations should probably altogether avoid *balut,* a hardboiled duck egg containing a partly developed embryo. But by and large the path to the enjoyment of Philippine foods is clear. There are no hot *sambal* booby traps, no *popeda* deadfalls and very few obstacle courses like the far-out lagoon delicacies of Samoa. And even though the Filipinos have been eating rice for more than 2,000 years, you do not have to like rice to eat and enjoy some of the best Philippine dishes.

So thoroughly have the centuries of colonial rule toned down the native Malay foods of the Philippines that when I arrived in Manila from Sumatra and Singapore, with the fiery brand of *lado* still on my tongue, the Philippine foods seemed blander and less interesting than I remembered from previous visits. But after a few days my palate recovered and I began to discern and enjoy again the distinctive flavors of Philippine cuisine. For Philippine cooking does have a unique and intriguing personality that can surprise a stranger without stunning him. This personality is marked by a few key traits: a range of sour and salty tastes, a predilection for frying with garlic and onions, and a tendency to cook several different kinds of foods together.

To achieve the cool, sour taste they like so much, the Filipinos cook many dishes with vinegar, or with the acidic pulp of the unripe tamarind pod, or with a sour cucumberlike fruit, native to the Philippines, called *kamias.* Even foods that have not been cooked in these acid agents are often seasoned at the table with a vinegar spiced with chili, or with the juice of the *calamansi,* a small, sour lime. Some vinegar uses —on noodles, for instance—may have come from China, but unlike the Chinese, the Filipinos do not fancy many sweet-and-sour dishes.

The distinctive sour taste of Philippine food attains its highest degree of perfection in *sinigang,* a soup of meat or fish cooked in water with sour fruits, tomatoes and vegetables. The variations of *sinigang* are subtle and nearly endless, depending on the meats used, on whether fish, fowl or prawns go into the pot, and on which sour fruits follow —tamarind, *kamias,* guava, green mango or something else. Any type of *sinigang* can be excellent, but to taste the best of them you have to follow the massive weekend exodus from Manila down to the historic shore resort of Cavite.

Admiral Dewey defeated the Spanish fleet off Cavite in the Battle of Manila Bay in 1898 and it was in that town that General Emilio Aguinaldo proclaimed Philippine independence from Spain a month and a half later. But the Filipinos who flock to Cavite today are more interested in food than in history. Middle-class Manilans pile their kids and cousins and huge food hampers into garishly painted jeepneys and head for Cavite's Lido Beach, where at any given moment on a hot afternoon, year-round, the number of people clustered in the thatched-roof picnic huts and feasting on home-cooked dishes is roughly equal to the number in the water. The mood of the beach is homey and somewhat prim; the women enter the water in knee-length cotton dresses to avoid the exposure of feminine flesh that still shocks family morality.

Such old-fashioned considerations do not seem to cramp the style of another contingent of Manilans that flocks to Cavite regularly. This is the high-living crowd that zips down to the shore in air-conditioned Mercedes sedans—and not usually in family groups. The jet set shuns the beach altogether and heads instead for Josephine's, a breezy pavilion restaurant purveying shrimp and oysters from the sea and prawns and catfish from its private fish ponds. At Josephine's the gourmets in the crowd will invariably call for *sinampalukan,* which can be classified as a *sinigang* in the same way, perhaps, that bouillabaisse can be called a fish stew.

On any table, in Marseilles or Cavite, *sinampalukan* would be a great soup. It comes steaming hot in a *palayok,* a quaint little earthenware pot, and you ladle it out with a large wooden spoon. Some people drench their rice with it, but the best way is to eat it like soup, making sure to get plenty of fish or chicken and vegetables, along with the rich, sour broth. A highly spicy soup can sometimes drown out the individual flavors of the ingredients; the *sinampalukan,* however, somehow preserves the integrity of its components within the overall sour flavor. And it is *really* sour, for *sinampalukan,* unlike ordinary *sinigang,* is made with the leaves—and often the blossoms—of the tamarind tree instead of the fruit. This taste of the tamarind, I should point out, is not the puckering sourness of a lemon. Rather, it recalls to me the clean, tart tang of the sour grass I loved to chew on as a boy. But until I tasted *sinampalukan* at Josephine's, in the middle of a sultry afternoon, it had never occurred to me that a piping hot, sour soup could cool and refresh me more thoroughly than a glass of cold beer or a carbonated drink. The *sinampalukan* also stimulates the appetite almost as effectively as a hot Indonesian *sambal,* which keeps the restaurant's nearby fish ponds busy. It is probably no coincidence that *sinampalukan* originated in Batangas province, south of Cavite. Batangueños are famous throughout the Philippines for their heroic capacity for *lambanog,* a sweet palm wine, and according to Josephine's proprietress, Mrs. Anita Masakayan, *sinampalukan* can take the sting out of a hangover —even a Batangas hangover—as quickly as any antidote known to the drinking fraternity.

For saltiness, the second prevailing Philippine taste, the Filipinos turn to their famous fish paste, *bagoong* (pronounced ba-go-ong), or to a clear liquid sauce called *patis.* Generally, *bagoong* tastes like anchovies, although there are dozens of varieties. It is made traditionally by putting salt and fresh fish or shrimp in a ceramic pot and letting the mixture ferment for days or weeks. In the Bicol region of southeastern Luzon, *bagoong*-making used to be a community enterprise. Netloads of tiny fish called *dilis* were dumped into a 20-foot-long canoe, which was then filled up with sea water. When most of the water had evaporated in the tropical sun, leaving the salt and fish, a dozen people would stamp around on the mixture in bare feet, pounding it into a uniform consistency. The salty fish paste would then ferment in vats that were

*Continued on page 130*

# A Seafood Feast for a Small Town Festival

Perched on piles at the edge of quiet Manila Bay, north of the capital, Isla de Balut is a typical Philippine coastal settlement. Festivals are never very splendid there—it is too small and poor—but they are welcome indeed, and the sea at least can be counted on to be generous. Thus while Santacruzan, the ancient Festival of the Holy Cross, has been forgotten in many parts of the country, here it is still celebrated every spring with some of the old traditions—including the election of a Reina Elena (after the Byzantine queen who took pieces of the True Cross to Rome) and a wonderful lot of eating. The festival fare, mainly seafood, is gathered by the men, cooked by the women, and eaten communally, to nourish both the diners and their town's spirit.

In preparation for the feast a man plucks mussels *(opposite)* from a stick on which they were cultivated in the ocean shallows, and the completed dishes are set out *(above)*. Then, attended by admirers, Reina Elena enjoys the meal *(below)*.

placed underground so that the paste would keep an even temperature.

Today *bagoong* comes out of commercial—and more sanitary—factories, and appears as a soft paste in which bits of fish are visible. The fish sauce *patis,* on the other hand, is a transparent amber liquid that has been strained, boiled and refined to a smooth consistency. Filipinos use it as Westerners use salt, and they relish its decidedly fishy aroma—although they will sometimes try to neutralize the smell with a dash of citrus juice. Both the *patis* bottle and the *bagoong* jar appear on every proper Philippine table and can be found in every kitchen, and both can be used by cook or diner. In general, *patis,* which blends well, finds its way into soups or dishes with broth, while *bagoong,* like a relish, is eaten with dry fish or chunky stews and sometimes, in poorer homes, with plain white rice.

But Filipinos almost never serve *bagoong* or *patis* to foreigners, even with dishes that cry out for one or the other. They regard the two products with a fierce, inverted pride, defying Westerners to eat them. One of the vivid memories of my stay in the Philippines is the crestfallen look on a waiter's face when I added some *bagoong* to my *adobo* and ate it with enjoyment; he seemed to feel that I had somehow violated his country's sovereignty. Actually, neither *bagoong* nor *patis* is as strong or as difficult to appreciate as the corresponding condiments of mainland Southeast Asia, such as Vietnam's famous *nuoc mam* or Thailand's *nam pla* and *kapi.* And even though the Indonesians, whose Muslim religion theoretically forbids the use of fermented products, use fish sauce sparingly, their *petis,* which is clearly related to *patis* in taste as well as name, comes on somewhat stronger than the Philippine sauce. Very possibly it is the Filipinos' long exposure to Spanish culinary standards that has gradually toned down and refined their fish sauce and fish paste.

Except for rice, and a few kinds of fish that may be broiled or grilled and served with *bagoong,* the Filipinos almost never cook anything by itself. Vegetables, meats, fish, chicken, noodles, all go into stews and soups and fonduelike concoctions that are served with rice; the diner mixes the rice and other foods together on his plate and adds *bagoong, patis* or *calamansi* juice according to taste. The repertoire of combinations is immense and imaginative, embracing almost all of the best Philippine dishes and often involving juxtapositions that seem strange to us—shellfish with pork or chicken, for instance, or chicken and pork together in the famous *adobo (Recipe Index).*

What makes the Philippine method of combining foods different from ours is that the Filipinos usually do not build these combinations around one central ingredient, as we would do with a lamb stew or a chicken soup. Instead, the various ingredients come to pot with equal status; none of them is central or essential. The combination itself, and the condiments and methods used, determine the outcome, not one prima donna ingredient. *Sinigang* can be made of fish or chicken and it is still *sinigang.* And *adobo* is *adobo* regardless of its basic ingredients, although chicken and pork are the most common.

*Adobo,* in fact, embodies all three of the distinctive cooking traits of the Philippines and therefore can claim to be the most typical dish of the country. Its ingredients are fried in garlic, it carries a fine sourish taste and it is a blend of several constituents that generally begin with chicken and pork, although fish and prawns are also frequently used. Like the Sumatran *rendang,* to which it seems to be related, *adobo* originated as a means of preserving meats during long journeys; a good *adobo,* it is said, will keep four or five days without refrigeration. Even now, with that need gone, Filipinos insist—and I agree—that *adobo* tastes best two or three days after it has been cooked. In fact, good Philippine cooks will always prepare their *adobo* at least a day before it is to be served. In any case, a fine *adobo*—with its rich, sour taste, chunks of tender meat and thick, brown sauce—lingers in the memory far longer than the dish itself lasts. Every Philippine cook knows how to make it, and although some versions of *adobo* that I had on my trip were better than others, only once was I given a poor one —and that was when my host, in a misguided attempt to pander to an American palate, deliberately held back on the essential garlic.

The distinguishing sour taste of *adobo* is achieved by first marinating chunks of meat in palm vinegar (which is not so sour as wine vinegar), usually with crushed garlic, bay leaves, salt and whole black peppercorns. Then the meat is boiled—in its own marinade plus soy sauce —until it is tender, fried in lard until brown, and finally simmered in the broth until the liquid turns to a thick sauce. In a first-rate *adobo* the flavor of the meats themselves can just be discerned through the good, sour tang.

In its many variations, *adobo* turns up everywhere. It can be cooked with coconut or *bagoong,* and seafood enthusiasts like a version using small squid along with the creatures' purplish, bitter "ink." The holiday picnickers at Cavite's beach devour *adobo,* and sugar plantation workers look forward to eating it after payday. I have found *adobo* on the menu at The Plaza, Manila's most opulent restaurant, at tiny *turo-turo* (point-point) cafeterias—so named because the customers point to what they want—and at an outdoor dinner on the terrace of a planter's mansion in Mindanao. And at a garish Manila nightclub-casino, customers who want to eat as well as drink, dance and gamble, are likely to order a standard *adobo* of chicken and pork.

The cooking of many foods together is probably an element of the Philippine legacy from Spain, which some experts feel accounts for about one third of the country's culinary ideas. This is not a surprising statistic, considering that Ferdinand Magellan, looking for spice routes, reached the Philippines (and was killed there) about a century before the Pilgrims landed at Plymouth. And some 40 years before the founding of Jamestown, Spanish missionaries established the first Roman Catholic church in the Philippines (which had been named for Spain's King Philip II). A few years later the Spaniards took over Manila, which was already a flourishing port for Chinese, Indian and Malay trading vessels, and soon established control over Luzon, the northernmost island of the Philippines, and most of the central islands. (Only in the south, where Islam had already gained a foothold, were the native popu-

*Overleaf:* Arrayed splendidly on an antique inlaid table, an unusually elegant Philippine *merienda* is ready for serving. Roughly comparable to high tea in England, the *merienda* can be anything from a simple snack to an elaborate spread like this, containing the following dishes, several of which are listed in the Recipe Index:

1 Fried *lumpia,* a kind of egg roll made with pork, chilies and vegetables
2 Sour sauce for the fried *lumpia*
3 *Bucayo,* a sticky coconut dessert
4 *Pancit luglug,* a noodle dish prepared in this case with shrimp
5 Fresh, or unfried, *lumpia*
6 Sweet sauce for the fresh *lumpia*
7 *Bibingka especial,* a dessert made from rice flour and sprinkled with cheese
8 Another type of *bibingka*
9 *Ukoy,* a vegetable and shrimp fritter
10 *Gulaman,* a soft dessert containing pineapple and coconut
11-12 *Puto maya,* sweet glutinous rice, surrounded by mounds of *cuchinta,* another glutinous rice confection

The people in the photograph, all attached to Philippine government offices in the United States, are *(from left)* the Misses Cynthia Evangelista, Brenda Duque and Ching Cruz, Mrs. Manuel Lozada and Mr. Gabi Ascalon.

lations able to resist effectively up to modern times.) For the next three centuries, despite attacks by Dutch and English fleets and raids by Muslim pirates, Spanish administrators and Spanish friars held fast to the islands, dispatching galleons laden with the wealth of the Orient to Mexico and Spain, and slowly depositing an ever-thickening crust of Spanish culture and customs on the Philippine towns.

Today the Spanish heritage is apparent in a number of ways besides religion. Most Filipinos bear Spanish names—not necessarily because they have Spanish ancestors but because late in the 19th Century the Spanish governor ordered them to adopt names from an official list. In every small city and town the community life focuses on a broad central plaza—a Mediterranean custom otherwise alien to Asia. In Manila the Basque game of jai-alai is one of the principal gambling sports; and all over the country Spanish dances such as the fandango and the jota have been incorporated into the lively and expressive Philippine repertoire of folk dances. On formal occasions, men and women don a "national costume" that is clearly influenced by Spain. For the women, this consists of the *terno,* a long dress with high, starched butterfly-winged shoulders; for the men, it is the *barong Tagalog,* a cool, sensible open-necked shirt made of pineapple fiber, embroidered with a lacy design that recalls the frills and ruffs of the Spanish grandees, and worn hanging loose over the trousers. And even today, no Filipino is considered really educated unless he knows Spanish as well as English. Without Spanish he can read neither the history of his country nor the works of the Philippines' great martyr-poet, José Rizal.

In the culinary realm, Spanish tastes and methods survive just as stubbornly. Dietary experts blame the Spaniards for the high fat and cholesterol content of Philippine cuisine—although the great majority of the populace works hard enough and eats little enough not to have to worry about weight or blood vessels. The Spaniards taught the Filipinos to sauté, in lard as well as olive oil, and fats and oils have become an integral element in Philippine cooking. Although many Filipinos use the rounded Chinese wok for their sautéing, they do not seem to have learned the Chinese knack of quick stir-frying, and they tend to leave the food in the oil longer, Spanish style.

Along with the general Spanish methodology came a number of specific Spanish dishes which the Filipinos now call their own. These include several *paellas;* a goat stew, *caldereta,* which derives from a Spanish fish stew of the same name; and chicken *relleno*—a whole chicken stuffed with boiled eggs, pork, sausage and spices *(Recipe Index)* —that has become a Philippine dish for fiestas and special occasions. One of the best examples of the Filipinos' inclination to mix foods is their *puchero,* which is a close cousin of the Spanish *cocido,* a beef, chicken and vegetable stew with a garlic sauce. In fact it could be said that *cocido* was the vehicle in which the basic notions of Spanish cooking traveled to the Philippines.

Both *puchero* and *cocido* remain popular today side by side, and one chef's *puchero* tastes like another's *cocido.* Generally *puchero* is a plebeian dish, and none of the restaurant versions I tasted could compare with those that came out of the housewives' kitchens. A home-cooked *puchero* can be an eminently satisfying meal in itself, as I discovered at one informal potluck dinner in Manila. For an appetizer, with glasses of the excellent San Miguel beer, we had a few slices of a fine *embutido,* a home-made spicy sausage that the Filipinos have adapted from the drier Spanish *galantina.* Then, heralded by a steamy, savory aroma, a large casserole of *puchero*—which, my hostess informed me, had been cooking all day on a low fire—was borne to table. Large chunks of what turned out to be pork, beef and sausage poked out of a thick sauce, reddish-yellow from sweet potatoes and tomatoes that had dissolved in it completely. Cabbage was in there too, and chick-peas and pieces of *saba* bananas (the sweet, cooking variety) and probably a few other vegetables I did not notice. We fell to, piling first rice on our plates, and then ladlefuls of *puchero* on top, then a teaspoon or two of a peppery and garlicky eggplant relish; and then mixing it all together. The result was a harmony of tastes: the vivid, sharp relish, the flavorsome meats and sweet potato, and a more muted accompaniment of cabbage, other vegetables and rice. Altogether, a rugged meal for big eaters and hard workers—but not for anyone who has any more work to do the same day. For dessert that night we had avocado-flavored ice cream, and I was hard put to find room for it.

Wisely, most Philippine families eat *puchero* for Sunday dinner only, when they can take their time and indulge in a long siesta afterward. In some homes Sunday *puchero* has become such an institution that the head of the household makes it a ritual, announcing in tones loud enough for the whole household to hear the entry of each ingredient into the pot. For thousands of Filipinos the Sunday *puchero* is a cherished childhood memory, and they complain that nowadays they cannot find a *puchero* like grandfather used to make.

If they do not have a sweet after their meal, and often even if they do, Filipinos like to end up with the excellent white cheese that they make from the milk of the ubiquitous long-horned carabao, or water buffalo, the work animal of all the islands. Since this is the only native cheese that I have ever encountered or heard of in East Asia and the Pacific, it would seem that the technique of cheese-making arrived with the Spaniards. Today imported Australian cheese and locally processed American cheese find their way even to small, neighborhood *sari-sari* (general) stores, and I had to go to market four or five times before I found a little banana-leaf packet of carabao cheese in stock. But it was worth the effort. Salty, mildly aromatic and slightly gamy, this light, white cheese has the texture of fine-grained cottage cheese and the consistency and delicacy of bean curd. Somewhere in Europe I once ate a fresh peasant cheese something like it; I cannot remember where but I suspect it was probably in Spain.

The Filipinos' Spanish masters altered the eating habits of the country as well as the actual eating. The Spanish custom of having dinner late in the evening has only recently succumbed to pressure from the American way of life, and among some proud families of Spanish descent the old tradition survives. Almost all Filipinos, though, still cling

to the custom of the *merienda,* the Spanish afternoon mini-meal of cakes, tarts and sweet fritters.

In the current Philippine version of the *merienda,* not just sweets but almost anything goes. As long as no fresh-cooked rice appears, the session does not qualify officially as a meal, no matter what or how much may be consumed. (By thus inversely showing the importance of rice, this concept proves that the Filipinos are essentially an Asian people despite their Spanish and Western culture.) Even *dinuguan,* a strong blood stew of beef entrails, turns up at *merienda*-time; but instead of eating it with fresh-cooked rice, as they would at dinner, the Filipinos take it with *puto,* a sweet, fluffy cake made of glutinous rice, sugar and sometimes coconut milk. Another dish that a Spaniard would be surprised to see on the *merienda* table is *ukoy (Recipe Index),* a deep-fried vegetables-and-shrimp creation rather like Japanese *tempura.* It is a fine food when properly prepared, but it is certainly not a sweet.

Although they have broadened the eligibility rules for the *merienda,* the Filipinos have by no means given up the idea of afternoon sweets. Included in the *merienda* is a galaxy of native treats, mostly made with coconut milk. Among them are *suman,* a mixture of glutinous rice, coconut milk and palm sugar steamed in banana leaves until gummy; *tsampurado,* an unlikely sounding but surprisingly compatible combination of chocolate and soft rice; and dozens of versions of *bibingka (Recipe Index),* a sweet, moist cake embellished with grated coconut, cheese and many other ingredients.

The luscious *halo-halo* (mix-mix), a liquid dessert that comes in a glass but is eaten with a spoon, also adds to the richness of the *merienda,* although it may appear as a dinner dessert and a sweet refreshment at any time of day. *Halo-halo* demonstrates once more the Philippine fondness for throwing all kinds of foods together, in that it consists of shaved ice and coconut milk mixed with a range of possible ingredients —including corn kernels, crisp fried rice grains, mung bean, pineapple jelly, sugar and boiled nipa-palm seeds—that ensure a variety of both taste and texture.

Many Filipinos credit the Japanese with evolving this jazzed-up version of what had been a less flamboyant traditional Philippine coconut-milk drink. In Manila I heard a fascinating story in connection with this theory. In the years before World War II, *halo-halo* parlors sprang up suddenly throughout the Philippines, all of them serving more or less the same product, and all of them owned and operated by Japanese. *Halo-halo* caught on quickly and the parlors became unofficial community hangouts, their proprietors attaining the popular status of friendly neighborhood pal, like an American candy store owner. Then, shortly before the war began, the parlors all closed and their owners vanished. At least one reputable Filipino swears that during the Japanese occupation he saw his friendly neighborhood *halo-halo* man striding down a street in the uniform of an officer of the Japanese political police. Whether this was a coincidence, or whether the Japanese government deliberately invented the easy-to-prepare *halo-halo* as an effective cover for its prewar agents, as this Filipino suggests, is a secret that may be

*Opposite:* An example of Spanish influence in the Philippine cuisine, *morcon* is flank steak stuffed with sausage and boiled eggs, then rolled and sliced. The objects shown with it also illustrate the distinctive conjunction of cultures in the Philippines. The carved wooden figures, *santos,* represent Catholic saints; the chest and betel-nut box, both inlaid with mother-of-pearl, are strictly Oriental.

lost forever. But *halo-halo* itself, as sweet and rich and peaceful as a malted milk, survives.

Long before the Spanish arrived, the Filipinos were adapting foods and learning cooking techniques from the vast culinary emporium of China, although it would be wrong to insist on too strong an influence. The Philippines stand outside the chopstick belt; the development of the islands' culture diverged from that of the Chinese many centuries ago, before the Chinese developed a sophisticated cuisine. So, although it shares with the Chinese many vegetables and a dependence on rice, to assert that Philippine cooking is basically Chinese is like saying European cooking comes from Mesopotamia because it uses wheat.

Nevertheless, Chinese traders and settlers have been in the Philippines for the past thousand years and through them the Filipinos were introduced to noodles, soy sauce, bean curd, bean sprouts and egg rolls. All these things they have adopted as their own. Philippine noodles are called *pancit (Recipe Index)*, and they come in a variety of styles and recipes. Very often, the Filipinos cook them in sautéed garlic, thus blending Spanish and Chinese techniques into a truly Philippine dish.

Probably the most ubiquitous version of this is *pancit luglug,* the word *luglug* referring to the sound made when the noodles are jerked back and forth in a bamboo skimmer to shake off the boiling water. Besides the sautéed garlic, *pancit luglug* is flavored with shrimp sauce, peppers, *patis* and *calamansi,* garnished with pork cracklings and boiled egg, and decorated with a red sauce made from the squeezings of the *achuete* (annatto) bean. Filipinos invariably serve *pancit luglug* at birthday parties, for the long rice noodle is said to symbolize long life. But it also turns up at fiestas, *meriendas,* restaurant buffets, and thousands of hole-in-the-wall *panciterias* in every town and city of the country.

In *lumpia (Recipe Index),* a rendition of the Chinese egg roll, the Filipinos have almost created a new dish. *Lumpia,* when fried, looks like egg roll, but the Filipinos also produce a soft, unfried version that does not, and neither one tastes like egg roll. The difference seems to be the presence of *ubod,* heart of palm, which offers little taste of its own but absorbs and relays the flavors of the other ingredients. *Lumpia* is most often served with a sweetened soy sauce or with chopped garlic. One of the most famous Philippine *lumpia* is that produced in Silay, on the island of Negros. Silay is a town of gambling establishments whose patrons like something to nibble on while placing their bets. The local *lumpia* keeps them satisfied—and prevents them from wandering away from the tables when they get hungry.

The influence of the Philippines' other neighbors, the Indian and Muslim worlds, brought spices and chilies to the islands, but for some reason only to certain areas. The Philippine Muslims in the south eat hot food that is similar to Sumatran cuisine, with the addition of such local delicacies as turtle eggs. And some quirk of history and migration has turned the province of Bicol, in southeastern Luzon, into a small enclave of chili-hot and spicy foods, with lots of coconut milk. Apparently Bicol was settled by a wave of migrants who brought with them tastes and textures developed in Sumatra, Java and Borneo. Since they made their home on the Pacific side of the Philippines, they must also have come into contact with Polynesian methods of leaf wrapping and coconut cooking. The excellent Bicol *pinangat* perfectly combines two extremes of the Pacific region: basically, it is a Polynesian *fafa,* chopped taro-type leaves in coconut milk, but it is cooked with *bagoong,* ginger, onion, garlic and chili, and it comes out nice and hot.

Stripping away these alien influences to find the truly native Philippine cuisine is a difficult and probably pointless task, but one that Filipinos like to muse on. Pigafetta, the chronicler of the Magellan expedition, reported in 1521 that the natives on Palawan "presented a gift of various foods all made only of rice, some in leaves made with rather long pieces like sugar-loaves, others like tarts with eggs and honey." The same foods, *suman, calamay* and *cuchinta,* can be found on Philippine *merienda* and picnic tables today. In many rural districts Filipinos still line their cooking pots with leaves before putting in rice, a technique that Pigafetta observed. And the basic dish of the common people is still *daing,* salt-dried fish, which Magellan and his men were offered in Mindanao. But my nomination for the best purely Philippine dish goes to *kari-kari (Recipe Index).*

It is presented in a *palayok,* the earthenware cooking pot, and it simmers on the table over a little charcoal brazier. The thick bubbling sauce is a gay orange hue, from the *achuete* bean; the prime ingredients are beef and oxtail (and sometimes tripe); and the predominant taste of the sauce, if you feel clinical enough to stop to analyze it, is of peanuts. With a *sandok,* a large bamboo spoon, you ladle it out over a plate of rice; *bagoong* sauce comes next, spiked with a little *calamansi* juice to kill any lingering fishiness. Then you settle in for a treat. The tender chunks of meat, the faint saltiness of the *bagoong,* the background flavor of peanut and the aroma from the cheery *palayok* add up to one of the finest concoctions from lowly ingredients that I have tasted anywhere.

Some Filipinos turn up their noses at *kari-kari,* preferring Spanish-style dishes or American steak. And *kari-kari* seldom appears at elegant restaurants. But food lovers know its value. My old friend Alfonso Calalang, the Governor of the Philippine Central Bank, is recognized as one of Manila's leading gourmets and amateur chefs. I had already been bewitched by *kari-kari* when I asked him what was the best purely Philippine dish. To my delight but not my surprise, the governor promptly and unhesitatingly cast his vote for *kari-kari* too.

Heaped before the earthenware *palayok* they will cook in are the ingredients for humble Philippine *kari-kari*.

### Kari-Kari (Philippines)
OXTAIL STEW WITH GREEN BEANS AND EGGPLANT

To serve 6

5- to 5½-pounds oxtail, cut into 3-inch lengths
1 tablespoon salt
3 tablespoons vegetable oil
2 tablespoons annatto oil *(Recipe Booklet)*
1 large onion, peeled and cut crosswise into paper-thin slices
2 teaspoons finely chopped garlic
4 quarts water
½ cup uncooked long- or medium-grain white rice
¼ cup salted skinned peanuts
1 pound fresh green string beans, washed and trimmed
A 1- to 1½-pound eggplant, washed, stemmed and cut lengthwise into 8 wedges

GARNISH (optional)
1 tablespoon thinly sliced scallions
1 tablespoon finely chopped celery leaves

Wipe the pieces of oxtail with a dampened towel, then sprinkle them with the salt. In a heavy 8- to 10-quart casserole, heat the vegetable oil over moderate heat until a light haze forms above it. Brown 5 to 6 pieces of oxtail at a time, turning them frequently with tongs and regulating the heat so that they color richly and evenly without burning. As they brown, transfer the pieces to a plate.

Pour off all the fat remaining in the casserole and in its place add the annatto oil. Drop in the onion and garlic and, stirring frequently to scrape in any brown particles that cling to the bottom and sides of the casserole, cook over moderate heat for 8 to 10 minutes until the onion is soft and a delicate golden color.

Return the pieces of oxtail and the liquid accumulated around them to the casserole and add 2½ quarts of the water. Bring to a boil over high heat, reduce the heat to low, and simmer partially covered for about 2½ hours, or until the meat can easily be pulled away from the bone with a small fork.

Meanwhile, place the rice in a small, heavy skillet or saucepan (preferably one with a non-stick cooking surface). Frequently sliding the pan gently back and forth over the burner, toast the rice over low heat for 20 or 30 minutes, or until the grains are golden brown. Pour the rice into the jar of an electric blender and blend at high speed until the rice is reduced to a flourlike powder. Pour it into a bowl. Pulverize the peanuts in the blender, then rub them through a fine sieve with the back of a spoon. Set the rice powder and peanuts aside. (To pulverize the rice and peanuts by hand, pound them as finely as possible with a mortar and pestle and force them through a medium meshed sieve with the back of a spoon.)

When the oxtail has cooked its allotted time, add the remaining 1½ quarts of water, the rice powder and pulverized peanuts. Mix well, then add the green beans and eggplant and turn them about in the stew with a large spoon. Bring to a boil over high heat and cook briskly, uncovered, stirring occasionally, for 10 to 15 minutes, or until the vegetables are tender but still intact.

Taste for seasoning and serve directly from the casserole or from a deep, heated bowl. If you like, garnish the top with scallions and celery leaves. *Kari-kari* may be accompanied by *patis (see Glossary)*.

### Garlic Sauce (Philippines)

To make about 1 cup

1 tablespoon finely chopped garlic
1 teaspoon salt
1 cup malt or distilled white vinegar

With a mortar and pestle, or in a small bowl with the back of a spoon, crush the garlic and salt together until they become a smooth paste. Pour in the vinegar and stir vigorously with a spoon to mix the ingredients thoroughly. Serve the sauce from a bowl or sauceboat as an accompaniment to fried *lumpia* and *ukoy (both, Recipe Index)*. Tightly covered, garlic sauce may be kept at room temperature for a day or so.

To make about 24 rolls

FILLING

A 2-pound chicken, cut into 6 or 8
    serving pieces
½ pound lean boneless pork butt,
    cut into 2 or 3 pieces
1 medium-sized onion, peeled and
    quartered
2 celery tops
1 medium-sized bay leaf
3 teaspoons salt
2 cups water
1 small green cabbage (about 1
    pound)
¼ pound slab bacon, trimmed of
    rind and cut into ¼-inch dice
1 small onion, peeled and cut
    crosswise into paper-thin slices
2 teaspoons finely chopped garlic
1½ pounds fresh green string
    beans, washed, trimmed and cut
    diagonally into ¼-inch lengths
¼ pound fresh bean sprouts,
    washed and husks removed, or
    substitute 1 cup drained, canned
    bean sprouts, washed in a sieve
    under cold running water
1 cup finely diced celery
2 tablespoons soy sauce, preferably
    Japanese

1 recipe *lumpia* wrappers *(page
    146)*
Vegetable oil for deep frying

## Lumpia *(Philippines)*
### DEEP-FRIED CHICKEN, PORK AND VEGETABLE ROLLS

Combine the chicken, pork, quartered onion, celery tops, bay leaf and 1 teaspoon of the salt in a heavy 3- to 4-quart saucepan. Pour in the water and bring to a boil over high heat. Reduce the heat to low, cover tightly and simmer for 20 to 30 minutes, or until the chicken and pork are almost tender and show only slight resistance when pierced with the point of a small, sharp knife.

Remove the chicken and pork and, when cool enough to handle, bone and skin the chicken and cut the meat and pork into ¼-inch dice. Strain the broth and reserve it.

Meanwhile, remove and discard the tough outer leaves of the cabbage and cut it into quarters. Then cut out the cores and slice the quarters crosswise into ⅛-inch-wide strips.

In a heavy 12-inch skillet, cook the bacon over moderate heat, stirring frequently, until it is crisp and has rendered all its fat. With a slotted spoon, transfer the bacon to paper towels to drain.

Drop the sliced onion and the garlic into the fat remaining in the skillet and, stirring frequently, cook over moderate heat for about 5 minutes until the onion slices are soft and transparent but not brown. Watch them carefully for any sign of burning and regulate the heat accordingly.

Add the pork and chicken and stir for 1 or 2 minutes, until the meats brown lightly. Then, in the following order and adding each vegetable a handful at a time, stir in the green beans, bean sprouts, celery and cabbage.

Add the bacon bits, ½ cup of the reserved broth, the remaining 2 teaspoons of salt and the soy sauce and, turning the vegetables about constantly with a spoon, cook over medium heat for 3 minutes longer. Transfer the entire contents of the skillet to a large colander and let the mixture drain for 10 to 15 minutes. Discard the liquid. (The filling may safely be kept at room temperature for 2 to 3 hours.)

To assemble each *lumpia,* shape about ⅓ cup of filling with your hands into a cylinder about 5 inches long and 1 inch in diameter, and place it in the center of the wrapper, leaving at least 1½ inches of the wrapper exposed at either side of the filling.

Lift the bottom of the wrapper over the filling and tuck it beneath it. Bring each of the side flaps, one at a time, up to the top of the enclosed filling and press them firmly in place. Then roll the cylinder up in the remaining section of the wrapper to make a neat package.

As they are filled, place the *lumpia* on a plate and cover them with a dry kitchen towel. If they must wait longer than about 30 minutes before being fried, cover them with foil or plastic wrap and place them in the refrigerator.

Preheat the oven to its lowest possible setting and line a large, shallow baking pan with a double thickness of paper towels. Set the pan in the middle of the oven.

Pour 3 cups of vegetable oil into a 12-inch wok or fill a deep fryer or large, heavy saucepan to a depth of 2 to 3 inches. Heat the oil until it reaches a temperature of 375° on a deep-frying thermometer. Place

3 or 4 *lumpia* at a time seam side down in the hot oil and deep-fry them for about 2 minutes, or until they are golden brown and crisp. As they brown, transfer them to the paper-lined pan to drain and keep warm while you proceed to deep-fry the rest.

Serve the *lumpia* as soon as possible, arranged attractively on a large heated platter and accompanied by garlic sauce *(Recipe Index)*.

NOTE: There is another version of this dish, in which the *lumpia* are not deep fried. To make fresh *lumpia,* prepare the filling mixture as described above and drain it thoroughly. Trim 2 heads of romaine lettuce, separate them into leaves and wash under cold running water. Pat the leaves completely dry with paper towels.

For each *lumpia,* shape ⅓ cup of the filling with your hands into a cylinder about 5 inches long and 1 inch in diameter and place it lengthwise in the center of a leaf of romaine lettuce. Lift the end of the leaf over the filling and bring the sides up and around it, enclosing the filling completely. Lay one end of the lettuce-covered *lumpia* in the center of a wrapper and fold the wrapper in half to cover it, then roll the sides of the wrapper snugly around the *lumpia.*

Serve the fresh *lumpia* at room temperature, accompanied by sweet sauce *(Recipe Index)*.

## Ukoy *(Philippines)*
### DEEP-FRIED SHRIMP, SWEET POTATO AND SQUASH CAKES

To make about 10 cakes

Combine the water, shrimp, annatto and salt in a heavy 1- to 1½-quart saucepan and bring to a boil over high heat. Reduce the heat to low and simmer for about 3 minutes, or until the shrimp are firm and pink. With a slotted spoon transfer the shrimp to paper towels to drain and strain the cooking liquid through a fine sieve into a bowl. Measure the liquid, add enough fresh water to make 1¼ cups and set aside. (Traditional Philippine cooks prefer to leave the shrimp in their shells, but you may prefer to shell and devein them.)

In a deep bowl, combine the flour and cornstarch. Pour in the shrimp cooking liquid and beat until the liquid is absorbed. Then add the grated sweet potato and squash and beat vigorously with a spoon until the mixture is well combined.

Pour the oil into a heavy 10- to 12-inch skillet. The oil should be about ½ inch deep; if necessary add more. Heat the oil until it is very hot but not smoking.

To make each cake, spoon about ⅓ cup of the vegetable mixture onto a saucer, sprinkle a teaspoon or two of the scallions on top and lightly press a shrimp into the center. Then holding the saucer close to the surface of the oil, slide the *ukoy* into it with the aid of a spoon. Fry the cakes, 3 or 4 at a time, for about 3 minutes, spooning the oil over each cake; then turn them carefully and fry them for another 3 minutes, regulating the heat so they color richly and evenly without burning. As each *ukoy* browns transfer it to paper towels to drain.

While they are still hot, arrange the *ukoy,* shrimp side up, on a heated platter and moisten each cake with a little of the garlic sauce. Pour the remaining sauce into a bowl or sauceboat. Serve at once.

½ cup boiling water
10 medium-sized raw shrimp in their shells (about 21 to 25 to the pound)
1 teaspoon annatto seeds
1 teaspoon salt
1 cup flour
1 cup cornstarch
A large sweet potato (about ½ pound), peeled and coarsely grated
A medium-sized acorn squash (about ¾ pound), peeled, halved, seeded and coarsely grated
2 cups vegetable oil
¼ cup finely chopped green scallion tops
Garlic sauce *(page 141)*

## A Shrimp Fillip for Fritters

In the Philippines, where frying and
deep-frying are popular cooking
techniques, fritters are a particularly
favorite food. The most unusual variety
is probably *ukoy* (shown ready for serving
at far right). The ingredients for *ukoy,*
assembled above, are sweet potatoes, acorn
squash, scallions, a mixture of flour and
cornstarch, shrimp and annatto seeds.
(The annatto colors the shrimp a brighter
pink than usual.) To make *ukoy,* boil
the shrimp, then mix its cooking liquid
with the flour and cornstarch, grated
squash and grated sweet potato. Spoon
about ⅓ cup of this combination onto a
saucer and shape it into a small, flat,
round cake like the one shown at right.

Now scatter a teaspoon of chopped scallions over the cake and center a boiled shrimp on top. Next, using a spoon to guide it, slide the *ukoy* cake gently off the saucer into hot oil. Allow each *ukoy* to fry for about 3 minutes, then gently flip it over with a slotted spatula and continue frying until the cake looks brown and crunchy on both sides. Depending on how fast you maneuver, you may be able to fry 3 or 4 cakes at a time. Drain the *ukoy* on paper towels and serve them hot—garnished, if you like, with whole scallions as shown in the picture below. The complete recipe is on page 143.

## Lumpia Wrappers (Philippines)

To make about 24 eight-inch round
   wrappers

2 cups instant all-purpose flour
2 cups cold water
Vegetable oil

Combine the flour and water in a deep bowl and stir vigorously until they form a smooth, fluid paste with the consistency of heavy cream.

Set a heavy 8-inch skillet, preferably one with a non-stick cooking surface, over moderate heat for about 30 seconds. Dip a pastry brush in the vegetable oil and spread a light film of oil evenly over the bottom and sides of the pan. Then immerse the tip of a 2-inch-wide paint brush in the flour paste and, with 5 or 6 slightly overlapping strokes, cover the entire bottom of the pan with a thin sheet of the paste. Cook the pastry for a few seconds until it begins to curl away from the edges of the pan. Immediately lift the wrapper out with your fingers and transfer it to a strip of lightly floured wax paper.

Brush the skillet with oil again and cook the next wrapper in the same fashion. Repeat until all of the paste is used, oiling the pan lightly before making each wrapper. The wrappers may be stacked one on top of the other, floured side down, then covered with foil or plastic wrap and kept at room temperature for no more than 2 hours.

## Rellenong Alimango (Philippines)
### DEEP-FRIED STUFFED CRABS

To make about 10

12 live blue crabs, each about 4
   inches wide and weighing about
   ½ pound, or substitute 1 pound
   fresh, canned or frozen crab meat
3 tablespoons plus 2 cups vegetable
   oil
½ cup thinly sliced scallions,
   including the green tops
1 teaspoon finely chopped garlic
1 small tomato, washed, stemmed
   and coarsely chopped
1¼ teaspoons salt
Freshly ground black pepper
2 egg whites
2 egg yolks
1 medium-sized head romaine
   lettuce washed, separated into
   leaves and chilled
1 firm ripe tomato, cut lengthwise
   into 6 wedges
2 lemons, each cut lengthwise into
   6 wedges

If you are using live crabs, bring 4 quarts of water and 2 tablespoons of salt to a boil in an 8- to 10-quart pot. Drop in the crabs and return the water to a boil. Reduce the heat to low, cover and simmer for 15 minutes, or until the shells are a deep pink or red.

Drain the crabs, then shell them in the following fashion: grasping the body of the crab firmly in one hand, break off the large claws and legs close to the body. Lift and pull off the pointed top shell or apron. With the tip of a small, sharp knife, loosen the large bottom shell from around the meat and cartilage, cutting near the edges where the legs were joined to the shell. Lift out the body of the crab, break it in half lengthwise, then with a small knife or lobster fork pick out the firm white pieces of meat. Discard the gray featherlike gills and tough bits of cartilage but save any pieces of orange roe. Crack the legs lengthwise with a cleaver or crush them with a nutcracker and pick out the meat inside them. Set the meat (and roe if any) aside. Wash the shells under cold water and invert them on paper towels to drain.

If you are using fresh, frozen or canned crab meat, drain it and pick over the pieces to remove all the bits of shell or cartilage.

In a heavy 8- to 10-inch skillet, heat the 3 tablespoons of oil over moderate heat until a light haze forms above it. Drop in the scallions and garlic and stir for 2 or 3 minutes. Watch carefully for any sign of burning and regulate the heat accordingly. When the scallions are soft and transparent, add the chopped tomato and stir for 5 minutes or so, until almost all the liquid in the pan evaporates. Mix in the crab meat, 1 teaspoon of salt and a few grindings of pepper and, stirring constantly, cook over low heat until the mixture is quite dry. Do not let the crab brown. Remove from the heat, taste for seasoning and set the mixture aside.

With a wire whisk or a rotary or electric beater, beat the egg whites and the remaining ¼ teaspoon of salt in a deep bowl until the whites

146

are stiff enough to form unwavering peaks on the beater when it is lifted from the bowl. In a separate bowl, with the same beater, beat the egg yolks until they thicken slightly. Use a rubber spatula to fold the egg yolks gently but thoroughly into the beaten whites.

To assemble each *alimango*, spoon about ¼ cup of the crab-meat mixture into the reserved crab shells or, if using fresh, frozen or canned crab meat, spoon mixture into natural scallop shells (not china or plastic), mounding the meat slightly in the center. With a rubber spatula, spread a 1-inch-thick layer of the egg mixture over the crab meat. Depending on the size and meatiness of the crabs, there may be only enough filling for 8 or 10 of the shells.

Pour the remaining 2 cups of oil into a heavy 10- to 12-inch skillet. The oil should be about ½ inch deep; if necessary add more. Heat until the oil is very hot but not smoking. Fry the *alimango* 3 or 4 at a time. Slide each one gently into the skillet, shell side down, and, constantly dribbling the hot oil over the top with a large spoon, cook for about 2 minutes, or until the tops are puffed and golden.

Serve the *rellenong alimango* hot. Arrange the lettuce on a platter, place the shells on them, and garnish with tomato and lemon wedges.

Crab shells are used both for cooking and serving the Philippine *rellenong alimango*. After the crabs have been boiled, the meat is picked out and seasoned, then stuffed back into the shells and spread with a fluffy meringuelike egg mixture *(left)*. As the crabs fry, oil is dribbled on each *(above)* until the top puffs and turns golden brown.

## Atsara *(Philippines)*
### BITTER MELON AND CUCUMBER SALAD

To serve 4 to 6

Wash the bitter melon under cold water and pat it dry with paper towels. Cut it in half lengthwise and scoop out the seeds by running the tip of a spoon down each half. With a small, sharp knife, cut V-shaped grooves, about ¼ inch deep and spaced ½ inch apart, the entire length of the cucumber. Then slice the melon and cucumber crosswise into ⅛-inch-thick half-rounds.

To remove some of the bitterness and moisture from the melon, place it in a deep bowl, add the salt and squeeze the melon vigorously with both hands. Let the melon rest at room temperature for 10 to 15 minutes. Wash it in a sieve under cold water. Squeeze the pieces dry.

Combine the melon, cucumbers and onions in a serving bowl, pour in the vinegar and toss gently but thoroughly together. Taste for seasoning. Refrigerate until ready to serve.

NOTE: Canned bitter melon may be substituted for the fresh. Simply slice it and toss with the onions, cucumber and vinegar in a bowl.

1 medium-sized bitter melon (about 1 to 1½ pounds)
1 medium-sized cucumber, peeled
4 teaspoons coarse salt, or substitute 1 tablespoon regular salt
½ cup finely chopped onions
3 tablespoons distilled white vinegar

## Rellenong Manok *(Philippines)*
### ROASTED BONED CHICKEN WITH PORK STUFFING

To serve 8 to 10

Preheat the oven to 350°. Bone the chicken following the directions in the Recipe Booklet. Combine the lemon juice and ½ teaspoon of the Worcestershire sauce and rub the mixture over the inside and outside surface of the bird. Set it aside while you prepare the stuffing.

Put the pork, frankfurters, ham and onion through the finest blade of a meat grinder and place the mixture in a deep bowl. Add the salt, raisins, raw eggs, gherkins, pimiento, 1 tablespoon of butter bits, and the remaining teaspoon of Worcestershire sauce. Knead vigorously with both hands, then beat with a wooden spoon until the mixture is smooth and fluffy. Before tasting for seasoning, fry a spoonful of the stuffing in a small skillet until the pork shows no traces of pink.

Lay the chicken cut side up and arrange two hard-cooked eggs end to end in each side of the large cavity. Spread the pork stuffing over and around the eggs, mounding it in the center and filling any empty space. Bring the sides of the chicken together and sew them securely with a large needle. Lift up and fasten the neck skin to the back of the chicken with a small skewer and gently pat the body of the chicken back into an approximation of its original shape.

Brush the chicken evenly with the remaining 2 tablespoons of softened butter. Place it breast side up on a rack set in a large, shallow pan and roast it in the middle of the oven for about 1 hour and 45 minutes. To test for doneness, pierce the thigh of the bird with the tip of a small, sharp knife. The juice that trickles out should be a clear yellow; if it is slightly pink, roast the bird for another 10 to 15 minutes.

Transfer the chicken to a large heated platter and let it rest for about 10 minutes for easier carving. To serve, slice the chicken in half lengthwise and lay each half cut side down. Cut off the legs, then slice the rest of the bird crosswise into ½-inch-thick pieces.

A 4½- to 5-pound chicken
1 teaspoon fresh lemon juice
1½ teaspoons Worcestershire sauce
1½ pounds boneless pork butt or loin, cut into small chunks
3 all-beef frankfurters, cut into small chunks
½ pound boneless boiled ham, cut into small chunks
1 large onion, peeled and coarsely chopped
1½ teaspoons salt
2 tablespoons seedless raisins
2 raw eggs
¼ cup finely chopped sweet gherkins
¼ finely chopped pimiento
1 tablespoon butter, cut into ¼-inch bits, plus 2 tablespoons butter, softened
4 peeled hard-cooked eggs

Boned and stuffed Philippine chicken *rellenong* is for special occasions. The plate, deftly made of sea shell, is special too, and is only for show.

# VIII

## *An Infinite Variety of Rice*

Curving down a deep-walled valley, the rice terraces of Banaue in northern Luzon gleam in the Philippine sun. The terraces represent rice production at its most demanding, with water channeled from mountain streams to provide the necessary wet conditions for the crop even on the sharpest inclines.

Chiseled into the steep mountainsides like stairways for a race of giants, the rice terraces of Banaue in the Philippines testify to Southeast Asia's ancient and continuing dependence on rice. About 2,000 years ago the tribesmen who had settled in the rugged mountains of northern Luzon began carving the first of these spectacular shelves out of the hillsides, and they have not yet finished the task. For mile after mile, curving, shimmering terraces line the narrow, winding valleys—60,000 acres of paddies dug out of nearly vertical ridges. The stone retaining walls, built without mortar to heights of four stories, have been repaired and extended through countless assaults of flood and earthquake; end to end they would stretch halfway around the world.

Stark necessity must have driven the Bronze Age Luzon tribesmen to undertake this colossal mutilation of nature. Rice was the mainstay of their diet, and the only way they knew to grow it was in water, in flat paddies. They had migrated from the fertile mainland of Southeast Asia, where rice cultivation was, and still is, as natural as the monsoons. In rice bowls such as the Mekong River Delta of southern Vietnam and the Chao Phraya Basin of Central Thailand, the original rice growers needed only to plow the level fields and await the monsoon rains; then the river would inundate the fields and the rice could be planted, and by the time the waters receded the rice would be nearly ripe.

To duplicate those growing conditions on the mountainous island of Luzon, the settlers built terraces, and over the centuries constructed intricate networks of sluices and ditches to carry a controlled flow of

151

water from springs and mountain streams far above down to and through the paddies. A massive complex of walls and conduits and small dams, the Banaue terraces have been compared to the pyramids and to the Great Wall of China, but unlike these other masterworks of ancient engineering the rice terraces still do the job they were built for. They are still being added to, terrace by terrace, hill by hill, for rice remains the most important food to all of Southeast Asia, and there is never enough of it to go around.

Expanding populations have strained the resources of all the rice lands of Asia, and only a few of the countries are truly self-sufficient in rice today. Every government in the region has embarked on a search for new ways to feed the growing number of mouths. Within 200 miles of the Banaue terraces, scientists of the International Rice Research Institute at Los Baños, after several years of careful crossbreeding and selection, have developed new "miracle rice" varieties that have so dramatically increased rice yields in Indonesia, Malaysia, India and about 20 other countries that the world's annual production of rice has risen by more than 10 percent. Some individual farmers who have planted such new strains as those designated IR5 and IR8 have produced five times as much rice as they did before. But the new rice varieties are not welcomed by everyone. Part of the problem is the natural conservatism of farmers whose ancestors have been growing one kind of rice, in one particular way, for thousands of years, and for whom the planting, harvesting and eating of rice is closely tied in with their religion and with all the ceremonies of their lives. More important is the matter of taste: most of the people of Southeast Asia just do not like the new rice, and generally only those families who are too poor to buy "good" rice will touch it.

The most common complaint is that IR8 gets hard after it cools, which means that you cannot cook it in the morning and eat it for lunch. This hardening occurs because the rice has a high proportion of a type of starch called amylose, which makes it expand as it cooks and become dry and fluffy. By contrast, grains of rices that are low in amylose tend to stick together. Glutinous rice, which is often called "sticky rice," is a type with no amylose at all; the grains blend together into what is nearly a dough, and if you cook it for too long you get something as sticky as glue.

Because cooked glutinous rice can keep for many days and tastes all right even when cold, it is the favorite portable food in Southeast Asia. In Bali, on the morning of a festival, graceful girls carry rice refreshments from miles around to the temple precincts. Balanced effortlessly on their heads are little tables and piled high on the tables are leaf-wrapped rolls of steamed glutinous rice to be eaten with peppery, chili-hot peanut and coconut sauces, all of it snack food for the hungry citizens who will come to see the dances and honor the gods.

Westerners aware of only one or two types of rice may find it hard to comprehend such fussiness over the stickiness of rice. But rice comes in thousands of varieties, differing in their characteristics: color, flavor, aroma and tenderness, as well as stickiness. Such distinctions may appear subtle and esoteric to us but they make the difference between enjoyment and dissatisfaction to the Asian. Every country of Asia seems to have its own standard of quality. The Malaysians and Vietnamese, for example, like rice that is very dry and flaky; the Japanese and many Chinese prefer it sticky and glossy; the Indonesians of Java and the Filipinos like it somewhere in between.

Even the method of boiling rice varies. I must have been told or shown ten "right" ways before I stopped taking notes. The Filipinos, for example, put their rice in cold water and then place it on the stove; the added soaking time makes the rice tender, they say, the way they like it. Most Malaysians squeeze their rice when washing it, and add it to water that is already boiling. Indonesians usually prefer steamed rice. The "stickier" the rice the more care must be taken in using just the right amount of water, for sticky rice can easily turn to mush. To judge the amount of water needed, experienced cooks in Pampanga, in the Philippines, swirl the rice and water together in the pan, and the way they move shows whether the proportion is right: a sluggish motion means there is too much water in the pot.

Aside from the not-so-simple process of boiling rice by itself, the cuisines of Southeast Asia produce a staggering variety of more complicated rice dishes. At a Philippine *merienda* I had a thick, milky rice gruel, *lugao,* and a sweet sticky mush of rice and chocolate called *tsampurado.* In Thailand there was *kao tung,* a crunchy cracker made from the brown crust you find at the bottom of the pan after rice has cooked a long time; the Thais love it with a hot sauce and little pork rolls. In Indonesia I frequently found *lontong* and *ketupat,* rice steamed in tightly-wrapped leaf rolls, that had been sliced or diced into sauces or spicy *sambal.* The Laotians use only glutinous rice, steaming it in attractive little coconut-frond baskets and dipping it into savory sauces before eating. The *nonya* cooks of Singapore boil rice with garlic or lentils, and the Vietnamese *com tay can* is an excellent rice dish cooked in an earthen pot with mushrooms, chicken and pork, and served with a tingling ginger sauce. And on both sides of the Malacca Strait, when a cook wants to take note of some special occasion, or just feels like devoting a little more time and effort to a meal, she will put together a *nasi samin* or another pilau called *nasi briani,* in which rice and chicken are cooked together with what seems to be a whole shelf of curry spices; this was originally an Indian dish, enriched and smoothed in Malaya by the addition of coconut cream.

In my travels through Southeast Asia I have felt the salubrious effects of at least five different kinds of rice wine and brandy, and have swallowed —on the morning after—a strong, sour tonic of rice, *kentjur* root, sugar and lime that *had* to be good for me, judging by the taste. I have spoiled my appetite for dinner by stuffing myself with too many little round *kanom krok,* the delectable Thai snack, a crusty shell of rice flour stuffed with pork or shrimp. In a restaurant where journalists gather in downtown Manila I devoured a tender fish that had been boiled, with vegetables and potatoes, in the starchy water used for washing rice, and in Makasar I found that rice steamed in hollowed-out bam-

These rice stalks, growing at the International Rice Research Institute at Los Baños, show three stages in the crossbreeding process that has created richly productive new varieties. At right is a normal stalk in flower. On the center stalk, the panicles—where fertilization takes place—have been clipped and their pollen has been replaced with pollen from another plant. The stalk at left, a result of the cross-pollination, has characteristics of both its parent varieties.

At the end of the day, a bare-legged Javanese farmer hurries to set out the last few seedlings in a new field of rice. The Malay word *padi,* from which paddy derives, actually refers not to the field but to the rice itself, in its newly harvested or threshed form.

boo somehow tastes fresher and more lively than other kinds. In every country I was dazzled by a rainbow of cakes and candies made basically of glutinous rice, coconut and palm sugar; the best of those I tried were some of Singapore's soft and jellylike *nonya kuey,* and a combination—prepared in Palembang, Sumatra—of glutinous rice and a semisweet custard pudding colored deep green with pandanus leaf.

As might be expected of a foodstuff that has sustained so many people for so many centuries, rice is subject to all sorts of customs and religious beliefs that enter into every aspect of its growing, cooking and eating. In Java, for instance, rice farmers traditionally harvest their rice with a small knife called *ani-ani,* which is sacred to their rice goddess, Dewi Sri, and they refuse to use more efficient modern cutting implements for fear they might anger the deity. To persuade these farmers to harvest the new Rice Research Institute varieties with ordinary sickles, officials pointed out that since these new strains came from the Philippines they could not possibly contain the soul of Dewi Sri and that therefore she would not be offended.

The notion that rice has a soul (and therefore must never be stolen even in the direst circumstances) is especially common around the Banaue terraces. Here pigs and chickens were once sacrificed to prevent the "death" of rice, and their entrails read for auguries of the success of the crop. Often the rice-soul is protected by hiding seeds in corners

154

of a house, where visitors cannot inadvertently sit on or walk over them; that, it is believed, would jinx their growth. In some Luzon villages farmers refrain from sexual activity during a four-day rice harvest ceremony. And in Malaysia, some rice farmers hide their cutting knives in their sleeves when they go out to harvest, lest the spirit of the rice be "frightened" and thereby lose its taste.

In Thailand, the rice goddess is known as Mother Posop. When the grain is ripening, farmers say that Mother Posop is "pregnant"; they place a little bamboo flag at the corner of the paddy to signify her condition—and to warn away evil spirits and human trespassers. In years gone by, after the rice was brought in from the fields, the farmers returned to the paddy to "invite" Mother Posop into the barns while they scoured the ground for stray grains. "O Mother Posop," they chanted, "come you up into the rice barn. Do not go astray in the meadows and fields for mice to bite you and birds to take you in their beaks. Go you to the happy place, to rear your children and grandchildren in prosperity." Then the fallen grains the farmers had gathered were stuffed into an effigy of the goddess and it was stored with the harvested rice; the following year these doubly sacred grains were mixed with the seed rice to insure its growth.

That particular custom has largely died out, but the King of Thailand himself still takes part in a yearly plowing and rice planting ceermony. At the Temple of the Emerald Buddha, he blesses a golden plow and helps consecrate the seed rice. The following morning, resplendent in a white uniform, he rides out with his beautiful queen in one of their canary yellow Rolls Royces to preside over the ritual of the First Plowing at the Pramane Ground, a square near the Grand Palace. A Brahmin priest leads a stately procession of conch-shell trumpeters, flower-decked oxen hauling the sacred plow, "celestial maidens" bearing gold and silver baskets of rice, and finally the Lord of the Plowing himself (usually the head of the Rice Department) in flowing robes of white, who casts the sacred seed into the new furrows. As soon as the royal party has departed, the common folk swarm onto the field, grabbing up every blessed grain. The farmers among them will mix the royal gleanings with their own seed rice to help it flourish, and the city people carefully deposit the precious grains in purses, in the belief that the sacred souvenir will make their money grow.

Rice is also the key element in Thailand's most important religious practice. Thais "win merit," so that their next incarnation will be on a higher and more comfortable plane, by giving alms to Buddhist monks. Every morning, thousands of saffron-robed monks leave their temple gates at dawn and fan out through the neighborhood with bowls in hand. Everyone, rich or poor, gives them at least a few grains of rice. In the northeast Thailand town of Nakhon Phanom, I once saw a curious early-morning procession. All along one street the housewives came out and stood in a row, each holding a pan of rice. The monks, looking neither right nor left, passed along the street in single file with their bowls held out, and each housewife, bowing for the honor and merit that she was earning for her whole family, placed a handful of rice into each bowl that came by. With similar intent, a Thai bride and groom feed each other mouthfuls of rice during the wedding ceremony and then complete the ritual by feeding more rice to the priest.

The marriage ceremony of the Menangkabau people of Sumatra has its own quite different rice custom. The bride's family prepares a huge *nasi kuning (Recipe Index)*, the yellow rice dish that brightens every joyous occasion. Within the *nasi kuning* they hide two wedding rings for which the bride and groom must search at the end of the ceremony—a rite symbolizing the search for fortune in married life. Whoever finds the first ring establishes moral superiority over the other. Naturally, the groom digs deeper and more frantically than his bride.

But it is Java's *tumpeng* rice cone, rich with the symbolism of mountains, gods and passions, that is perhaps the most revealing token of the Southeast Asian reverence for rice. The white of its cooked rice, representing purity and virtue, is the cone's most important symbol. At the birth of a baby an all-white, all-rice *tumpeng* is placed beside the bed in the hope that this representation of the mastery of reason over passion may be the first object seen by the newborn child.

Whether he glimpses the *tumpeng* or not, anyone born in Southeast Asia is going to see plenty of white rice before he is laid to rest. If he is poor, it will be plain rice and he will be grateful for as much as he can get; if he is more fortunate he will feast on variations of rice dishes that seem to have no end.

Most often, perhaps, if he lives in Indonesia and Malaysia, he will enjoy *nasi goreng*, fried rice, since it is probably the most ubiquitous of all the variations on plain boiled rice. Fried rice may have come from China, but the Chinese begin by boiling the rice, mincing their meats and garnishes into tiny pieces and frying all this together. In *nasi goreng*, the meats and vegetables are fried separately, in larger chunks; the rice is then fried in the same oil, and only near the end of the process do all the ingredients join each other in the simmering pan. The result is less of a blend than the Chinese rendition; it is rather a parliament of flavors that vie with one another while at the same time obeying some supreme culinary rules of order. It is almost impossible to list what may go into a *nasi goreng*, because more than any other dish of Southeast Asia its composition depends on the tastes of the diners, the conditions of the marketplace, and the identity and mood of the cook.

No two *nasi goreng* are ever quite the same. What they have in common is that versatile and enduring grain that holds together all the people of Southeast Asia in a tacit brotherhood. From Bali to Bangkok (and beyond), from the steep valleys of Banaue to the even greener, lusher terraces of Java, on the sampans that carry the rice down the Mekong and the Chao Phraya Rivers, in Thai villages that are cut off from their neighbors when the water floods the fields, the peoples of this region all appreciate and understand the delicate beauty of young rice stalks reflected on a still paddy, the back-breaking labor of rice planting, and the spiritual satisfaction and sensual pleasure that can be found in a simple mound of white, warm, wonderful rice.

*Opposite:* The planting, cultivation, harvesting and processing of rice is a complicated occupation, and most countries with a rice culture have traditions carefully defining the roles men and women play in it. These Indonesian women of west Sumatra, for example, have the jobs of pounding rice with a wooden pestle to loosen the hulls from the grains and tossing them in a scoop to get rid of the chaff.

156

## Com Chien Thap Cam *(Vietnam)*
### FRIED RICE WITH SAUSAGE, SHRIMP AND CRAB MEAT

**To serve 4 to 6**

1⅔ cups long- or medium-grain white rice

6 dried Chinese mushrooms, each 1 to 1½ inches in diameter

2 Chinese sausages, sliced crosswise into 1⅛-inch-thick rounds

¼ pound uncooked medium-sized shrimp (about 21 to 25 to the pound)

¼ cup plus 1 tablespoon vegetable oil

1 medium-sized onion, peeled, cut in half lengthwise and sliced lengthwise into ¼-inch-wide strips

1 tablespoon fish's gravy *(see Glossary)*

½ pound fresh, frozen or canned crab meat, thoroughly drained, picked over to remove all bits of shell and cartilage, and broken into small bits

2 eggs

2 large scallions including the green tops, trimmed, cut crosswise into 1-inch pieces and sliced lengthwise into ¼-inch-wide strips

Starting a day ahead, prepare the rice in the following way: Bring 6 quarts of unsalted water to a boil over high heat in a large, heavy pot. Stirring constantly, slowly pour in the rice in a thin stream. Then reduce the heat to moderate and let the rice boil uncovered for about 15 minutes, or until the grains are somewhat tender but are still slightly firm to the bite.

Drain the rice in a large sieve or colander, meanwhile fluffing it with a fork. Transfer the rice to a large bowl and set it aside to cool to room temperature. Cover the bowl tightly with aluminum foil or plastic wrap and refrigerate the rice overnight or for at least 12 hours.

Before frying the rice, place the dried Chinese mushrooms in a small bowl, pour in 1½ cups of hot water and let them soak for at least 30 minutes. Remove the mushrooms with a slotted spoon and discard the water. With a cleaver or sharp knife, cut away and discard the tough stems of the mushrooms and slice each of the caps crosswise into ¼-inch-wide strips.

Meanwhile, in an 8- to 10-inch skillet, fry the sausages over moderate heat, stirring constantly for about 2 minutes, or until the slices are delicately browned on both sides and the edges are crisp. Drain the sausages on paper towels.

Shell the shrimp. Devein them by making a shallow incision down their backs with a small, sharp knife and lifting out the black or white intestinal veins with the point of the knife. Chop the shrimp into ¼-inch bits and set aside.

Heat ¼ cup of the oil in a heavy 12-inch skillet over moderate heat until a light haze forms above it. Drop in the onions and, stirring constantly, cook for 2 or 3 minutes, or until they are soft and transparent but not brown. Watch carefully for any sign of burning and regulate the heat accordingly.

Add the mushrooms, then the chilled rice and, stirring constantly with a fork, cook for about 3 minutes, or until the rice is heated through. Stir in the fish's gravy.

With the fork, push the rice to the edges of the pan to make a well in the center. Pour the remaining tablespoon of oil into the well and drop the shrimp into it. Without disturbing the rice, cook the shrimp for about 2 minutes, turning them carefully about with the fork until they are firm and pink.

Mix the shrimp into the rice and, still stirring frequently, cook over moderate heat for 5 minutes. Do not let the rice brown. Stir in the crab meat and the sausage and cook for 2 minutes, then break in the eggs one at a time, stirring well after each addition.

Mix in the scallions and taste for seasoning; add salt or more fish's gravy if the rice seems too bland. Serve the *com chien thap cam* mounded on a large heated platter or in a bowl.

The secret of *com chien thap cam,* a Vietnamese fried-rice dish, is to boil the rice a day ahead and refrigerate it overnight.

### Deep-fried Shrimp with Rice-Stick Coating  *(Hawaii)*

Carefully shell the shrimp, but leave the last shell segment and the tail attached. With a small, sharp knife, devein the shrimp by cutting halfway through them down their backs and lifting out the black and white intestinal veins with the point of the knife. Wash the shrimp under cold running water and pat them dry with paper towels. Sprinkle them with the salt and pepper.

Pour the oil into a deep fryer or large heavy saucepan to a depth of about 3 inches and heat the oil until it reaches a temperature of 350° on a deep-frying thermometer.

One at a time, dip the shrimp into the flour and shake off the excess. Then immerse each shrimp in the beaten eggs, roll it in the crumbled rice sticks to coat it all over and drop it into the hot oil. Fry the shrimp, in batches of 5 or 6, for 2 or 3 minutes, turning them frequently with a slotted spoon until they are golden brown and crisp. As they brown transfer them to paper towels to drain while you deep-fry the rest. Serve at once.

To serve 6 as a first course

1 pound uncooked medium-sized
   shrimp (21 to 25 to the pound)
½ teaspoon salt
¼ teaspoon freshly ground black
   pepper
Vegetable oil for deep-frying
1 cup flour
2 eggs, lightly beaten
1 cup *py mei fun* (Chinese rice
   sticks, *see Glossary)* broken into
   pieces ⅛ to ¼ inch long

## RICE CONE

½ cup vegetable oil

1 cup finely chopped onions

1 tablespoon finely chopped garlic

2 blades fresh lemon grass, tied
together, or ¼ teaspoon
powdered *sereh (see Glossary)*

4 *salam* leaves *(see Glossary)*

4 *djeruk* leaves *(see Glossary)*

4 teaspoons turmeric

1 tablespoon salt

3 cups uncooked white rice

6 cups fresh coconut milk made
from 6 cups coarsely chopped
coconut and 6 cups hot water
*(page 61)*

## GARNISH

3 fresh hot red chilies, each about
4 inches long, stemmed and
seeded *(caution: see page 69)*

3 cups plus 1 tablespoon vegetable
oil

½ cup medium-sized shallots,
peeled and sliced paper thin

2 eggs, lightly beaten

1 tablespoon finely chopped celery
leaves

12 to 15 ti leaves, or substitute 1
head of romaine lettuce, trimmed,
washed and separated into leaves

2 large cucumbers, scrubbed but
not peeled, scored lengthwise
with the tines of a fork and
sliced into ¼-inch-thick rounds

7 hard-cooked eggs, preferably
tinted with various hues of
vegetable coloring

## SIDE DISHES (RECIPE INDEX)

*Udang asam garem* (tamarind
shrimp)

*Rempejek* (peanut wafers)

*Rempah* (coconut patties)

*Sambelan goring kentang* (deep-
fried potato rounds)

*Atjar kuning* (yellow pickles)

*Serundeng katjang* (toasted spiced
coconut with peanuts)

*Ajam ungkap* (deep-fried tamarind-
marinated chicken)

## *Nasi Kuning Lengkap* (Indonesia)
### SPICED BAKED RICE CONE DINNER

First prepare the rice cone in the following way: Preheat the oven to 350°. In a heavy 4- to 5-quart casserole, heat the oil over moderate heat until a light haze forms above it. Drop in the onions and garlic and, stirring frequently, cook for about 5 minutes, or until they are soft and transparent but not brown. Watch carefully for any sign of burning and regulate the heat accordingly. Mix in the lemon grass or powdered *sereh, salam* leaves, *djeruk* leaves, turmeric and salt, and cook for a minute or so. Then add the rice and stir for 2 or 3 minutes, until all the grains are evenly coated, but do not let the rice brown.

Pour in the coconut milk and cook over moderate heat until small bubbles appear around the edge of the pan. Do not let the coconut milk boil. Cover tightly and bake in the middle of the oven for about 35 minutes, or until the rice is tender and has absorbed all liquid in the pan. Remove the lemon grass, if you have used it, and the *salam* and *djeruk* leaves. While still hot, pack the rice tightly, a cup at a time, into an Indonesian cone mold or a conical sieve about 8½ inches deep and 7½ inches in diameter. Place a large serving plate upside down over the mold or sieve and, grasping them together firmly, invert them. Rap the plate on a table and the rice cone should slide out easily.

While the rice is baking, prepare the garnishes. Cut 2 of the chilies lengthwise into strips about ¼ inch wide and 2 inches long. Shape the remaining chili into a fringed "cap" by slicing it lengthwise at ¼-inch intervals from the stem end to within about 1 inch of the other end.

Pour 3 cups of oil into a 12-inch wok or fill a deep fryer or large, heavy saucepan to a depth of 2 inches. Heat the oil until it is very hot but not smoking. Drop the chili strips into the hot oil and, stirring constantly with a slotted spoon, fry them for a minute or so, until they are delicately brown and somewhat crisp around the edges. With the slotted spoon, transfer them to paper towels to drain. Add the shallots to the oil and stir them for 20 or 30 seconds until they are brown and crisp; remove them with the spoon and drain them on paper towels.

In a heavy 8-inch skillet, heat 1 tablespoon of oil over moderate heat until a light haze forms above it. Pour in the beaten eggs and cook undisturbed for 1 minute, or until the bottom is lightly browned. Turn the egg pancake over, cook for another minute, slide it onto a plate and cut it into strips about ¼ inch wide and 2 inches long.

To assemble the *nasi kuning lengkap,* place the chili pepper "cap" on top of the rice cone and scatter the chili strips, shallots, pancake strips and chopped celery leaves decoratively around the base. Arrange the ti or romaine leaves in a spokelike pattern around the cone, overlapping the leaves to cover the outer edge of the plate completely. Arrange the seven side dishes in mounds on the leaves, encircling the rice cone. Separate the side dishes from one another with rows of overlapping cucumber rounds, and place a hard-cooked egg on the rim of the plate at the end of each row.

NOTE: The name *nasi kuning lengkap* means, literally, yellow rice, complete. Even in Indonesia, the side dishes vary in type and number from three or four to dozens. You may decide to make only a few of the side dishes listed above and shown in the photograph on page 91, or you may omit them altogether and use any of the other Indonesian meat, poultry, seafood or vegetable recipes in their place. The *atjar kuning* and *serundeng katjang* may be prepared a day in advance if you like. The *rempejek*, the *sambelan goring kentang* and the *ajam ungkap* may be cooked an hour or so in advance and served at room temperature or kept warm in a 250° oven. The *udang asam garem* and *rempah*, however, should be made at the last possible moment—perhaps while the rice is baking.

## Rempah *(Java)*
### COCONUT-BEEF PATTIES

Combine the ground beef, coconut, egg, coriander, garlic, cumin, salt and pepper in a deep bowl and knead vigorously with both hands. Then beat the mixture with a wooden spoon until it is smooth and fluffy. For each patty scoop up about ¼ cup of the coconut-beef mixture with your hand and pat it into a round cake about 2 inches in diameter and ½ inch thick.

Preheat the oven to the lowest setting and line a large, shallow baking pan with a double thickness of paper towels. Set the pan on the middle shelf of the oven.

Pour the vegetable oil into a heavy 10- to 12-inch skillet. The oil should be at least 1 inch deep; if necessary, add more. Heat the oil over moderate heat until it is very hot but not smoking. Fry the patties, 5 or 6 at a time, for about 5 minutes on each side, or until they are crisp and richly browned. As they brown, transfer them to the paper-lined pan to keep warm while you fry the rest.

Arrange the *rempah* on a heated platter and serve as soon as possible. *Rempah* are traditionally served with *nasi kuning lengkap (opposite)*.

To make about 20 two-inch round patties

1 pound lean ground beef, preferably chuck
4 cups finely grated fresh coconut *(page 61)*
1 egg
2 teaspoons ground coriander
½ teaspoon finely chopped garlic
⅛ teaspoon ground cumin
2 teaspoons salt
¼ teaspoon white pepper
2 cups vegetable oil

## Rempejek *(Indonesia)*
### PEANUT-AND-COCONUT-MILK WAFERS

Combine the garlic, *kentjur* and salt in a deep bowl and mash them with the back of a spoon into a fairly smooth paste. Mix in the all-purpose flour and rice flour, then add the coconut milk and egg and beat with a wire whisk or large spoon until the mixture becomes a smooth thin batter. Stir in the peanuts.

Pour the oil into a heavy 10- to 12-inch skillet. The oil should be about ½ inch deep; if necessary add more. Heat the oil until it is very hot but not smoking. For each wafer, ladle in about 3 to 4 tablespoons of the batter. Cook 2 or 3 wafers at a time, leaving enough space between them so that they can spread into 3- to 4-inch rounds. Fry the *rempejek* about 2½ minutes, turn them over with a slotted spatula and fry for 30 seconds more, or until they are crisp and golden on both sides. As they brown, transfer the wafers to paper towels to drain.

Serve the *rempejek* warm or at room temperature. *Rempejek* is considered a bread and is often served with *nasi kuning lengkap (opposite)*.

To make about 12 three-inch round wafers

¼ teaspoon finely chopped garlic
⅛ teaspoon crushed *kentjur (see Glossary)*, pulverized with the flat of a large, heavy knife
½ teaspoon salt
5 tablespoons all-purpose flour
1 tablespoon rice flour *(see Glossary)*
2 cups fresh coconut milk, made from 2 cups coarsely chopped coconut and 2 cups hot water *(page 61)*
1 egg
¾ cup shelled raw (unroasted) peanuts
2 cups vegetable oil

# IX

# The Unconquerable Vietnamese Cuisine

An enterprising young Vietnamese sugar-cane merchant checks out the Sunday traffic on Binh Loi Bridge in Gia Dinh Province. When buses, cars and motorbikes are backed up at the narrow one-way bridge, he darts out to peddle his bouquets of sweet, juicy cane chunks, ingeniously skewered on split bamboo sticks.

For obvious and tragic reasons, the Southeast Asian country most familiar to the world at large today is Vietnam, though our minds have been so occupied with the war there as to make it difficult to think of that long-ravaged land in any terms other than terror and death. But Vietnam is much more than a collection of jungle villages, rice paddies and pajamaed peasants caught up in the vortex of catastrophe. It is a complex and sophisticated nation, with a language and identity that go back more than 2,000 years, with a university older than any in Europe, and with a people steeped in the legends of their ancient heroes and devoted to their religions and theater—and to their foods as well.

Beneath the helicopter gunships breathing fire on the Mekong Delta battlefields in the 1960s the ancient cycle of planting and harvesting continued; even after rocket attacks on Saigon—now called Ho Chi Minh City—small boys were soon in the streets again peddling sugar cane, and old women appeared selling a cane-and-shrimp paste delicacy called *chao tom*. Every winter, whenever the shooting ceased to allow for the observance of Tet, the lunar new year, every Vietnamese who could manage it went home to remind himself of the enduring values of his land and ancestors. At Tet, in both North and South Vietnam, briefly reunited families feasted on their traditional, ceremonial holiday fare: a squid soup, sometimes a special sharp fin soup, pork with lotus root, glutinous rice cakes filled with meat and beans and boiled in banana leaves.

The Vietnamese, who originally came from Indonesia, Southern China and elsewhere, have been struggling to maintain their independence ever since about 100 B.C. At that time China, coveting the rich rice-growing areas of the Mekong and Red Rivers, first conquered the young kingdom of Nam Viet. For a thousand years or more, broken only by a few short-lived rebellions which Vietnamese legend still celebrates, the Chinese emperor kept his southern neighbors in thrall. Even after the Vietnamese set up the first of their own dynasties in 938 and established a nation that was able to repel further invasion for 900 years, the Chinese influence persisted in the written language, in methods of administration, and in art and architecture. Throughout this long process of assimilation, however, the Vietnamese culture has tenaciously retained its own character. The Chinese institutions have been distinctively modified by a people who are intensely proud of their individuality, and who feel they have little in common with their northern neighbor—which has been more often enemy than friend.

Still, there are certain unmistakable signs of the long Chinese presence in Vietnam. One of the most obvious is in the manner of eating: the Vietnamese are the only people of Southeast Asia or anywhere in the region covered by this book (except for Singapore's *nonya* and other emigré Chinese) who eat with chopsticks. One can actually trace the line of Chinese penetration in some Vietnamese highland villages, for example, by noting where chopsticks disappear and finger eating begins.

Other echoes of the Chinese past in the Vietnamese cuisine are the tendency to eat plain white rice and other foods separately rather than mixing them together, and the popular practice of stir-frying vegetables in pots similar to the Chinese-style wok.

The excellence of Vietnamese cooking owes a great deal to the example of China—and, in more recent generations, to that of France, which ruled the country for most of the past century. Many Vietnamese still esteem both of these cuisines, and when they eat out it is usually at a Chinese or French restaurant. As a result there are few quality restaurants serving Vietnamese food. But a multitude of ordinary food stalls offer a varied assortment of pleasing, filling dishes that you need try only once to realize that as much as the cooks of Vietnam may have borrowed from the Chinese or French, they still do honor to their own distinctive panoply of flavors.

Probably the most popular of these everyday dishes is a delicate beef-and-noodle soup called *pho,* a particular favorite of the marketplace. Before dawn, in the market area of a Vietnamese town, the steam is already rising from great simmering cauldrons of *pho;* it must cook for hours, and the laborers, the vegetable vendors arriving from their farms, and later the shoppers and the tradesmen will be demanding it all day long. The cooking of *pho* involves such a long period on the stove that it is impractical for preparation at home. One Vietnamese cookbook calmly advises that after beef, beef bones, onions, ginger and cinnamon have been added to a pot of water, you bring it to a boil, reduce the heat to low, and then "simmer all day, or all night if you have to work during the day." But you cannot sleep while it cooks: "Add more water, whenever necessary, because lots of it will boil away." Furthermore, *pho* would be difficult to prepare for the simul-

164

taneous servings required in the home because the final stage of cooking must be done in each bowl separately, one portion at a time, and must be deferred until just a few moments before eating. For these reasons, *pho* is far better suited as a dish for a food stall with a small, steady flow of customers. I suspect, in fact, that *pho* must have evolved long ago precisely to meet the needs of an Oriental market.

While the beef is simmering in its seasoned broth, the *pho* chef (who may spend his lifetime cooking this dish and nothing else) cuts up scallions and some more onions, slices some more beef very thin, and then briefly boils thin white rice noodles. With everything ready, and the customer poised for a treat, the chef begins a rapid two-handed shuffle that looks like some kind of culinary shell game. With one hand he dips a strainer full of the cooked noodles, mixed with bean sprouts, into a pot of boiling water—just long enough to warm the noodles and blanch the sprouts. With the other hand he picks up a ladle filled with the sliced beef and vegetables and immerses it in the long-simmering soup until the beef begins to change color. Then the noodles and bean sprouts are emptied into a soup bowl, followed immediately by a ladleful of the soup-beef-vegetable mixture. A few drops of Vietnam's salty *nuoc mam,* or fish sauce, may be added for flavor, as well as a few coriander leaves. This flashy legerdemain not only dazzles the eye but produces a sort of soup-with-salad in which the delicate flavor of the broth contrasts and vies with the fresh, natural tastes and textures of the other ingredients without blotting them out. Thousands of Vietnamese insist on partaking in the performance at least once a day.

While it is true that *pho* must be encountered on its home ground, and has therefore been pretty much out of bounds to all but local Vietnamese for many years, other Vietnamese foods can be enjoyed at any Western table. Included among them are several soups that are as good as or better than *pho*. My own favorite is *mien ga (Recipe Index),* which means simply chicken noodle. But any relationship between *mien ga* and a chicken noodle soup sold in cans is purely coincidental. For one thing, *mien ga* arrives with the taste of chicken but without the oily fat, mostly because the chickens of Vietnam are so lean. The Vietnamese like them that way; indeed they like their foods as fat-free as possible, and use vegetable oil instead of lard for frying. (Their dislike of fat is one reason Vietnamese boil so many of their foods.) The noodles of *mien ga* are the "cellophane" type made of mung beans, cut up into short strips; mushrooms and scallions are additional essential ingredients. The overall impression is of a light, rather willowy soup with a subtle flavor that seems to shift a bit with each spoonful.

Lightness and subtlety, as exemplified in *pho* and *mien ga,* are the characteristics that most distinguish Vietnamese from Chinese cooking. Frequently one comes across a Vietnamese dish that looks like something Chinese and even suggests some familiar Chinese aroma, only to discover upon eating it a delicacy and clarity of taste that might be entirely wasted on someone who is accustomed to Chinese food alone. One might say that the difference between the Chinese and the Vietnamese

Lemon grass, otherwise known as citronella grass, contributes its distinctive sweetish-lemon flavor to many Vietnamese dishes. The lower part of the stem, below the grass blade, is generally sliced thinly crosswise like a scallion before being added to a soup or sauce.

cuisine parallels the difference between symphonic and chamber music.

A more easily pinpointed characteristic of Vietnamese cooking is the use of the fish sauce, *nuoc mam,* a salty condiment similar to but considerably stronger than the Philippine *patis.* The Vietnamese use *nuoc mam* so extensively, in every kind of dish, and wartime exigencies have long forced them to rely on such cheap raw grades of the sauce, that many Westerners in Vietnam are frightened away from Vietnamese food by what they regard as the fishy reek of it. This is a pity, for properly handled, the quality grades of *nuoc mam* add a fine piquancy to Vietnamese foods that cannot be duplicated by salt alone. And what is *nuoc mam?* Essentially, it is the liquid that is drained off from wooden casks in which alternating layers of fresh fish and salt have been tightly packed and allowed to ferment. The best grade, marketed in the United States in Philippine and Chinese markets as "Fish's Gravy," comes from the first sauce which seeps off naturally; the cheaper, more redolent sauce is then obtained by adding more salt and pressing out what remains in the barrels, and only Vietnamese who can not find or afford anything else will use it.

The Vietnamese put *nuoc mam* into just about every cooked dish, but as long as the proper amounts are used, the sauce no more dominates the taste of Vietnamese dishes than salt dominates Western dishes. In fact, *nuoc mam* serves the same function as salt and behaves in the same way: if the right amount has been included, you do not notice it; if there is not enough, you know something is missing. To take care of the latter eventuality, soups like *pho* and *mien ga* are often accompanied by a little bottle of *nuoc mam* from which the diner may add a few drops to suit his taste. Somehow, salt alone will never produce the same effect as *nuoc mam,* the one essential element in Vietnamese cooking. "Give me some *nuoc mam* and anything else," says one expert Vietnamese cook, "and I'll cook you a Vietnamese dish."

By adding a number of other condiments to *nuoc mam,* the Vietnamese transform it into an exciting hot sauce called *nuoc cham,* which may be regarded as Vietnam's rendition of the Indonesian *sambal.* Every cook has his own formula for *nuoc cham,* and the versions vary according to the foods with which they are to be eaten. The most common mixtures contain ground chili, vinegar, sugar, garlic and some kind of citrus fruit juice. For the simplest possible meal, the equivalent of bread and butter, a Vietnamese peasant might get along with a bowl of rice and a few spoonfuls of *nuoc cham.* At another level, this hot sauce can be used to spice up almost any cooked dish and as a dressing for salads.

A frequent role for *nuoc cham* is as a dipping sauce for an assortment of casual snack-type foods, the best of which is *cha gio (Recipe Index).* These are little thumb-sized rolls usually consisting of minced pork, crab meat, mushrooms and vegetables wrapped in a thin rice-paper blanket and deep fried until crisp and golden brown. Just before eating, you wrap a *cha gio* roll in a leaf of Chinese lettuce, add a few sprigs of coriander leaf and a kind of sweet basil, and perhaps a slice of pickle, then dip the whole leafy bundle into your chili-hot

166

*Continued on page 172*

# Mrs. Mai's Cook-It-Yourself Beef Stars at a Vietnamese Family Dinner

Making dinner for a Vietnamese family as large as that of Tran Xuan Mai, who lives with his wife, five daughters and two sons in a small house on the outskirts of Ho Chi Minh City, requires considerable preparation and a bit of ingenuity. For this Saturday meal, Mrs. Mai went to the market to select the meat, fish and vegetables she would need. Then she and her daughters got to work slicing, paring and grinding. By mealtime everything was ready, including an unusual cook-it-yourself beef dish that neatly solved the dilemma of preparing meat to suit nine different palates.

As Mrs. Mai thin-slices raw beef, three of her daughters cut sheets of rice paper and arrange serving plates. Since many of the ingredients will be taken to the table raw, it is especially important that they be set out as attractively as possible. The kitchen of the Mai home is in a separate building, a traditional arrangement aimed at minimizing fire hazard.

In olden times—and to this day among poorer Vietnamese—the normal cooking device was an open hearth with three stones upon which a pot could rest. The spirits of the hearth symbolically resided in the three stones. Far more common now is the kerosene or bottled gas burner, though slightly more conservative cooks like Mrs. Mai prefer the Chinese-style clay brazier stoked with glowing charcoal. Above, she precooks pork rolled in cabbage for one of the two soups being served. The other, made of salt pork and eggs with coconut milk, simmers on a brazier at right.

Thanh Luong, 12, the Mais' youngest daughter, prepares to sample the vinegar-soaked beef appetizer, which is cooked to taste by each diner at the table. A slice of lean raw beef is dipped into a boiling broth of vinegar and water flavored with lemon grass and sugar. It cooks quickly. Then it is rolled up in a piece of rice paper along with various bits of vegetables and fruit, and dunked in *nuoc mam*, a fish sauce, before eating.

Having heaped it with a fragrant pile of spices, vegetables, noodles and seasonings, Mrs. Mai prepares to steam a fish.

In her deep Chinese-style wok, Mrs. Mai rapidly stir-fries a mixture of leeks, carrots, onions and cauliflower with shrimp. Her cooking techniques, as well as her use of chopsticks, are evidence of the historical influence of Vietnam's huge neighbor, and sometime conqueror, to the north.

Seated at a large round table in their gaily painted dining room, the Mai family share the feast, which includes pork, fish and shrimp dishes. Tran Xuan Mai and his two sons drink beer, the women soft drinks. On the doorposts beyond the table a classical poem is inscribed in Chinese characters, and family photographs hang on the wall.

171

*nuoc cham.* Each bite thus brings you a broad and satisfying range of tastes and textures; the fresh leaves somehow blunt the sharpness of the spices without actually lessening their flavor. Just as *sambal* making is the Indonesian's classic test of a young girl's homemaking skill, every Vietnamese bride is supposed to know how to produce a *cha gio* of exactly the right crispness, color and taste. Making *cha gio* rice-paper wrappers is a delicate and difficult process that most housewives avoid by purchasing dried wrappers at the market. The Vietnamese insist that no other country's rice paper is so good as theirs. I hesitate to offer my own verdict on this ticklish issue, but in any event the matter remains largely academic because unfortunately Vietnamese rice paper—or any other kind of rice paper for that matter—is extremely hard to find in the United States. Other kinds of wrappers for *cha gio,* however, can be improvised.

Similar to *cha gio* in content, but steamed instead of deep-fried, is a soft little dumpling called *banh cuon.* This, like *pho,* is another marketplace favorite. To prepare it, the cook spreads a spoonful of rice paste (rice flour and water) on a drum-tight circle of cheesecloth placed over a pot of boiling water. The rising steam cooks and softens the dough, which is next rolled around cooked minced meats, mushrooms, onions and shrimp, then dipped in a hot *nuoc cham* and eaten immediately. *Banh cuon* is something like the Chinese *dim sum* dumpling—softer and chewier but just as beguiling.

Many southern Vietnamese delicacies besides *cha gio* are often served on some leafy vegetable in which the diner assembles his own little packet. In some of these a tiny charcoal-grilled pork patty is featured; in others boiled beef, shrimp or noodles may be the central ingredient. Each of these dishes rates its own special hot sauce, often containing some form of peanuts, as in the *saté* sauces of Sumatra.

This handy, informal do-it-yourself leaf-wrapping custom crops up in several parts of Southeast Asia. Probably the practice is an ancient one, indigenous to the area, for in Vietnam it is found primarily in the south, where customs have been least influenced by China.

The southern Vietnamese, like the inhabitants of most of the regions discussed in this book, consume a great deal of fresh fruit and raw vegetables. Being a tropical people, they traditionally prefer spicier food than the Vietnamese in the north do; they also use a lot of coconut and enjoy quick and simple dishes. The northerners regard the southerners as rustics, and tend to consider southern foods as at least garish, and certainly less subtle than their own; they prefer their vegetables cooked and tend to seek out more complex and delicate flavors. Southerners, on the other hand, tend to think most northern Vietnamese food is flat and uninteresting.

Some excellent northern dishes include a delectable soup *(Recipe Index)* of crab and asparagus (called "western bamboo" by the Vietnamese), a sweet-and-sour fish with a sauce far thinner than Chinese versions, and *nuoc mam*-flavored bean curd stuffed with chopped pork, onions and mushrooms that is so light on the tongue it seems to be all flavor and no substance.

But despite their differences, the North and South share many tastes. During the winter in the North, which is mild by some standards but noticeable enough to them, people like to gather around a charcoal-fired table brazier, cooking individual portions of meat by swishing them around with chopsticks in a boiling liquid. At first glance this looks like Chinese "hot pot" cookery, but the taste is purely Vietnamese: the boiling liquid contains pork and chicken bones, and the dipping sauce, of course, is a hot *nuoc cham.* In the South, though there is practically no seasonal change of temperature, the same congenial custom prevails.

In both North and South, the Vietnamese rely on fish for their main source of protein and for some of their most interesting dishes, such as fish stewed with *nuoc mam,* barbecued fish, and minced fish meat cakes of several sorts. As for beef, they have learned from the French how garlic can enhance its flavor—and have applied this acquired knowledge to the preparation of their own traditional beef dishes. They do wonders with pork as well, making omelettes with it and cooking it with *nuoc mam;* they also have a fine pork sausage called *cha lua* (silky sausage) which bears a texture to match its name. To vary the plain white rice they use so extensively, they sometimes boil it in an earthen pot with mushrooms, chicken and pork and serve it with a ginger sauce. They use in moderation almost all of the spices in Southeast Asia and most of the fruits, and have discovered many subtle and various uses of the delicate tang of lemon grass to perk up what might otherwise be ordinary dishes.

Their skills have earned the Vietnamese an international reputation as cooks. Paris boasts a selection of excellent Vietnamese restaurants and a goodly number of Vietnamese chefs, whose exposure to both French and Chinese techniques have well equipped them to cook for Paris' cosmopolitan tastes. And to those who know this reputation, it was not surprising that a Vietnamese chef was invited to preside over the White House kitchens by President John F. Kennedy.

It is no wonder that most Vietnamese are enthusiastic to the point of chauvinism about their foods. In the perhaps prejudiced opinion of one well-traveled Vietnamese cook, "the Chinese use too much grease, the Japanese are more interested in the appearance of the food than in taste and enjoyment, Indian and Thai foods taste too strong and too many have coconut milk and turmeric, and some countries avoid certain meats and ingredients. But we use everything and employ every method in our cuisine—and that's why it's the best."

To serve 4 to 6

A 2½- to 3-pound red snapper, cleaned but with head and tail left on

2 teaspoons salt

½ teaspoon white pepper

20 dried tiger lily buds *(see Glossary)*

4 dried Chinese mushrooms, about 1 to 1½ inches in diameter

½ cup chicken stock, fresh or canned

½ cup distilled white vinegar

2 tablespoons sugar

2 tablespoons fish's gravy *(see Glossary)*

1 tablespoon coarsely chopped garlic

1 teaspoon cornstarch

6 pickled scallions *(see Glossary)*, cut lengthwise into ⅛-inch-wide strips

A 1-inch length of fresh hot chili, seeded and cut into paper-thin rings *(caution: see page 69)*

3 tablespoons plus 2 cups vegetable oil

1 small onion, peeled and cut lengthwise into ¼-inch-wide strips

1 medium-sized carrot, scraped and cut lengthwise into strips ¼ inch wide and 1½ inches long

1 celery stalk, cut lengthwise into strips ¼ inch wide and 1½ inches long

3 small fresh scallions, trimmed and cut into strips ¼ inch wide and 1½ inches long

½ small firm ripe tomato, sliced ¼ inch thick and each slice cut in half crosswise

GARNISH

Fresh coriander leaves

1 small scallion including the green top, trimmed

## *Ca Ran Chua Ngot* (Vietnam)
### SWEET-AND-SOUR FISH

Wash the red snapper under cold running water and pat it completely dry with paper towels. Rub it inside and out with the salt and white pepper and set it aside to rest for 30 minutes or so.

In a deep bowl, combine the tiger lily buds, dried mushrooms and 2 cups of warm water. Soak for about 30 minutes; then drain and discard the water. Wash the lily buds and mushrooms under cold running water. With a cleaver or sharp knife, cut away and discard the hard ends of the lily buds and tie a knot in the center of each. Cut away and discard the tough stems of the mushrooms and slice the caps crosswise into ¼-inch-wide strips.

Combine the chicken stock, vinegar, sugar, fish's gravy, garlic and cornstarch in a deep bowl and beat vigorously with a whisk or table fork until the sugar and cornstarch are dissolved. Drop in the pickled scallions and chili rings and let them marinate for at least 10 minutes. With a slotted spoon, transfer the scallions and chilies to a plate. Reserve the marinade.

In a heavy 2- to 3-quart saucepan, heat 3 tablespoons of the vegetable oil over moderate heat until a light haze forms above it. Stirring for about 30 seconds after each addition, drop in the onion strips, the mushrooms, the carrots, the celery, the lily buds, the fresh scallion strips and finally the tomato slices.

Add the reserved marinade and, stirring constantly, bring to a boil over high heat. Still stirring, cook briskly for 2 or 3 minutes, until the sauce thickens and clears. Then remove the pan from the heat and taste the sauce for seasoning.

Pat the fish dry once more with paper towels to remove the excess salt. Then pour the remaining 2 cups of oil into a heavy skillet or shallow roasting pan large enough to hold the fish comfortably. The oil should be at least ½ inch deep; if necessary, add more. Heat the oil until it is very hot but not smoking.

Fry the fish in the hot oil for 8 to 10 minutes on each side, or until the fish is firm and delicately browned, turning it carefully with a slotted spoon or spatula.

Transfer the fish to a large, heated platter. Add the reserved pickled scallions and chili rings to the sauce and, stirring constantly but gently, reheat it for a minute or two. Pour the sauce over the fish, spreading the vegetables attractively on top. Garnish with coriander leaves and a whole scallion, and serve at once.

To carve the fish, slide the vegetable and scallion garnish to the side of the platter. Divide the top layer of the fish into individual portions with a fish server without cutting through the spine. Leave the head and tail intact. Lift out the portions with the fish server and a fork, and serve them, or arrange them attractively on another platter. Then gently remove the backbone in one piece, discard it, and divide the bottom layer of fish into individual portions as before.

Coriander leaves and a whole scallion garnish Vietnamese *ca ran chua ngot,* a fried red snapper in sweet-and-sour sauce.

## *Mang Tay Nau Cua* (Vietnam)
### CRAB AND ASPARAGUS SOUP

To serve 6

Cover the dried mushrooms with 1 cup of warm water and let them soak for 30 minutes. Drain them and save the water. With a sharp knife, cut away the tough stems, then slice the caps into strips ¼ inch wide.

In a heavy 3- to 4-quart saucepan, combine the reserved mushroom water, the stock and onions. Bring to a boil over high heat, reduce the heat to low and simmer for 3 or 4 minutes, until the onions are soft. Stir in the crab meat, asparagus and mushroom strips and bring the soup to a boil again. Then reduce the heat. Combine the cornstarch with ½ cup of cold water, stir well, and pour it into the soup. Stirring constantly but gently, simmer until the soup thickens and is clear.

Taste for seasoning and serve at once from a heated tureen or in individual soup plates. Just before serving, crumble the salted egg yolk into small bits and sprinkle the yolk and scallions on top of the soup.

5 dried Chinese mushrooms
6 cups chicken stock, fresh or canned
1 small onion, cut lengthwise into ¼-inch-wide strips
1 pound fresh or canned crab meat, thoroughly picked over
A 2-pound can white asparagus spears, cut into 1½-inch lengths
1 teaspoon cornstarch
1 Chinese salted duck egg yolk *(see Glossary)*
2 scallions, cut in 1-inch lengths

# X

# Thailand, a Realm of Exotic Flavors

Loaded with fruits and vegetables from market gardens upstream, boats choke the Bangkhoontein *klong* (canal) in Thorburi, a city across the Chao Phraya River from Bangkok. Commerce, travel and daily life all depend on the *klong* network, which veins much of central Thailand.

In the shadowed garden the black waters of a lotus pond reflect the yellow glimmer of lantern light. From an upper floor of the stately teak-beamed house, flutes and drums and a *ranad,* a Thai instrument resembling a xylophone, begin to play a pulsing, insistent melody. Summoned to the feast, we finish our drinks and the last little leaf-wrapped appetizers, remove our shoes and ascend to the dining area. Thick carpets cushion our feet, and we arrange ourselves on red pillows around low tables that gleam with lacquer and gold inlay. There we are led through an opulent pageant of sensory delights: for the ear, the tinkle and boom and wail of the unfamiliar yet strangely intimate music; for the eye, the spidery, elegant movements of classic dancers in glittering brocade, and the greens and yellows and reds of the curries and sauces that decorate our table like shafts of light from a prism; and for the tongue and nostrils, a galaxy of flavors, aromas and textures: spicy and sour, mild and meaty, soft and crunchy, leafy and smooth.

All the foods that night at Bangkok's Baan Thai restaurant arrived together and, as is the custom of Thailand, we ate them in random order, putting a little bit of each on our plates of rice, tasting and enjoying it, and then, according to whim, trying more of the same or succumbing to the lure of another bit with a different color or texture or fragrance. I made no effort to memorize the entire array, but I do recall the *kaeng tom kha kai,* a superb lemony chicken soup, thick and creamy with coconut milk and flavored with *laos* (known as *kha* in Thailand) and with the jungle redolence of coriander leaves. There was a beef curry, hot and red with chilies, and a turmeric-yellow curry of chicken in a spice-laden sauce. To soothe our chili-seared palates we turned to sweet *mee krob (Recipe Index),* a famous Thai dish of fried noodles coated with caramelized meat sauce—and it provided not only a change of pace in flavor but a brittle texture to contrast with the satin smoothness of the curries.

We had a fish dish with a hot sauce of its own, then a salad of pineapple and peanuts that came with a saucy sidekick—and quite a kick it had. And when all these foods had disappeared, when the dancers had retired, then the smiling waiters delivered to each of us a dish full of intricately carved fruits: pineapple slices fashioned in the form of tiny fans, juicy melons shaped into zinnia blossoms, and a luscious sapodilla that looked like a rose.

Before I finished this extraordinary meal I realized that the cuisine of Thailand—at least that which comes from sophisticated kitchens of the upper class—is more coherent than any other in Southeast Asia. Unlike the hodgepodge cooking styles of some of the other countries, which have produced marvelous dishes seemingly by accident, this cuisine is an integrated, harmonious whole, following definite rules, selecting with care the foreign ideas it will accept and catering to eye as well as palate.

This is not surprising in view of Thailand's history. Alone among the countries covered in this book, Thailand, formerly known as Siam, has never been subject to European colonial rule, and only rarely and briefly has it been overrun by other Asian nations. Adept at Western technology, following Indian religions, speaking a language akin to Chinese and writing it with a Sanskritic script adapted from the Khmers, the ancient Cambodians, the Thais are obviously a cosmopolitan people. At the same time they have managed to retain their own imperturbable character and their deeply religious culture.

Driven from their original homeland in South China by the expanding Mongol Empire, the Thai people began migrating slowly southward as early as the Eighth Century; by about 1300 they had carved out a new homeland between the Burmese on the northwest and the Khmers, the builders of the great temples at Angkor, on the southeast. Incursions by the Khmers and the Burmese twice forced the autocratic Thai kings to move their capital—including their sacred white elephants, their harems and slaves, and their kitchens—but always they kept control of the fertile Chao Phraya River basin, which they were developing into one of the world's greatest rice-producing areas.

In the mid-19th Century the shrewd and progressive King Mongkut, who reigned from 1851 to 1868, was able to maintain his jeweled throne and his independence by playing the French and British against each other, making concessions in turn to each but giving little of importance to either. Mongkut learned Latin and English, studied Western astronomy and mathematics, and confounded his court astrologers by correctly predicting a solar eclipse. Anxious to make allies, he once offered to send President Lincoln some battle elephants to help him fight the Civil War. Nothing irritates modern Thais more than the widespread Western notion, created by the romanticized play and movie

"The King and I," that an English schoolteacher opened Mongkut's eyes to the modern Western world. The King, they point out, was better read in European affairs than Anna Leonowens was, and her very presence in Thailand was one result of his long-standing effort to bring Siam into the 19th Century. The Thais doubt that Anna ever spoke more than a few polite words at a time to the King.

Mongkut's son, Chulalongkorn, who was one of Anna's pupils, abolished slavery, and he permitted his subjects to appear before him without groveling in the dust. But old ways and traditions die hard in Thailand: even Chulalongkorn had many wives and retained all the old royal powers. Not until 1932 did a coup end the absolute monarchy of Siam. And even today the placid, lethargic pace of the old life has barely been ruffled by the traffic and commerce and new buildings in downtown Bangkok. Almost every Thai male still spends some time as a Buddhist monk, living for a few months a life of austerity and meditation, setting out from his monastery every morning at dawn, clad in a saffron robe, to collect alms of rice from neighborhood householders. Elephants, no longer needed for war, still haul teak logs from the forests in the north to the headwaters of the Chao Phraya. The great river remains the country's chief source of wealth and power and its main artery of transportation and communication. Huge deep-draft sampans carry rice and salt for hundreds of miles along the Chao Phraya, and a network of narrow *klongs,* or canals, reaches out to nearly every village in Central Thailand.

Recently, many *klongs* within Bangkok itself have been filled in to make roads, but across the river in the capital's twin city of Thonburi one can still get about more easily by water than on land. There, every morning, hundreds of small sampans loaded with produce and propelled by women in bright *panungs* and conical "lampshade" hats make their way through the *klongs* to the famous "floating market"; and all day long, sampan peddlers selling everything from coconuts to ice cream, from hot coffee to steaming noodles, paddle through the *klongs,* stopping to honk their horns and hawk their wares at little steep-roofed houses perched on stilts between the flame trees along the banks of the crowded waterway.

Protected from outside invaders, safe from domestic turmoil, the conservative court and nobility of Siam developed over the centuries many elegant traditions, including refined arts of the kitchen that eventually seeped down to the lower classes. In a very special fashion, moreover, the kings of old Siam became patrons of cooking; this was especially true of Chulalongkorn, a redoubtable trencherman who liked to whip up a hot sauce or a curry himself.

Each of Chulalongkorn's 32 wives lived in her own apartment in the palace, attended by her own servants. At the New Year, each wife's kitchen had to furnish one dish for a lavish party that actually amounted to a cooking contest in which the monarch himself judged the foods and dispensed the prizes. Whenever the King dined in his own apartments he ordered his meal from the kitchens of his principal wives, and he usually could tell which dish came from whom because

In a pond beside the Friendship Highway north of Bangkok, an elderly Thai woman plucks lotus flowers. The lotus blossom has enormous symbolic importance in Oriental religions, and the plant's everyday importance is equally great: the root is a vegetable, the seeds are consumed as a salted or sweet snack, and even the dried leaf finds use as cigarette papers.

Monks at a *wat* (temple) in downtown Bangkok prepare to enjoy a rare feast. Cooked at home by a number of local housewives, the meal was presented to the monks as an offering, and includes such dishes as roast duck, eggs and pork, and herring. But the monks, who beg for rice daily as part of their ascetic regimen, do not usually eat so well—and no matter what food is available, they are not permitted to touch it after noon.

the cooks were expected to deliver their food in person and stand by while the King ate it—a routine precaution against poisoning. The real test, however, came when the King went to spend the night with a wife, expecting, among other things, to be fed; while the chosen queen prepared to please the royal person her loyal cooks did everything in their power to captivate the royal palate—for failure in either department could bring disaster.

Out of this culinary competition—on which fortunes and lives depended—there arose a complex and formal cuisine rich in subtleties of taste and texture, concerned with the appearance of food as well as its flavor (for if the food did not *look* good the King might not even try it), and bound by rules about the condiments to be used with certain foods. The court kitchens also were responsible for the fact that the best cooks in the land were women, for no man but the King or his sons was permitted to enter the inner palace.

Nothing illustrates the organization of Thai cooking better than the spectrum of dishes called *kaeng* (pronounced "kang"). The word means liquid, and refers to any cooked food served as a liquid or with a great deal of sauce, such as a soup or a curry. A *kaeng,* in other words, is something you can mix with your rice—and most Thais still do just that despite the tut-tutting of a few finicky, Westernized aristocrats who consider the custom untidy and backward. In old Siam, of course, even the King mixed his *kaeng* with his rice, and ate with his fingers. (Now most Thais eat with fork and spoon.) Cooked foods that come to the table dry, or with a sauce too thick to run, are known as *krueng kieng,* or side dishes.

In general, *kaeng* soups are mild or lemony. *Kaeng chud,* for example, is a downright bland, clear broth, in which any of a number of ingredients, such as chicken or squid or vegetables *(Recipe Index)*, may play a principal role. *Kaeng chud* is essential to any well-balanced Thai meal, and I frequently found myself reaching for it frantically when my mouth was burning from some hot chili preparation. *Kaeng tom yam kung (Recipe Index)*, a superb lemony shrimp soup that I was served during my first Bangkok meal on this trip and many times thereafter, can also calm the palate even though it contains chili. This is due to the gumdrop sourness of lemon grass, the fragrance of basil and the musky aroma of coriander leaves, which all add up to a healing balm. Sometimes this soup comes to the table bubbling away on a brazier, with shrimp so tender that they are ready to dissolve with the first gentle bite. Another *kaeng tom yam* may be made with chicken, while other *kaeng* soups rely on different soothing combinations of leaves and herbs; those with lemon grass seem to be most successful.

Most dishes called *kaeng,* however, can be described as curries rather than soups. Like the soups, *kaeng* curries make ingenious use of herbs and aromatic leaves. In fact some Thai *kaeng* curries contain none of the pungent curry spices at all, relying entirely on herbs—plus chili, shallots and sometimes garlic—to provide the zing that a curry should have. Some experts say that this herb-with-chili kind of *kaeng,* used mainly for meats and vegetables, is the original, native Thai curry, to which the Indian influence later added a broader range of spicery. However, the *kaeng* dishes I like best are those that did develop from the Indian curries. It is a mark of Thailand's cultural independence that authentic Indian curries are seldom found on Thai tables. The Thai adaptations differ from the originals in their magical blending of sharp and pungent spices with the mellow fragrance of a number of aromatic leaves. These *kaeng* curries always come in established colors, each color representing a particular blend of spices and herbs. (The overall spiciness of the dish may be adjusted, of course, by varying the proportion of the blend to other ingredients.)

*Kaeng kari,* for example, is a yellow curry; it contains most of the Indian spices and herbs (coriander, cardamom, fennel, anise, nutmeg, mace, cinnamon, turmeric, to name a few) along with palm sugar and *nam pla,* a fish sauce. The *kaeng kari* takes its color from turmeric and is made with dried chilies, not so fiery as the fresh ones. Generally used for chicken or beef, it tastes more like an Indian curry than any other *kaeng* but is not nearly so spicy as the Indian product.

Moving up the thermometer of spiciness, the next *kaeng* we meet is *kaeng phed,* a common vehicle for fowl, eels and a sour fish ball called *luk chin.* Tiny fresh red chilies endow *kaeng phed* with a bright red color and a red-hot power to match—especially if an uncrushed bit of chili finds its way to the tongue. When making their *kaeng* curries the Thais let the coconut milk boil; this separates the oil from the milk and decorates the sauce with swirls of darker and lighter shades, an effect that is particularly attractive in the red *kaeng phed.* The hot blast of spices and spicy roots in this *kaeng* is tempered by the mellowing presence of basil leaves, but *kaeng phed* is about as far up the scale as most Western visitors want to go.

*Overleaf:* A selection of typical Thai fruits, some familiar in the West and others highly unusual, is shown in artful display at one of the finest of Bangkok's many restaurants, the Baan Thai, or Thai House. The fruits include a spiky, ineffably flavored durian at right; a carved watermelon with watermelon balls; a large basket of mixed fruit containing bristly orange rambutans; a pink and white rose apple carved into the shape of a flower; an opened lotus pod beneath a bouquet of skewered lotus seeds and rose apple slices; and several strawberrylike *rakam.* The white rosettes are carved yam beans.

The Thais, however, consider *kaeng phed* a fairly mild curry, and so it is—compared to the green variety, *kaeng keao wan*. The hottest Thai chilies of all are a small green variety, and these are what give this dish its deceptively innocent pale green tint. I first tangled with *kaeng keao wan* at a dinner in Bangkok's modern commercial district, at a popular middle-class restaurant noted more for its good food than its decor. When we arrived at the jammed, brightly lit Chitpochana, nose-tingling cooking aromas, the babble of conversation and a beer-hall atmosphere of good cheer were spilling out to the sidewalk. In the hot climate of Thailand, restaurants like this one need no front wall and it seemed that the passing throng outside was continuing mingling with the customers within. All the zinc-topped tables were full, waiters bearing large trays plunged recklessly through the narrow spaces between them, and the diners were so obviously having a good time that it seemed unlikely anyone would ever yield place to us.

But then my interpreter-guide, a vivacious descendant of King Mongkut, spotted some friends and we were invited to join their table. Before sitting down we studied the array of foods set out under a glass case along one wall: grilled fish and fowl, a patchwork of *kaeng,* many side dishes and the sauces for them. We picked out, among other things, a pale green *kaeng keao wan* of chicken.

At the table of young people, Thai and foreign, the conversation was lively; and then several dishes arrived at once, and everyone tried some of what everyone else had ordered. Nobody had really planned the meal but we seemed to have received a good variety. There was a fine yellow *kaeng* of snails with coriander leaves, a side dish of a small catfish called *pla duk* grilled with hot spices and sweet basil leaves, a vegetable *kaeng chud* and a perfect tender crab cooked in a clay pot and accompanied by a sweetly hot, vinegared soy sauce. Then my chicken *kaeng keao wan* appeared and was passed around, and all the foreigners suddenly stopped talking and reached for the mild soup. But even as I told myself that a dish that looked like nothing more than vichyssoise had no business creating such blazing havoc in my mouth, the compensating light fragrance of the sweet basil leaves within the *kaeng keao wan* began to placate and restore my palate. The herb-spice combination took over and despite the superhot green chilies I began to appreciate this distinctively Thai duet of flavors.

The spice ingredients of the *kaeng* curries (and I have only mentioned some of the basic combinations) are marketed throughout Thailand in paste and powder form, premixed in the right proportions. Fussy chefs insist on preparing their own mixtures but most housewives, and even many good restaurants, save time and trouble in the first stage of *kaeng* curry making by simply frying the proper premixed paste with coconut cream. Additional spices, seasonings such as fish sauce and onions, and herb leaves are added later. Although the methods of curry making are many and complex, one interesting principle generally holds good for them all: both coconut milk and coconut cream are prepared and the meat or chicken is first boiled in the milk. Then the curry paste is fried in the cream; the stock, meat and seasoning are added gradually and the mixture is further cooked until the oil rises. This makes a thick *kaeng,* the way the Thais like it. For her foreign guests who often prefer a thinner sauce, M. L. Nravadi Chaixanien, the food supervisor of the opulent Baan Thai restaurant, sets some of the coconut milk aside during most of the process and adds it at the last minute. (Cooking thickens coconut milk, so this last bit is cooked only for a moment or so, to keep the sauce thin.) The herb leaves that go into these *kaeng* must also be added near the end of the cooking process lest their fragrance dissipate in steam.

Having said all this about coconut milk, I must mention one Thai curry that uses vegetable oil instead. This is a *kaeng phed nok kaeng bha,* a red curry of a tiny bird that lives in the rice paddies. Why this bird is never curried with coconut milk is a mystery that probably lies buried with some ancient palace cook. I suspect she devised the dish as a culinary tour de force, because without the smoothing, blending presence of the coconut milk, the chilies, coriander seeds and all the spices in the red curry paste could be expected to come out harsh and raw. But they do not, possibly because of the sweet basil leaves that go into the dish, or possibly because of some technique I was not told about. At any rate this rice-bird curry, hot yet delicate, demonstrated to me again the sophisticated Thai blending of spices and herbs.

Like everyone else in Southeast Asia, the Thais rely heavily for basic salting on a fish sauce, *nam pla,* which resembles Vietnam's *nuoc mam,* and a fish or shrimp paste, *kapi,* which somewhat resembles the Indonesian *trassi.* Both *nam pla* and *kapi* are essential to the preparation of many *kaeng* and side dishes, but their most important function is to serve as the base for an all-but-infinite number of hot sauces, or *nam prik.* To say that *nam prik* is the Thai equivalent of Indonesia's *sambal* or Vietnam's *nuoc cham,* is to state only part of the truth. In usage, it parallels both of them, and since it contains fish sauce it is indeed related to *nuoc cham.* But it seems to me that the Thais have carried the idea further, with more variety and precision.

A simple, basic *nam prik* may contain some combination of *nam pla,* roasted *kapi,* dried salted shrimp, garlic, chili, sugar, lime juice and a few sweet-sour berries of a Southeast Asian plant the Thais call *ma-uk.* The proportions can vary according to the cook and the purpose. In addition to these ingredients, any of a long list of foodstuffs may be included: tamarind, peanuts, shallots, herbs, egg yolks, coriander leaves, even coconut cream. Some jaded epicures insist on adding, for flavor as they say, a particular type of water bug, ground up.

The many kinds of *nam prik* came at me so thick and fast that I soon gave up trying to distinguish between them or to figure out which ones went with what kind of food. Mostly I got them with a *yam* salad: fresh vegetables that you roll up in a leafy package, dip and eat, as is the Vietnamese fashion. However I also remember, at a lunch at the Baan Thai restaurant, being served a *nam prik* to accompany a dish of noodles with papaya, banana flowers and several unfamiliar Thai vegetables fried in batter. One particularly hot sauce enlivened a crab and papaya salad I had at a tiny lunch stall in Bangkok's Pratuman market.

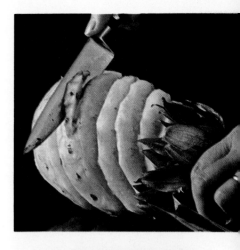

**ARTFUL PINEAPPLE PEELING**
Here is a decorative way to remove a pineapple's "eyes" without wasting edible fruit. The eyes grow in a series of spiral rows. When the outer skin of the fruit has been shaved off with a sharp knife, the spirals show clearly and are easy to excise *(top),* leaving intact the pulp between rows. Use a sharp knife to undercut the eyes, top and bottom, at about a 45° angle. Lift out the wedges, and the fruit is ready to eat.

At a more luxurious establishment I ate *tot num pla,* a tiny fish dumpling dipped in a peanut-flavored *nam prik* that reminded me happily of the *saté* sauces I had enjoyed in Singapore. At the same meal another rice-bird dish, not a curry, was grilled in soy sauce and served to be dipped in a *nam prik.* And on several occasions—once at the mansion of a grandson of King Chulalongkorn, another time in a small farming village far from Bangkok—I have eaten the most basic meal of the Thais: a *pla tu,* a small unpretentious salted mackerel fried brown and served up with a bowl of rice and little round saucers of a red, fiery and altogether stimulating *nam prik.*

Every good Thai cook can whip up a few dozen *nam prik* with no trouble at all, but perhaps none ever did it so well as an octogenarian lady, a minor princess in her own right, who once was a cook for one of King Chulalongkorn's wives. Tiny and withered, but still gracious and alert, Princess Chongchit recalled for me the day long ago when the King, feeling poorly and lacking an appetite, came to visit "my queen." Then and there Princess Chongchit invented a new and special *nam prik* for the King. He ate it, with fish and vegetables, quickly recovered both his appetite and his health, and conferred a royal decoration on the Princess. With that, her reputation was established, and she became the recognized authority on *nam prik.* Did His Majesty, the present King, I wondered, sometimes request her expert services? Princess Chongchit sighed and shook her head; King Bhumibol, who was educated in Switzerland and who plays a jazz clarinet, has developed a worldly taste for Western and Chinese food.

Unfortunately for me, Princess Chongchit is no longer up to cooking for informal visitors, so I could not sample her sauces. But while I was in Bangkok another Princess introduced me to the cuisine of a neighboring country. Mrs. Sanda Simms, the wife of an English journalist, Peter Simms, is a Princess of the Shan states of northern Burma, and a first-rate cook. One evening soon after my arrival the Simmses invited me to their home for a dinner that even to them was out-of-the-ordinary fare. Sanda herself prepared several Shan dishes, a Burmese friend of theirs cooked three Burmese specialties, and one of the Simms's cooks produced several dishes common to northern Thailand and Laos.

As Sanda was the first to point out, Shan cooking is less varied than Thailand's and more closely related to China's. Living on the Burma-China border, the Shans use soy sauce instead of the fish sauces and pastes of the Burmese and Thais, and instead of making thick-sauced curries they eat either soups or dry, fried dishes. Among the Shan specialties we sampled that night was pork cooked with bamboo shoots, fried fish with a soy bean cake, and, the best of the lot, something Sanda called "three-layer pork": chunks of skin, fat and meat from a cut of bacon fried in garlic, ginger and shallots.

Located between Thailand and India, the Burmese share culinary preferences with both areas: their curries resemble those of India and their fish sauces and pastes are nearly identical with Thailand's. But the Burmese dislike coconut oil and prefer to cook in sesame or peanut oil and without many aromatic herbs; this makes their curries less smooth and

*Opposite:* The curries of Thailand are identified by color, and three of the most popular are shown here in front of a benign Buddha. The green shrimp curry, *kaeng keao wan kung,* in the foreground gets its color from green chilies; the chicken curry, *kaeng phed cai,* in the center bowl is colored by red chili powder; the beef curry, *kaeng kari nau,* has the yellow tinge of turmeric. The other dish is *mee krob,* a superb Thai creation of rice noodles, egg, pork and shrimp.

1 With your hand, dribble a tablespoon of lightly beaten egg over the surface of hot vegetable oil. The egg will coagulate.

2 When the lace formed by the egg has browned on both sides, remove it to paper towels to drain. Repeat with the rest of the egg.

3 Reheat the oil and add the *py mei fun,* or rice-stick noodles. Turn gently until the sputtering stops. Remove to paper towels.

6 Combine the pan's contents with the *py mei fun* little by little. Toss them together lightly, being careful not to crush the noodles.

7 Mound the mixture on a plate and spread the egg lace over the top. Put the bean sprouts around the *mee krob,* garnish with scallions and chilies and place a fringed chili "cap" on top *(opposite).*

4  Add onions, garlic, pork, shrimp, bean sauce
and tomato paste to ⅓ cup of the oil, one ingredient
at a time, stirring after each addition. Bring the
sauce to a boil, then stir in the sugar.

5  As the mixture boils, the liquid
will form a thick, glossy syrup. At
this stage, begin to add the tamarind
water and fish's gravy.

sweet, though just as hot as those of Thailand. The best of the Burmese dishes I tasted at the Simmses was *hin lay,* a strong, down-to-earth pork curry with pickled mango, fragrant with all the curry spices and suggesting the manifold flavors of India.

Linguistically, culturally and gastronomically, the peoples of northern Thailand have less in common with their own countrymen around Bangkok than with their neighbors in Laos. Ethnically the Laotians are Thais too, but they and the people of northern Thailand arrived from China later than the central Thais and never quite united with their cousins in the Chao Phraya basin. The international border between Thailand and Laos is another unnatural line drawn by an accident of colonial history; Laos used to be a French colony (like Cambodia and Vietnam a part of French Indo-China) and the border simply marks the limit of French colonial expansion.

One of the favorite foods of the Thais and Laotians on both sides of that border is a pickled, uncooked pork sausage called *nam.* In deference to our Western stomachs, Sanda's northern Thai cook had fried it, but later I ventured to try the uncompromised version at a Bangkok restaurant. Heavily spiced, served with ginger, peanuts, scallions and tiny hot raw chilies, it made an excellent salty snack to nibble while drinking; the spices, the chili and the alcohol would protect me from the raw pork, I reasoned, and I was right—or lucky. Besides the fried *nam,* the Simms's selection of north Thai dishes included an excellent spiced beef, chopped fine and served with a *nam prik* type of sauce and coriander leaves, and a crisp salad of green papaya and tomato combined with just enough fresh chili to make it interesting.

For reasons I have been unable to determine, every meal the Laotians eat features the glutinous rice that other peoples of the area save for special occasions or for cakes and sweets. The rice is steamed in small cylindrical baskets and then sliced up to be eaten with a hot sauce. Since they do not touch plain white rice, it is not surprising that the Laotians have no curries. Another peculiarity of their cooking is the painstaking way they go about preparing a dish with several ingredients: each spice, the ginger, the garlic, and each vegetable is fried separately, usually in lard, and then set aside to wait until all is ready.

But the oddest of all Laotian idiosyncrasies is a preference for a breakfast soup, called *furr,* containing noodles, pork, garlic and the common Laotian leaf that once made the remote little country a haven for hippies from all over the world: marijuana.

It is in Thailand itself, I realized as I prepared to leave Bangkok, that the foods and cooking styles of the vast region I had traveled reach a sort of culmination. Do Hawaii and Tahiti and Bali boast of their fruits? I have never tasted pineapple better than Thailand's, and the Thai *pomelo,* which looks like a grapefruit and tastes something like a blackberry, is one of nature's wonders. The Pacific islanders and the Indonesians do remarkable things with coconut milk, and I think when it comes down to it that I like the west Sumatran *gulai* better than Thai curries, but the Thais know how to make their curries *look* as good and exciting as they taste. Wrapping food in leaves may be an

East Indian and Polynesian art, but making food of leaves, as the Thais do it, is an even worthier accomplishment. Are the Malayans superb spicers? Yes, but the Thai curry pastes are so expertly and thoughtfully prepared, so easy to handle that even Nancy Rutgers, my Tahiti hostess, asked me to send her some from Bangkok. And as for the *sambal* of Indonesia, well, Thailand's *nam prik* is on the same high level.

Moreover, Thailand's blending of Indian and Chinese culinary ideas with such native Southeast Asian specialties as fish sauce has been done so thoroughly and so expertly that there are no rough edges. Seldom does one find at a Thai meal a dish that proclaims its foreign origins; everything has been changed, adapted, fitted carefully into the scheme of the Thai cuisine. The cooks I watched in Samoa were carefree and spontaneous, casually substituting an available ingredient for what was missing; the Indonesians frequently enjoy dishes from several of their differing cuisines at a single sitting—and occasionally a Dutch stew as well. But the Thais are purists who seem to feel that if a food is worth cooking it is worth cooking right and that dishes of obviously foreign origin spoil the balance of a good meal.

On my way to the airport for the flight back home I stopped in at the Baan Thai restaurant to thank the doe-eyed, fragile-looking food director, M. L. Nravadi Chaixanien, for her assistance. We had a drink, and she offered me a tiny leaf-wrapped snack made with shrimp, spiced pork and other wondrous ingredients. It was a morsel I had not tasted before and I realized with a pang how few foods of Thailand I had really had time to eat, and how many yet untried combinations of tastes await my next visit to the fair, green islands of the Pacific and the teeming lands of Southeast Asia.

## *Kaeng Keao Wan Kung* (*Thailand*)
### GREEN SHRIMP CURRY

Shell the shrimp. Then devein them by making a shallow incision down the backs with a small, sharp knife and lifting out the black or white intestinal vein with the point of the knife. Wash the shrimp under cold running water and pat them completely dry with paper towels. Set them aside.

Prepare the coconut milk and let it rest at room temperature or in the refrigerator for an hour or so, until the rich top milk rises to the surface. With a large spoon, skim 1 cup off the top and transfer it to a heavy 3- to 4-quart saucepan. Set the remaining coconut milk aside.

Stirring frequently, bring the top milk to a boil over high heat. Reduce the heat to low and, stirring occasionally, simmer uncovered until coconut oil begins to bubble to the surface and the liquid has been reduced to about ¼ cup. Add the green curry paste and the pulverized *kachai*, and cook briskly, still stirring from time to time, until most of the liquid in the pan has evaporated.

Add the shrimp and turn them about with a spoon for 3 or 4 minutes, or until they are firm and pink. Stir in the remaining coconut milk and the fish's gravy and, stirring occasionally, simmer uncovered for 10 minutes. Taste for seasoning and garnish with the chili strips and fresh basil leaves.

Serve at once from a deep heated platter or large bowl. *Kaeng keao wan kung* is traditionally accompanied by hot boiled rice.

**To serve 4 to 6**

1½ pounds medium-sized uncooked shrimp (21 to 25 to the pound)
3 cups fresh coconut milk made from 3 cups coarsely chopped coconut and 3 cups hot water (*page 61*)
2 tablespoons green curry paste (*Recipe Booklet*)
1 tablespoon crushed *kachai* (*see Glossary*), pulverized with the flat of a heavy knife or with a mortar and pestle
2 tablespoons fish's gravy (*see Glossary*)
1 tablespoon fresh hot green chili strips about 1 inch long and ⅛ inch wide (*caution: see page 69*)
4 fresh basil leaves

## *Kaeng Kari Nua* (*Thailand*)
### YELLOW BEEF CURRY

Prepare the coconut milk and let it rest at room temperature or in the refrigerator for an hour or so, until the rich top milk rises to the surface. With a large spoon, skim off 1 cup of the top milk and transfer it to a heavy 3- to 4-quart saucepan. Set the rest of the coconut milk aside.

Stirring frequently, bring the top milk to a boil over high heat. Reduce the heat to low and, stirring occasionally, simmer uncovered until coconut oil begins to bubble to the surface and the liquid has been reduced to about ¼ cup. Add the curry paste and turmeric, and cook briskly, still stirring, until most of the liquid in the pan has evaporated.

Stir in the star anise, cinnamon and bay leaves, then add the beef and turn it about with a spoon until it is evenly coated with the spice mixture. Add the potatoes, onions and the reserved coconut milk. Stirring occasionally and regulating the heat so that the sauce does not boil rapidly, cook partially covered for 30 to 40 minutes, or until the meat and potatoes are tender but still intact.

Taste for seasoning and serve from a deep heated platter or large bowl. *Kaeng kari nua* is traditionally accompanied by hot boiled rice.

**To serve 4 to 6**

3 cups fresh coconut milk made from 3 cups coarsely chopped coconut and 3 cups hot water (*page 61*)
2 tablespoons red curry paste (*Recipe Booklet*)
2 teaspoons turmeric
2 star anise (*see Glossary*)
A 2-inch piece of stick cinnamon
2 medium-sized bay leaves
1½ pounds lean beef chuck, trimmed of excess fat and cut into 1-inch cubes
3 medium-sized potatoes, peeled and cut into 1-inch cubes
3 medium-sized onions, peeled, cut lengthwise into quarters and then crosswise into 1-inch-thick slices

Three memorable Thai soups are: *kaeng chud woon sen,* with cellophane noodles and vegetables; *kaeng chud pla muk,* with pork and stuffed squid; and *kaeng tom yam kung,* a lemony broth with shrimp.

½ cup dried tiger lily buds *(see Glossary)*

2 tablespoons dried cloud ears *(see Glossary)*

2 ounces cellophane noodles *(see Glossary)*

½ pound small uncooked shrimp (at least 30 to the pound)

1 tablespoon finely chopped garlic

1 tablespoon finely chopped fresh coriander roots

½ teaspoon freshly ground black pepper

2 tablespoons vegetable oil

1 large onion, peeled and cut lengthwise into ½-inch-wide strips

¼ pound pork shoulder, cut into strips 1 inch by ½ inch

2 quarts boiling water

5 small scallions, cut into 3-inch lengths

3 tablespoons fish's gravy *(see Glossary)*

2 to 4 tablespoons sugar

1 tablespoon Japanese soy sauce

2 eggs, lightly beaten

1 tablespoon finely cut fresh coriander leaves

To serve 6

1½ pounds medium-sized uncooked shrimp (21 to 25 to the pound)

2½ quarts water

6 small *makrut* leaves *(see Glossary)*

1 tablespoon *takrai* (dried lemon grass sticks, *see Glossary*), cut into 1-inch lengths

⅓ cup strained fresh lime juice

⅓ cup fish's gravy *(see Glossary)*

¼ cup finely cut fresh coriander leaves

¼ cup thinly sliced scallion tops cut into strips about ⅛ inch wide and 1½ inch long

12 fresh hot red chili strips, each about ⅛ inch wide and 1 inch long *(caution: see page 69)*

## *Kaeng Chud Woon Sen*  (Thailand)
### CELLOPHANE NOODLE AND VEGETABLE SOUP

In a deep bowl, combine the tiger lily buds and cloud ears, and cover them with 4 cups of warm water. In a separate bowl, cover the cellophane noodles with 2 cups of cold water. Soak for 30 minutes; then drain and discard the water.

Wash the drained lily buds and cloud ears under cold running water. Then cut away and discard the hard ends of the lily buds and tie a knot in the center of each. If the cloud ears are large, cut them into ½-inch pieces. Cut the noodles into ½-inch-long pieces.

Meanwhile, shell the shrimp. Then devein them by making a shallow incision down their backs with a small, sharp knife and lifting out the intestinal vein with the point of the knife. Wash the shrimp under cold water and set them aside on paper towels to drain.

With a mortar and pestle, or in a small bowl with the back of a spoon, mash the garlic, coriander roots and pepper to a smooth paste.

To make the soup, heat the oil in a heavy 4- to 6-quart casserole over moderate heat until a light haze forms above it. Drop in the onions and, stirring frequently, cook for about 5 minutes until they are soft and transparent but not brown. Watch carefully for any sign of burning and regulate the heat accordingly. Stir in the garlic mixture, then add the pork and shrimp. Stirring constantly, cook for 4 or 5 minutes, or until the shrimp are pink.

Pour in the 2 quarts of boiling water and add the lily buds, cloud ears and noodles. Bring to a boil again, then stir in the scallion tops, fish's gravy, 2 tablespoons of the sugar and the soy sauce. Taste for seasoning and add up to 2 tablespoons more sugar if you prefer the soup sweet as the Thais do. Stirring constantly, slowly pour the beaten eggs in a thin stream into the boiling soup. They will instantly form firm threads. Remove from the heat immediately lest the eggs overcook.

Serve at once from a heated tureen or in individual soup plates. Just before serving, garnish the soup with the coriander leaves.

## *Kaeng Tom Yam Kung*  (Thailand)
### LEMONY SHRIMP SOUP

Shell the shrimp carefully, leaving the tails attached. Then devein them by making a shallow incision down their backs with a small, sharp knife and lifting out the black or white intestinal vein with the point of the knife. Wash the shrimp under cold running water and pat them completely dry with paper towels.

In a heavy 4- to 6-quart casserole, bring the water to a boil over high heat. Drop in the *makrut* and *takrai* and boil uncovered for about 10 minutes, or until the leaves become somewhat yellow.

Stir in the lime juice and fish's gravy and boil the soup for 5 minutes more. Reduce the heat to moderate, drop in the shrimp, and cook for 4 or 5 minutes longer, or until the shrimp are firm and pink. Add the fresh coriander leaves, scallion tops and red chili strips, and taste for seasoning.

Serve at once from a heated tureen or in individual soup plates.

## Mee Krob (Thailand)
CRISP NOODLES WITH SHRIMP-AND-PORK SAUCE

To serve 6 to 8

First make scallion "brushes" in the following way: Wash the scallions under cold running water. With a small, sharp knife, trim off the roots and cut off all but about 2 inches of the green tops, leaving firm stalks 3 or 4 inches long. Holding each stalk firmly in the center, make 4 intersecting cuts about 1 inch deep into each end. Place the scallions in ice water and refrigerate them.

Shell the shrimp and devein them by making a deep incision down their backs with a small, sharp knife and lifting out the black or white intestinal vein with the point of the knife. Wash the shrimp under cold water and set them aside on paper towels to drain.

Pour 4 cups of vegetable oil into a 12-inch wok and heat until the oil reaches a temperature of 350° on a deep-frying thermometer.

Scoop about a tablespoon of the beaten eggs with your fingers and, moving your hand in a circle over the wok, dribble the egg into the hot oil as shown in the photograph on page 188. The eggs will instantly coagulate into irregular lacy shapes. Fry for 30 seconds, then turn the egg lace gently with a slotted spatula, and continue frying for 30 seconds longer, or until golden brown. Transfer to paper towels to drain. Dip your hand in cold water and repeat the process until the remaining eggs have been fried. As you proceed, lay each batch on the towels.

Raise the heat of the oil to 400°. Drop in one piece of *py mei fun;* it will immediately begin to splutter and within a moment will have swelled to 3 or 4 times its original size. Fry about one minute; turn the piece gently with two spoons and fry for 30 seconds longer, or until the spluttering stops and the *py mei fun* browns lightly. Carefully transfer it to drain on a double thickness of paper towels. In a similar fashion, deep-fry each of the remaining 3 pieces of *py mei fun* and set them side by side on the towels.

Pour off all but ⅓ cup of the oil and return the wok to high heat. Stirring for about 1 minute after each addition, add the onions and garlic, the pork, shrimp, bean sauce and tomato paste. Bring the sauce to a boil, then stir in the sugar and as soon as the liquids become a thick glossy syrup, begin to add the tamarind water and fish's gravy. Reduce the heat to low and, stirring occasionally, simmer uncovered for about 25 minutes, or until almost all of the liquid in the pan has evaporated and the mixture is thick enough to hold its shape almost solidly in a spoon. Stir in the lemon juice and lemon peel and simmer for 4 or 5 minutes longer until the peel is limp. Remove the pan from the heat.

To assemble, place about ¼ of the *py mei fun* in a large, deep bowl and pour about ½ cup of the sauce over it. With two table forks, toss them together gently but thoroughly, taking care not to crush the noodles. Add another quarter of the noodles, and ½ cup of the sauce, toss them with the mixture in the bowl and repeat the procedure twice more until all the noodles and sauce are combined.

Mound the *mee krob* on a large platter, spread the egg lace attractively over it and arrange the bean sprouts in a ring around the edge. Place the chili "cap" on top of the *mee krob*. Then drain the scallion brushes and garnish the platter with the scallions and chili strips.

6 to 8 medium-sized scallions

1 pound medium-sized uncooked shrimp (21 to 25 to the pound)

Vegetable oil for deep-frying

2 eggs, lightly beaten

½ pound or 2 layers of *py mei fun* (rice stick noodles, *see Glossary*), each layer pulled gently in half lengthwise

¼ cup finely chopped onions

1 tablespoon finely chopped garlic

½ pound lean boneless pork, sliced ¼ inch thick and then cut into strips 2 inches long and ¼ inch wide

¼ cup yellow bean paste or thick bean sauce *(see Glossary)*

2 tablespoons tomato paste

¾ cup sugar

¼ cup tamarind water *(page 63)*

¼ cup fish's gravy *(see Glossary)*

½ cup strained fresh lemon juice

1 tablespoon fresh lemon peel, cut into slivers about 1 inch long and ⅛ inch wide

½ pound fresh young bean sprouts, washed and with husks removed, or substitute 4 cups drained, canned bean sprouts, washed in a sieve under cold water

2 fresh hot red chilies, washed and seeded, one cut lengthwise into strips about 1 inch long and ⅛ inch wide and one shaped into a fringed "cap" by slicing it lengthwise at ¼-inch intervals to within 1 inch of the top *(caution: see page 69)*

# The Foods of Australia and New Zealand

*This discussion of the foods of Australasia is based primarily on research provided by Gordon Bedson, chef, wine expert and restaurateur on the Queensland Gold Coast, and by Miss Tui Flower, cookbook author and columnist and home economist for Auckland's "New Zealand Woman's Weekly." Selected recipes from Australia and New Zealand are listed in the Recipe Index and will be found in the Recipe Booklet.*

Far off in their remote corner of the Pacific the 15 million people of Australia and New Zealand have created a hearty style of life and a distinctive culture of their own. But, although they can claim some interesting dishes, they have not yet produced a highly developed cuisine.

This culinary deficiency—which they themselves would be the first to admit—may seem strange, considering how richly endowed Australasia is with fertile land and teeming seas as well as with generous climates, subtropical and temperate, that have made foodstuffs a major industry and principal export. But a fine cuisine is slow in maturing. It needs leisure to evolve and—if it is to be a high cuisine—a leisured class to appreciate and support it. The Australians and New Zealanders have been there for only a century and a half. They are still pioneers, too busy mastering and exploiting their patrimony to bother with epicurean refinements; their eating habits are mostly the same simple, substantial ones they arrived with as working-class settlers from Britain. For the average Australian or New Zealander, food is still a matter of steak and eggs doused with tomato sauce, or boiled lamb and cabbage, or roast beef and Yorkshire pudding, followed even in hot weather by sweet pastry and tea.

Yet, in recent years there have been signs of a gastronomic awakening. Part of it comes from overseas: the governments have been actively promoting immigration, and hundreds of thousands of newcomers, most of them from Europe, have brought their own cuisines with them. As a result, espresso parlors and shops stocked with foreign food items have sprung up in the bigger cities, and the menus of better restaurants in Melbourne and Sydney have blossomed with *Königsberger Klopse, crêpes suzettes* and *saltimbocca*. These cosmopolitan novelties are gradually making people more food-conscious and more willing to experiment with foods.

## Australia

When it comes to native cuisine, Australians feel most at home outdoors—where their more interesting dishes are prepared. Barbecues are a national custom, as might be expected among a people accustomed to roughing it in the outback; and the plain traditional fare has been enlivened by a number of tasty specialties—steaks stuffed with oysters, prawns grilled slowly over charcoal with a little brandy to flame; fish fresh from the surf and roasted in foil. Any of these dishes may be garnished with the tropical fruits like bananas and pineapples that are so plentiful in Australia.

Australians are fond of seafood, and although paradoxically they still import most of their fish from Britain, Canada and the United States, they are turning more and more to the dozens of varieties of fish that shoal exclusively in Australasian waters. Bream and snapper are the same as anywhere else; but the five local types of whiting, none of them related to the Atlantic variety, are among the most delicious fish in the world. A species of trout is being farmed on an increasing scale for restaurants; and tailor, an Australian variety

of bluefish which is pursued by surf-casters, is excellent eaten fresh, fried in an oatmeal-and-egg batter.

These are mostly cool-water fish. Warm-water fish from the Great Barrier Reef are often edible also, but they must be eaten fresh because they lose their flavor when frozen. One of the pleasures of northern Queensland is to dine on fried fillets of barramundi (a kind of tropical perch), egged and crumbed with locally grown macadamia nuts *(Recipe Index)*. The fillets are quite thin, and two of them may look a little stingy on a plate; but the egg and nut coating adds a rich and filling touch and the sweetness of the macadamias brings out the flavor of the fish.

Australia's long coasts also abound in crustaceans—crabs, crayfish, prawns, rock lobsters (but no genuine lobsters). Prawns have lately become a major industry, being exported to Japan as well as consumed on a large scale at home. There are no less than five varieties, large and small, and the usual method is to serve them fried in light batter or simply grilled or barbecued.

Each region of Australia has its local crustacean delicacies, but Queensland has the best, such as the Moreton Bay bug, which looks like a cross between a crab and crayfish and tastes a lot better than its name sounds. Its tail, deep fried in light batter, is as delectable as the best Mediterranean scampi. Even better, and worthy to cross feelers with any crustacean anywhere, is the humbly named Queensland mud crab. Expensive and not always easy to find, the mud crab's flesh is so sweet and delicate that it should be eaten with nothing more than a few drops of lemon juice or wine vinegar.

Another Australian seafood that is worthy of international acclaim is the Sydney rock oyster—a misnomer, since the original breed died out in an epidemic around 1900 and was replaced by a new species imported from New Zealand and cultivated many miles inland from Sydney in riverbeds in New South Wales. Still, the oysters have taken well to their new habitat and can be enjoyed the year around, for Australia has no closed season on oysters.

Despite the popularity of seafood, meat is the mainstay of the Australian diet—as befits one of the world's largest meat-producing countries. Beef heads the list of favorites, and a substantial old-fashioned roast with the traditional trimmings is a fixture on Australian dinner tables. One beef dish, however, combines Australia's best from land and sea. This is carpetbagger steak *(Recipe Index)*, a thick tender steak stuffed with raw oysters and lightly sautéed, or grilled over charcoal. Carpetbagger steak is a specialty also of San Francisco; but it cannot compare with the Australian variety, in which the beef is grassfed and the oysters are the famous Sydney rock oysters. The silky texture of the shellfish and the firmer flesh of the beef go together in a succulent and sumptuous combination.

Next to beef in popularity come lamb, pork and veal—chicken and turkey being more expensive and therefore rating as comparative luxuries. Australians seldom eat mutton; their lamb is of the same age, about 6 to 8 months old, and prepared in the same ways as in the United States. A fine dish in good Australian restaurants is a rack of spring lamb, roasted slowly after having been rubbed with rosemary and a few sprigs of spearmint from the garden.

One kind of meat which is not readily available anywhere else, and which is a curiosity to many Australians themselves, is kangaroo. Frontiersmen in the outback boil or roast the legs, which look something like ham, and are especially good when spiked with bacon. City folk consider kangaroo meat beneath notice and much of it is canned for pet food. But one part of the animal, the tail, is the base for a rich and heavy soup that is thought to be quite a delicacy.

Australia is a prolific producer of vegetables, berries and fruits of almost every variety, from strawberry mangoes and other tropical fruits in Queensland to blackberries, currants and apples in the brisker southern climate of Tasmania. Australians consume them in quantity and do not fuss much over their preparation; but lately the idea has caught on of mixing fruits and vegetables in combination salads to accompany grilled meat at barbecues.

Whatever the Australians may have lacked in imagination and enterprise in the preparation of food, they have amply compensated for in their beverages. Australian beers are uniformly excellent, with real bite and flavor, and are served well-chilled as in America, not cool as in England. But the real surprise, and one of the little-known facts about Australia, is the high quality of its wines. Over the generations hundreds of cuttings from European grapes have been taken to Australia by wine lovers, beginning with the first governor, Arthur Phillip, who planted the continent's first vines in his own garden.

Australia's vineyards now extend in a broad band across the southern part of the continent from Brisbane to Perth. For a long time the emphasis was on strong, sweet muscatels and ports which were more to the liking of the early British immigrants. In recent times, with the growing sophistication of public taste, the vineyards have concentrated on producing high-quality dry red and white table wines and some superb champagnes, sherries and brandies.

Though they come from the same stock as European wines, Australian wines tend to be heavier and fruitier, but are by no means inferior. A great deal of Australian *vin ordinaire* is a good cut above many of its French counterparts, and some of the best Australian vintages so closely resemble the noblest wines of France that even connoisseurs have trouble telling them apart. If anything presages future glory for the Australian cuisine, it is the presence of fine wines and excellent oysters. Not many of the great cuisines of the world have had that much to start with.

## New Zealand

New Zealand cooking has evolved pretty much along the same lines as Australia's—a solid meat-and-potatoes foundation, a topping since World War II of international dishes (chiefly Dutch-Indonesian and Chinese), and a marginal embellishment of exotic local specialties. In contrast to Australia it is lamb rather than beef that takes first place among the meats. Lamb is so ubiquitous that New Zealanders even stuff it like fowl and serve it up roasted as "colonial goose" *(Recipe Index)*. New Zealanders are fussy about the age of their lamb. The most tender is baby spring lamb, which is considerably younger and more delicate in flavor than United States lamb; this specialty is now being exported frozen to America as a treat for epicures. Next in age, and most often eaten in New Zealand, is hogget—aged from 12 to 18 months. Finally, there is mutton, cherished by Englishmen but spurned by most New Zealanders.

Whatever the age of the lamb, New Zealanders like to serve it accompanied by a tart sauce. Most of the time it is the traditional British mint sauce, but an interesting variation is an orange-juice sauce in which shoulder chops are simmered, and which accompanies them to the table *(Recipe Index)*.

It is in baking that New Zealand cooks have learned to express themselves most imaginatively, building on the traditional British love of tea cakes and pastries. Country fairs feature baking competitions, and tables at teatime or at dinner (which is also called "tea" by New Zealanders) are regularly laden with a board-sagging display of buttery scones, biscuits, and sponge cakes thick with cream. The perennial favorite is a confection known as Pavlova *(Recipe Index)*, named after the famous ballet dancer who took New Zealand by storm on a tour in 1926; Pavlova, popular also in Australia, is a dessert cake made entirely of meringue, baked to bare crispness on the outside, soft and marshmallowy on the inside, smothered in whipped cream and garnished with any fruit that happens to be in season.

In the recipe offered in this book, the Pavlova is garnished with kiwi fruit, or "Chinese gooseberry." This is a New Zealand specialty with a hairy brown exterior that conceals the tenderest and juiciest interior imaginable, pale green and aromatic like a miniature melon. Another New Zealand favorite is the *tamarillo,* an egg-shaped, red or yellow fruit with tart flesh that is either eaten as a fruit or served as a tomatolike vegetable. Among the true vegetables popular with New Zealanders are the kumara, a species of yam that was the staple food of the aboriginal Maoris before the Europeans came, and the pumpkin. Both are most often served roasted and are popular accompaniments for the roast meat that is an obligatory staple of Sunday dinner.

As in Australia, some of New Zealand's finest local delicacies come from the sea. For a few months each year the little silver whitebait, netted at the mouths of rivers where they were spawned, appear at steep prices in fish stalls, to be fried and eaten whole. Much rarer and more highly prized is a flat, clamlike mollusk known as the toheroa. Too tough to be eaten whole or even chopped, toheroas are minced, puréed and used in the making of a rich, heavy green soup whose celebrated flavor has all the taste of the sea in it. Tohereoas are found only on certain stretches of beach on New Zealand's western shore, and even there appear only sporadically, vanishing for years in between. When the season on them opens, crowds of eager diggers rush down to the sea with wooden shovels—metal ones being banned by law.

Although New Zealanders are as traditional and conservative as Australians in their eating habits, they have unbent to the extent of borrowing at least one specialty dish—or rather, cooking technique—from their Polynesian predecessors, the Maoris. This is the communal outdoor steam-roast known by its Maori name of *haangi,* and here Polynesia and its cuisine have at last succeeded in breaching the stern Anglo-Saxon bastions of New Zealand cooking. For the *haangi* is the local version of the cooking technique that is practiced by islanders across the Pacific as far as Hawaii. It starts out with a shallow pit—like the *imu, umu* or *hima'a* of the more eastern islands—and a pile of firewood covered over with large stones. After the fire has burned down to glowing embers and the stones are good and hot, meat or poultry and then potatoes, kumaras, pumpkin, corn, and baskets of eels and shellfish are all quickly piled on. Water is splashed over the stones and the food is covered completely with clean sacks and earth to hold in the clouds of rising steam. About an hour and a half later the covering is lifted off and a mélange of delicious aromas summons the hungry to a heroic feast.

# Glossary

**ANNATTO SEED** (*achiote* or *achuete*): Rusty-red dried seed of the fruit of a tropical West Indian or South American tree. When used as a seasoning, it is an inexpensive substitute, both in flavor and for the orange color it imparts, for the more expensive saffron. Available in packages or jars at Latin American groceries.

**BAGOONG:** Salty fermented fish paste used in or to accompany many Philippine dishes. *Bagoong-alamang* is a similar paste of salted and fermented shrimp. Both are sold in jars or cans in Oriental groceries.

**BEAN CURD, FRESH:** Custardlike squares of pressed puréed soybeans. Sold fresh by the cake, usually ½ to ¾ inch thick and 3 inches square, in Oriental specialty stores. The Chinese variety is generally firmer in texture than the Japanese and more suitable for deep-frying. To store the cake, drain, cover with fresh water, refrigerate in a covered jar for up to 2 weeks, changing water daily. No substitute.

**BEAN PASTE, YELLOW** (thick bean sauce; yellow bean sauce): Viscous, pungent sauce of yellow beans, salt and water, used to flavor and preserve food. Sold canned in Oriental grocery stores. Keeps for months after opening when stored tightly covered in the refrigerator.

**BITTER MELON** (balsam pear): Small, pale green, tapered melon 6 or 7 inches long with furrowed or bumpy skin. Slightly bitter, but refreshingly cool. Sold fresh by weight or in cans in Chinese groceries.

**BOK CHOY:** A crisp, mild-tasting variety of Chinese cabbage that grows somewhat like celery but has 12- to 16-inch-long smooth white stalks and large dark-green leaves. Sold fresh in Oriental specialty stores. Substitute celery cabbage or Swiss chard.

**BREADFRUIT:** Fruit of a tree native to Pacific islands, but also grown in the West Indies. It may weigh up to 10 pounds, and has a warty or prickly hide. When used slightly immature as a starchy vegetable, its texture and flavor resemble that of grainy bread. It is always cooked before eating. Occasionally available fresh in mainland markets.

**CARAMBOLA** (star fruit): Tropical fruit of an ornamental shrub of Asian origin, about 4 inches long, with thin, waxy, yellow-green rind and star-shaped in cross section. The mild-tasting watery pulp may be sweet or sour according to variety. Best eaten raw or used in iced drinks. Occasionally available in Florida and Southern California markets.

**CELLOPHANE NOODLES** (mung bean threads): Thin translucent noodles made from ground mung beans. Dried in looped skeins and sold in 2- to 6-ounce packages in Oriental specialty stores. Cover with foil or plastic wrap to store. No substitute.

**CHINESE EGG NOODLES, FRESH:** Long thin noodles no more than ⅛ inch wide, made of wheat flour, eggs and water. Sold by weight in Oriental specialty stores. May be stored in plastic bags in the freezer for months or in the refrigerator for a week. Substitute dried Chinese egg noodles or any other narrow egg noodle, cooked according to package instructions.

**CHINESE PARSLEY:** *See* **CORIANDER, FRESH.**

**CHINESE SAUSAGE:** Sweet, mildly seasoned cured sausage of fat and lean pork, thumb-thick and about 6 inches long. Sold by weight (about 4 pairs per pound) in Oriental markets. No substitute.

**CITRUS LEAVES:** *See* **DJERUK PURUT.**

**CLOUD EAR:** Small, crinkly, dried fungus, about 1 inch long. Sold by weight in Oriental specialty shops. Store in a covered jar. No substitute.

**COCONUT SYRUP:** Heavy opaque caramelized syrup of sugar and coconut milk. Available bottled at gourmet food stores.

**CORIANDER, FRESH** (Chinese parsley; *cilantro*): Aromatic herb of the parsley family, much more pungent than the flat-leaf parsley it resembles. Sold by the bunch in Oriental or Latin American markets. Store refrigerated in a plastic bag or wrapped in a damp paper towel, without washing or removing roots.

**DAUN DJERUK:** *See* **DJERUK PURUT.**

**DAUN SALAM:** *See* **SALAM.**

**DJERUK PURUT** (citrus leaves, *daun djeruk purut*, dried lime leaves, *makrut*): Dried leaves of Far Eastern wild lime tree. Sold whole in small packets by importers of Indonesian specialties or in some Oriental food stores.

**FISH'S GRAVY** (fish sauce, *nam pla*): Thin brownish sauce produced by fermentation of salted fresh fish. Extremely salty and smells strongly of fish, but when used with moderation, it provides a surprisingly subtle flavor. Used in much the same way as soy sauce. Available bottled as "fish's gravy" in most Oriental groceries.

**GINGER ROOT, FRESH:** Gnarled brown root, about 3 inches long. Sold by weight in Oriental and Puerto Rican specialty shops. Whole ginger root will keep for a few weeks wrapped in paper towels in the refrigerator. Peeled, sliced fresh ginger root, placed in a jar of dry sherry and refrigerated, can safely be kept for several months without losing or changing its flavor. Peeled, sliced ginger root in brine, available in cans, may be substituted; ground or crystallized ginger may not.

**GOLDEN SYRUP:** Popular British product, a lightly caramelized syrup of refined cane sugar, sold in gourmet shops. Substitute a mixture of 1 part molasses to 5 parts light corn syrup.

**JACK FRUIT** (*jaca*; jakfruit): Irregularly shaped fruit of a tropical tree related to the breadfruit, sometimes weighing as much as 70 pounds. Its yellowish-green hide is covered with closely set spines. When immature, its fibrous pulp is used as a vegetable, in soups or curries; when riper and sweeter it may be used in sherbets or fruit salads. Sometimes available in Latin American markets.

**KANG KUNG** (Chinese spinach): Leafy greens of a water-grown Oriental plant, sold in summer in some Oriental markets. Substitute spinach.

**KENTJUR** (*kachai*): Thick root of a tropical Asian plant of the ginger family. Sold dried, sliced or chopped, in jars, by importers of Indonesian specialty foods or in some Oriental food stores.

**KIWI** ("Chinese gooseberry"): Fruit of a climbing shrub originally from China, now grown commercially in New Zealand. Named for that country's flightless, hairy-feathered bird, the kiwi (from which New Zealanders also derive their nickname for themselves). The fruit is from 2 to 3 inches long and about ¾ inch in diameter, with a light-brown fuzzy skin and sweet, juicy pale-green pulp, with flavor and texture reminiscent of honeydew melon. Available in gourmet shops and fancy fruit markets during a 2- to 3-month season beginning in June or July. May occasionally be found canned.

**KRUPUK:** Dried, mildly spiced wafers made of shrimp and tapioca flour, which when deep-fried swell to many times their original size. They are served as crisp appetizers or accompaniments to many Indonesian dishes. Sold dried in boxes or tins in Oriental specialty shops or from suppliers of Indonesian foods.

**LAOS** (java root, *lengkuas, kha*): Thick root of a Malayan plant of the ginger family. Sold in powdered form or as dried stem pieces in Indonesian or Oriental specialty stores.

**LEMON GRASS** (*sereh; takrai*): Aromatic, lemon-flavored tropical grass, widely used in Indonesian and Southeast Asian cooking. It is available fresh in Hawaii and Puerto Rico; though it is not sold in mainland U.S. markets, it can easily be grown from clipped rooted plants available by mail in limited quantities from select greenhouses or nurseries (*see Shopping Guide*). Three to six roots will multiply fast enough to provide an adequate household supply. Grow outdoors in warm climates; in cooler climates, grow outdoors during warm months and potted indoors when it is cold. Available dried as a powder or as dried blades (*daun sereh*) from Indonesian and some Oriental specialty shops.

**LITCHI:** Small, oval, sweet but slightly tart fruit with thin red shell, white juicy pulp and large pit. Sold fresh in July in Oriental specialty stores, or canned, in gourmet shops and Chinese stores.

**LENGKUAS:** *See* **LAOS.**

**MAKRUT:** *See* **DJERUK PURUT.**

**MUSTARD GREENS, PICKLED:** Green variety of Chinese cabbage pickled in brine and fermented. Sold in jars and cans and from barrels in Oriental specialty stores. Store in refrigerator. Substitute rinsed sauerkraut.

**MUSHROOMS, CHINESE DRIED:** Strongly flavored dried mushrooms from ¾ to 2 inches in diameter. Sold by weight or already packaged in Oriental specialty shops. Can be stored indefinitely at room temperature in a covered jar. Substitute Japanese dried mushrooms but not the European variety.

**N**AM PLA: *See* FISH'S GRAVY.
**NUOC MAM:** A salty extract of pickled fish widely used to season Vietnamese dishes. Similar to fish's gravy.

**P**ATIS: Philippine fish sauce, a salty clear brownish liquid used like soy sauce as a universal condiment. Sold bottled in some Oriental specialty stores.
**PICKLED DUCK EGG YOLKS** (salted eggs): Yolks of duck eggs precooked and soaked in brine for a month or more. Sold in packages of 4 in Oriental specialty stores. Store in refrigerator or freezer. You may also buy whole pickled duck eggs, sold singly, and hard-cook them; do not substitute hard-cooked fresh egg yolks.
**PY MEI FUN:** *See* RICE STICK NOODLES.

**R**ICE FLOUR, GLUTINOUS OR SWEET: *See* SWEET RICE FLOUR.
**RICE STICK NOODLES** (Chinese rice sticks, *py mei fun*): Thin, brittle white rice noodles, dried in 8-inch looped skeins. Packaged in layers, sold by weight in Oriental specialty stores.

**S**ALAM (*daun salam*, Indonesian laurel leaves): Dried Far Eastern bay leaves, sold in small bundles by importers of Indonesian foods and in some Oriental food stores.
**SCALLIONS, PICKLED:** Pickled olive-sized white bulbs of small green onions, available in jars in Oriental specialty shops.
**SEREH:** *See* LEMON GRASS.
**SHRIMP PASTE:** *See* BAGOONG, TRASSI.
**STAR ANISE:** Dry, brown, licorice-flavored spice resembling an 8-pointed star, about 1 inch across. Sold whole (though often the sections break apart) by weight in Oriental specialty stores. Store indefinitely in tightly covered containers.
**STAR FRUIT:** *See* CARAMBOLA.
**SWEET RICE FLOUR** (glutinous rice flour): Waxy type of flour made from glutinous or sticky rice. Sold by weight in Japanese markets and as glutinous rice flour in Chinese markets.

**T**AKRAI: *See* LEMON GRASS.
**TAMARIND:** Tart, brown fruit of the tamarind tree. The dried pulp from the pod is available in gourmet food stores, Indian and Latin American groceries.
**TI LEAVES:** Shiny oblong leaves of the ti plant, abundant in Hawaii and other Pacific islands, used to ornament or wrap foods for cooking. The leaves (which measure 2 to 6 inches wide and up to 24 inches long) are available in the mainland United States through florists, who may take a week or two to get them on special order. The leaves may be refrigerated up to 3 months in perforated plastic bags. Do not dampen. Substitute foil or vegetable parchment.
**TIGER LILY BUDS, DRIED:** Pale gold, stringy lily buds about 2 to 3 inches long. Sold by weight in Oriental specialty shops. Store in a covered container. No substitute.
**TRASSI** (Indonesian shrimp paste): Thick, dark brown, salty shrimp paste, sold in small sausagelike rolls by sources specializing in Philippine or Indonesian foods or in some Oriental groceries. Because it is strong smelling, cover or wrap it tightly to store. Will keep almost indefinitely.

**V**EGETABLE PEAR (*chayote*; *christophine*): Round or pear-shaped white to dark-green tropical squash, 3 to 8 inches long. It may be smooth or corrugated and is sometimes covered with soft spines. The firm, crisp flesh is more delicate in flavor than the familiar summer squash. Available year round in some Latin American markets.

**W**ATER CHESTNUTS: Walnut-sized bulbs with tough, brown skins and crisp, white meat. Sold fresh by weight in Oriental specialty shops and canned (whole, sliced or diced) in supermarkets as well. Store fresh ones refrigerated for several days. After opening canned water chestnuts, drain and refrigerate them in water in a covered jar for as long as a month, changing the water daily.

**Y**ARD BEANS (Chinese long beans; yard-long beans): Far Eastern species of bean prized for the tenderness of the slender young green pods, ½ inch wide, often growing to 3 feet long. Available seasonally in some Oriental vegetable markets.

## Mail-Order Sources

The following firms accept mail orders for herbs, spices and other dried or canned ingredients called for in this book. Some sell utensils as well. Write to those marked "I" for Indonesian foods and to those marked "O" for Oriental foods; the others handle both types of foods. Consult the Glossary when you plan to order. Because policies differ and managements change, check with the store nearest you to determine what it has in stock, the current prices, and how best to buy the items you are interested in. Some stores require a minimum amount on mail orders, ranging from $5.00 to $10.

The firm below is a mail-order house only, and handles an extensive range of Indonesian products:

Indonesian Foods (I)
Mrs. De Wildt
R.D. #3—Box 3385
Bangor, Pa. 18013

Listed below are retail stores that handle mail orders as well. They are grouped by regions:

### East

Cambridge Coffee, Tea and Spice House (O)
1765 Massachusetts Ave.
Cambridge, Mass. 02140

Cardullo Gourmet Shop
6 Brattle St., Cambridge, Mass. 02138

Toko Garuda (I)
997 1st Ave., New York, N.Y. 10022

Trinacria Importing Co.
415 3rd Ave., New York, N.Y. 10016

### South

Antone's
Box 3352, Houston, Tex. 77001

Chinese Food Products Co. (O)
1119 Jackson St.
Houston, Tex. 77003

Chinese American Co. (O)
719 Royal St., New Orleans, La. 70116

### Midwest

Holland Dutch (I)
6911 W. Roosevelt Rd.
Berwyn, Ill. 60402

Shiroma (O)
1058 W. Argyle, Chicago, Ill.

Wah Lee Co.
3409 Cass Ave., Detroit, Mich. 48201

Asia Food Products
1509 Delmar Blvd.
St. Louis, Mo. 63103

### West

Granada Fish Market
1919 Lawrence St.
Denver, Colo. 80202

Holland American Market
10343 E. Artesia Blvd.
Bellflower, Calif. 90406

The Hollinda Co. (I)
9544 Las Tunas Dr.
Temple City, Calif. 91780

Wing Chong Lung Co. (O)
922 S. San Pedro St.
Los Angeles, Calif. 90015

Haig's (I)
441 Clement St.
San Francisco, Calif. 94118

Sang Wo & Co. (O)
867 Grant Ave.
San Francisco, Calif. 94108

House of Rice
4112 University Way N.E.
Seattle, Wash. 98105

Wah Young Co. (O)
717 S. King St., Seattle, Wash. 98104

### Canada

The Dutch Mill (I)
5216 Côte des Neiges Rd.
Montreal 249, Quebec

Leong Jung Co. (O)
999 Clark St., Montreal 128, Quebec

Pirri's Dixieland Market
1108 Pharmacy Ave.
Scarborough 731, Ontario

Lemon grass plants may be ordered from the following places:

Logee's Greenhouses
55 North St., Danielson, Conn. 02369

Manis Brothers
13601 Old Cutler Rd., Miami, Fla. 33165

Mathews Nursery
12100 S. W. 43rd St., Miami, Fla. 33165

# Recipe Index: English

NOTE: An R preceding a page refers to the Recipe Booklet.

# Recipe Index: Foreign

# General Index

# Credits and Acknowledgments

**BLAKE**

**BURROWS**

**ELISOFON**

**LYON**

**RENTMEESTER**

**THE PHOTOGRAPHERS:** Anthony Blake came from England to make the studio photographs for this book. He also photographed *The Cooking of the British Isles* for FOODS OF THE WORLD. Still-life materials for his photographs were selected by Mrs. Paddy Folkard. Larry Burrows did the photography in Vietnam. Eliot Elisofon, who traveled in much of the area covered by the book, also photographed in other countries for this library. Fred Lyon, who made the Hawaiian pictures, was the photographer for *The Cooking of Italy* and *The Cooking of Vienna's Empire.* Co Rentmeester went to the spice areas of Indonesia for this book. Their specific credits appear below.

**PICTURE CREDITS:** The sources for the illustrations in this book are shown below:
Photographs by Anthony Blake: Cover; pages 9, 24, 25, 31, 43, 47, 60, 61, 63, 73, 88, 91, 104, 105, 122, 123, 132, 133, 136, 140, 144, 145, 147, 148, 159, 175, 185, 186, 188, 189, 192.
Photographs by Larry Burrows: pages 162, 167, 168, 169, 170, 171.
Photographs by Eliot Elisofon: pages 32, 35, 38, 39, 40, 41, 64, 86, 103, 108, 154, 157, 176, 179, 180, 182, 183.
Photographs by Fred Lyon from Rapho Guillumette: pages 13, 16, 17, 18, 19, 21, 48, 52, 53, 54, 55, 165.
Photographs by Co Rentmeester: pages 50, 51, 76, 77, 78, 79, 80, 81, 82, 83, 94, 96, 98, 100, 101, 102, 113, 114 (left), 115 (top), 116, 117, 124, 128, 129.
All other photographs: page 4, Walter Daran except bottom right Jon Brenneis. 10, 11—Map by Jerome Kuhl. 28, 29—Richard Jeffery. 44, 45 —Drawings by Matt Greene. 114—Right Rafael Steinberg. 115 —Bottom Rafael Steinberg. 150—Ted Spiegel from Rapho Guillumette. 153—Dick Swanson from Black Star. 208—Philip Dowell, Larry Burrows, Henry Groskinsky, courtesy Fred Lyon, Co Rentmeester.

In addition to the consultants listed on page 4, the following experts on various cuisines of the Pacific and Southeast Asia also contributed recipes used in this book and helped test them in the FOODS OF THE WORLD kitchen: Louis Loh, executive chef at Trader Vic's Restaurant in New York, assisted with Polynesian recipes. Mrs. Manuel Lozada, wife of a Philippine Consulate official, has cooked for special occasions at both the Philippine Consulate in New York and at the Mission to the United Nations. Udom Chaipipat and Dang Lueamrung, natives of Thailand, operate a catering service in New York. Miss Samsong Somrejprasong, a student in New York, also helped with Thai recipes. Miss Jenny T. Hoang, who teaches Vietnamese in New York, grew up in Vietnam where her mother taught her to cook.

The editors wish to thank numerous individuals who gave assistance to members of the staff as well as to the author and photographers of this book. Among them are: *in New York,* Art Asia; Algonquin Hotel; James A. Beard; Bonniers, Inc.; Nellie Burgos, Philippine Tourist and Travel Assn.; Dr. Samuel R. Freiberg, International Research Institute; Hoffritz Cutlery; Hammacher-Schlemmer; Jean's Silversmiths, Inc.; Sek-Hiang Lie; Florence Lin; Carolina Moulton, Philippine Consulate General; Macy's; Rastro Importers; To Tuyet; José Wilson; Harry Wong, Trader Vic's; *in*

*Florida,* W. E. Manis; *in Washington,* Deirdre Mead Ryan; *in Hawaii,* Joan Abramson; Jim Becker; Dora Derby; David W. and Cynthia Eyre; Iris Halloran, Pat's Restaurant; Clarence Hohu; Moki Kawaha, Halekulani Hotel; Glenn Kukahiko, Polynesian Cultural Center; Kenneth Lum; Emmie Matua; Jill Nhu Huong Miller; Henry S. Morita; Kathleen Perry, The Willows; Helen Sheard; Oliana Tautu; Josiah Tavaiqia II; *in Tahiti and Moorea,* Max Estorez; Lala Hall; Tau Neti; Nick and Nancy Rutgers; Arii Tupea; Crista Winkelstroeter Teihotu, Aiméo Hotel; Jeanne Winkelstroeter, Royal Tahitian Hotel; W. K. S. Wonghen *dit* Atchoun; *in Samoa,* Bill Barrett; Laki Stehlin; Chief Sua of Iliili; Palagi Sua; Chief Tuatesi of Malaeloa; Mauga and Caroline Tapusoa; Chief Afoa Fou Vale; *in Fiji,* George and Edna Cathcart, Gateway Hotel, Nandi; Jeremiah Tavaiqia; Josiah Tavaiqia; Opetaia Tuivuya; Tony Wilkinson, *Fiji Times; in Indonesia,* Ibu Asnawi Mangku Alam; Chaidir Anwar; Siegfried Beil, Bali Beach Hotel; Darlis; Professor Djadiguna; Zaimuddin Djuragan; The Tjoeng Eng; Kartini Erwan; Tommy Graciano; Bob Hargrove; Puri Suling; Harry Hersubeno; Mawardi Junus, Andales University; Mr. and Mrs. Mohamad Kaboel, NITOUR; Raymond G. Khalife; Palok Le Majeur; Mrs. Junus Mili; K. Musa; Dr. Raden Moerdowo; Gan Tjiam Nio; Mme. Oen, Toko Oen; Jim Pandy; Richard Ponggawa; Tung Piet San; N. P. Scholte, Catz International N.V.; S. Sinai; Z. M. Sitanala; Ita Sjamsuddin; Tom Spooner; Ibu Suhardjo; President and Mme. Suharto; Tjokorda Agung Sukawati; S. Supit; Colonel Sutikno, Presidential Secretary; Tan Heng Siak; Tatia and Wija Waworuntu, Tanjung Sari, Bali; Ieke Wener; *in Singapore and Malaysia,* Mariam Abdullah; Alwee Hussein Alkaff; Rejal Arbee; Marian Emery; Chin Koon Lee; Ivy Siow; Lee Lang Tan, Kolek Restaurant; Mr. and Mrs. Ali Yussuff; *in the Philippines,* Augustus Africa; Hector Alvarez; Lucila P. Aspiras; Senator Helen Benitez; Alfonso Calalang; Dante Calma; Maria Isabella Diaz, Barandilla Restaurant; Steve Espie; William and Doreen Fernandez; Lagrima Martires; Myrna Martires; Anita Masakayan, Josephine's Restaurant; A. Colin McClung and other members of International Rice Research Institute at Los Baños; Tita de Ocampo; Luz Oñate; Mr. and Mrs. Benjamin Osias; Deanna Palma-Bautista; Gosta Peterson; Faith, Engracia, Imelda and Joseph Reyes, Plaza Restaurant; Gertrude Stewart; Chona Trinidad; Mrs. Valencia, *Manila Chronicle; in Vietnam,* Germaine Loc; *in Thailand,* Pimsai Amranand; Sala Dasananda; M. L. Nravadi Chaixanien, Baan Thai Restaurant; H. S. H. Chongchit Thanom Diskul; Anne de Henning Michaëlis; Char Lerm Pol, Chitpochana; H. S. H. Piya Rangsit; Vipy Rangsit; H. S. H. Wibhawadi Rangsit; Sanda Simms; Jimmy Aung Than; Kim Willenson; Terb Xoonsai.

Printed in U.S.A.